THE PAGODA:
A Lesbian Community by the Sea

THE PAGODA:

A LESBIAN COMMUNITY BY THE SEA

ROSE NORMAN

A Sapphic Classic from
Sinister Wisdom

Copyeditor: Trent Duffy
Editor: Julie R. Enszer, Sinister Wisdom
Indexer: Holly Knowles

Sinister Wisdom, Inc.
2333 McIntosh Road - Dover, FL 33527
sinisterwisdom@gmail.com - www.sinisterwisdom.org

Designed by Nieves Guerra.

Cover drawing by Rainbow Williams; colorized by Nieves Guerra

Title Font: Movement Direct and Movement Indirect font
designed by María Ramos and Noel Pretorius, available at Libre
Fonts by Womxn, https://www.design-research.be/by-womxn/

Other Fonts: Montserrat, designed by Julieta Ulanovsky; Gara-
mond, and Corbel.

First edition, January 2024
Simultaneously published as *Sinister Wisdom* 131.
ISBN-13: 978-1-944981-63-1

Printed in the U.S. on recycled paper.

Contents

Chronicles

Backmatter

Introduction

This Pagoda Motel postcard shows the building that became for twenty-two years the Pagoda cultural center and guesthouse, the Center.

Uncredited postcard provided by Emily Greene

Rainbow Williams drove me to the Pagoda my first time there. It was November 2013, and she had just sold her Pagoda cottage the day before. We parked near that cottage, Amelia, at the end of Beachcomber Way where the narrow sand path through the dunes to the beach begins. A short walk down that path, banked by sea oats on both sides, leads to the ocean. Wildflowers bloom in the dunes year round, in summer and fall purple Clitoria and a yellow flower that locals call Ponce de Leon daisies or sea daisies. The beach is sandy with patches of coquina, tiny seashells often used in the old days in building construction. The sand is the color of oyster shells, mottled white and gray. To the north, the beach extends as far as I can see, lined with houses. To the south, more houses, then jagged rocks bordering an inlet to the Intracoastal Waterway. Straight ahead, the rolling waves of the Atlantic Ocean, vast and variable, its tides a constant background.

This beach was the backyard of a small community of women who came to create a woman's world. The ocean casts a spell. It seems boundless, powerful, inviting. Every day it is different. Sometimes calm seas break on a flat hard beach with little or no coquina. Other days, rough waters crash on deep, soft sand that is hard to walk on except near the water. One Pagoda visitor titled a story about her initial visit, the weekend of the second Pagoda birthday celebration on November 11, 1979, "Coming Home to Mother Ocean." "Here at Mother Ocean all is peace," she writes. "Waves break one after another sighing and cresting and rushing in as if the water were making love to the earth."[1]

In those days, no houses lined the beachfront, and you could see the St. Augustine skyline across the river to the southwest. The Pagoda women enjoyed nude sunbathing on a sundeck in the dunes, fire circles on the beach, pool parties with live music, variety shows with bellydancing, poetry readings, and comedy sketches, and regular concerts by feminist musicians in a private theatre. They produced feminist plays about Cinderella's after-story and sketch comedy by Positively Revolting Hags. They hosted celebrations of the Goddess, Tarot readings, and psychic workshops. At its height, the place known as "The Pagoda" was a Goddess church, cultural center with a private theatre, and guesthouse surrounded by twelve tiny, custom-built, knotty pine cottages and a duplex, all owned by lesbians. The cultural center and guesthouse lasted twenty-two years as an active operation run by the incorporated, tax-exempt Pagoda-temple of Love in the closing decades of the twentieth century, and another sixteen years after that shepherded by Fairy Godmothers, Inc., four women with a different vision for the space. This is the story of how all that happened, and of the women who made that community a place for lesbian culture to bloom and grow.

The story begins with a feminist dance theatre troupe called Terpsichore, named for the goddess of dance. Terpsichore was two lesbian couples living in St. Augustine and touring Florida with original shows like *Moonwomb*, combining dance, mime, and theatre to celebrate women and making their entrance through a giant vagina. Morgana MacVicar was a bellydancer, Rena Carney an actor and speech pathologist, Kathleen Clementson,[2] a visual artist, and Suzanne "Suzi" Chance a social worker. They found the beach cottages that had been a seaside motel, the Pagoda, and began the process of transforming them into the base for a cultural center operating out of a two-story house that had been the owner's home, built over a three-car garage.

The Pagoda story is one long series of amazing synchronicities, happy chances, and friendship bound up with a love of art, music, dance, theatre, and one another. The mixture of romance, spirituality, and feminist politics spurred the women running the Pagoda to rapid growth over the next twenty-two years as a succession of women found the Pagoda, saw its potential, and contributed to the brew. The organization never had a formal business plan or a mission statement, but that did not stop these enterprising women from starting the Pagoda Playhouse, then a women's resort, and then transforming that to a residential community connected to the guesthouse and cultural center, the latter sustained by a Goddess church receiving monthly donations from a growing list of supporters.

It began in 1977, when those four lesbians bought four cottages, leased the two-story house in front of them, and began producing feminist plays and concerts. By 1988, the property had expanded to become a residential community with twelve cottages, a duplex, and three beachfront lots (one with a house). The Goddess church, Pagoda-temple of Love, owned and managed the cultural center, the swimming pool next to it, and an adjacent space known as Persephone's Garden. Individuals privately owned all the rest, many of them sharing mortgages.

The complex arrangement that was the Pagoda is unique in the annals of lesbian herstory. There have been lesbian guesthouses and residential communities and cultural centers and Goddess churches, but never before or since has a lesbian residential community evolved around a Goddess-church-supported cultural center that anchored the community while also drawing visitors from far and wide. Some cottage owners came from well-to-do families, but most were from the middle class or working class, and several were trying to make a living as artists. There was never a lot of money, but things got done.

Throughout its history, the Pagoda cultural center was under-resourced because it relied almost entirely on many individual donors, rather than on a few major backers. While this egalitarian model of support fit with the women's feminist goals, it meant they were constantly fund-raising. Time and again their supporters came through for them.

The three-car garage became a fifty-seat theatre where the group produced feminist plays by a lesbian playwright who was in residence there for three years. For twenty-two years, that stage hosted intimate performances by lesbian icons like Alix Dobkin, Kay Gardner, and Holly Near, as well as many other touring women musicians and local performers. Performers often stayed on the premises as part of their fee, and guests rented space in various nooks and crannies in the main building, including the attic, accessed by a built-in ladder. In the Center building, the group operated a popular discount natural food store that also sold women's music and women-made crafts and jewelry. They built a library of books by and about women, plus an enviable video collection. The Pagoda hosted feminist art exhibits, study groups, and workshops on sign language, bellydancing, Gestalt therapy, psychic development, astrology, sexuality, music and healing (with Kay Gardner), and theatre. The Southeastern Regional Conference for Matriarchy was held there. Filmmaker Barbara Hammer stayed a week in the tiny room behind the stage and showed one of her films. Adrienne Rich led a five-day poetry workshop. All were women-only events; prices were low and on a sliding scale. Once they were a formal church, in order to sustain these activities, the Pagoda-temple of Love recruited supporters making tax-exempt donations of ten to twenty dollars a month.

The year it all began, 1977, was an important moment in the women's movement. The federally funded National Women's Conference launched in Houston, attended by two thousand delegates, thirty-two thousand observers, and First Lady Rosalynn Carter—along with two former first ladies, Betty Ford and Lady Bird Johnson—as well as activists like Coretta Scott King, Betty Friedan, and Bella Abzug. The feminist movement was entering the mainstream, making great strides toward women's liberation, especially in changing laws affecting employment discrimination, domestic violence, reproductive rights, and access to higher education and sports. The National Organization for Women (NOW) was pushing hard for the Equal Rights Amendment (ERA), electing pro-ERA state legislators in unratified states. Thirty-five of the necessary thirty-eight states had ratified the amendment by 1977, and feminist activists secured an extension of the deadline for the last three states needed to make the provision part of the U.S. Constitution. NOW elected a president, Ellie Smeal, who led an effort to add gay rights to the group's action plan. The Combahee River Collective issued a landmark Black lesbian-feminist statement, introducing the term "identity politics" and the concept that "major systems of oppression are interlocking," now theorized as "intersectionality."[3] Two years earlier, in California in 1975, Zsuzsanna "Z" Budapest had incorporated the first Goddess church in the country. The rise in feminist spirituality groups coincided with feminist bookstores opening across the country, as well as with women's land groups forming. Feminist consciousness-raising groups had done their work, and women were rising up demanding change. The women of the Pagoda took part in all of that and more.

The Pagoda was a cauldron of all that was going on in the women's movement in the last three decades of the twentieth century. Its foundation was feminist spirituality, especially the Dianic Wicca introduced in the United States by Z Budapest. Morgana had read Budapest before founding the Pagoda, and her teachings informed the credo of the Pagoda-temple of

Love. Morgana expressed spirituality through cultural activism, especially dance, which fueled her feminist political activism. She understood bellydancing as both a dance of birth and of female empowerment, women controlling their bodies. From that spiritual grounding in female empowerment, the women of the Pagoda processed and sometimes developed policies about controversial topics familiar to lesbian-feminists everywhere, including separatism, bisexuality, and consensual sadomasochism. They found ways to address important issues of the day: drug and alcohol abuse, battering, racism, economic and other oppressions. They borrowed money to make their cultural center wheelchair-accessible, and often provided sign language interpretation for plays, concerts, and other events. They discussed and addressed a variety of issues, but they always kept a low profile politically. They advertised in *Lesbian Connection* and in feminist newsletters and newspapers around the country, but they avoided publicity that would draw undesirable attention to their private enclave. The strong spiritual and cultural component at the Pagoda made that political work possible.

This cauldron of feminist activism established itself on a rustic patch of beach real estate. The Pagoda property was just over an acre and a half at its maximum expansion, including vacant lots, and the cottages were small and very close together.[4] Having been built as a motel, the cottages and cultural center shared many utilities, and some cottages were originally zoned commercial. For the first ten years or so, the couple who sold them the cottages owned and lived in the four cottages on the north border, and still owned the swimming pool, although the Pagoda women usually had access to the pool. Everything about owning the property was complicated, and it would get more so legally as cottages changed hands and the Cottage Association worked to keep them affordable to new buyers.

Complications never deterred these women. They were on a beautiful beach, most of them were in their twenties and thirties, and they had the spunk and enthusiasm of youth. They also had magic. Morgana was a practicing witch with psychic abilities. She read Tarot cards, organized circles for holy days, and often produced ritual theatre. Many events at the Pagoda began by raising a cone of power and sending out healing energy. No stranger to the law as the daughter of a federal judge, Morgana led the move to becoming a legally recognized Goddess church. Nearly all Pagoda residents participated in Wicca-inspired rituals and were committed to healing and growth through feminist spirituality. Becoming an incorporated Goddess church with tax-exempt status formalized the spirituality that had always been there and provided some financial stability. The women were in business, providing sleep space and producing lesbian-feminist entertainment at a place that some would experience as "Lesbian Paradise."[5]

St. Augustine is not the first place you would expect to find Lesbian Paradise. A small tourist town on Florida's northeast coast with a population of about 12,000 in the 1970s, St. Augustine is celebrated for its long multicultural history as the oldest city of European origin in the United States, having been colonized by Spanish explorers in 1565.[6] Today, historic preservation brings millions of tourists to St. Augustine to view restored eighteenth- and nineteenth-century buildings, a Catholic basilica built in 1793, and the remains of a 350-year-old masonry fort, now a National Monument, the Castillo de San Marcos. Downtown also features magnificent examples of Spanish Renaissance architecture, enormous structures commissioned by the millionaire industrialist Henry Flagler at the end of the nineteenth century as grand hotels, now housing city hall, the Lightner Museum, and Flagler College.

Despite its multicultural heritage, St. Augustine, like the rest of north Florida, was as deeply conservative as neighboring Georgia and Alabama, with a population that was 83.5 percent white non-Hispanic. Until 2020, a thirty-foot statue of a Confederate general stood in St. Augustine's downtown plaza, where a historic marker still identifies the remains of a slave market.[7] *Crossing St. Augustine*, a two-part documentary film about U.S. Ambassador Andrew Young's brutal encounter with mob violence during a peaceful protest in St. Augustine in 1964, shows just how racist this place had been.[8] Legal segregation had ended by the 1970s, but vestiges remained, as in most cities throughout the country. A lesbian-separatist community and a cultural center supported by a Goddess church are not what one would expect to find in this historic town in the Deep South in the 1970s.

St. Augustine is a town that appeals strongly to artists, like the many artists drawn to the Pagoda. Tourism brings many opportunities for artists and craftspeople to sell their wares, and the city has many art galleries as well as shops selling locally made jewelry, pottery, paintings, and souvenirs. Artists appreciate the quality of the light reflected in the many waterways. Several rivers converge at St. Augustine, flowing out to the Atlantic Ocean. These are spanned by several bridges. The oldest is the Bridge of Lions, spanning the Matanzas River and connecting the downtown plaza to Anastasia Island and St. Augustine Beach, the most developed beach in the area. North of the Bridge of Lions and visible from downtown is the Francis and Mary Usina Bridge, an impressive structure built in 1995 over the Tolomato River to link St. Augustine to Vilano Beach. The western end of the Usina Bridge is near the Fountain of Youth, a privately owned archaeological park, and leads to State Road A1A, disgorging motorists at the entrance to the Pagoda.

The new bridge replaced a much smaller drawbridge that led to Vilano Road, a block south of the Pagoda. It was that old drawbridge to Vilano Beach that the members of Terpsichore crossed when they went out to look at the beach cottages for sale for six thousand dollars in 1977. Real estate was still relatively cheap on Vilano Beach, then very much a backwater and known as the "hippie beach," with a few old motels and a scattering of homes. The beach community is at the south end of a peninsula running between the Tolomato River (now the Intracoastal Waterway) and the Atlantic Ocean. Nested at the south end of that peninsula, the Pagoda cottages had excellent views of sunrise and sunset.

The early efforts to develop the peninsula focused on railroad and ferry connections, and these foundered until the 1920s, when improved roadways and an automobile bridge made it more accessible to cars.[9] Then August Heckscher, a New York industrialist, named the area Vilano Beach and built an entertainment palace there, the Grand Vilano Casino (not a gambling operation). Heckscher's plans went awry when the casino was irreparably damaged by strong storms in 1937 and 1938.[10] The casino was still drawing crowds when a professional pilot named Lucius "Shorty" Rees (1896–1988) bought property a few blocks away and began building what would become Rees's Seashore Motel Cottages, then the Pagoda Motel, and then Pagoda-temple of Love.

Shorty Rees was a colorful character, celebrated for having flown with Lindbergh, and for a time chauffeur to a Flagler heiress. In 1934, he built a two-story house for himself, facing the highway, with its main entrance on the second floor and a garage/workshop on the ground floor. In 1936, he began building small cottages on Lot 3, behind his house. He built the first four that year and began renting each out as soon as he finished it. He did a lot of the work himself, and his mother and two sisters contributed to the design.[11]

Aerial view after 1970, showing a swimming pool on Lot 2, next to the Center building. Shorty Rees had bought lots platted as five strips, all the same size, labeled 1 to 5, GG and ZZ. The ZZ designates the beachfront lots, separated from GG by a sand road then called Ocean Boulevard. Lots 1–4 GG became first Rees' Seashore Motel Cottages, then the Pagoda Motel, then the Pagoda lesbian-feminist residential community. When a St. Augustine couple, the Schillings, bought the motel from Shorty Rees, they added the swimming pool on the A1A end of Lot 2, but that lot still has no cottages. All the beachfront lots now have houses, and the path at the end of Beachcomber Way provides public beach access.

Each cottage had a living room, bedroom, galley kitchen, bathroom, and garage. Rees built with knotty pine (including ceilings) and maximized space with a pull-down dining table and a Murphy bed (a pulldown bed). Over the years, he built eight more cottages, four more on Lot 4 GG, and the last four, about a third larger, on the north lot, Lot 1 GG, next to the beach access road, Beachcomber Way.[12] Rees named each cottage after a bird or seashell, and every cottage had a plaque over the front door bearing its name. The first four were Sandpiper, Seagull, Flamingo, and Pelican. Rees also built a two-story duplex for his sister on Lot 4 near the highway. By 1949, he was advertising the complex as Rees's Seashore Motel Cottages.

This scale drawing of cottage 4 shows the original garage enclosed as a bedroom (later, a half bath and laundry were added), and an addition on the ocean side, used first as a screen porch and later as a TV room. Not counting the addition, all the cottages on Lots 3 and 4 use this floor plan, which is 440 square feet, including the garage. The Murphy bed had been on the garage wall.

In about 1970, Shorty Rees sold the property to Jane and Frederic Schilling, who remodeled the buildings with a pagoda theme and changed the name to the Pagoda Motel. They painted all of the cottages burnt orange, added curved ornaments to the roofline (Pagoda women called them horns), and replaced the sign out front.[13] After adding a swimming pool, they changed the name from Pagoda Motel to Pagoda Ocean Cottages. We don't know why Jane Schilling chose the pagoda theme, but it strongly appealed to Morgana and Rena's spirituality. A pagoda is a religious building with multiple tiers. They immediately construed it as a temple, and in the early years experimented with various Asian-themed designs in their publicity and for a T-shirt. Later they would use Rainbow Williams's drawings in their publicity, but always held to the association of "pagoda" with a religious temple.

The Schillings were longtime St. Augustine residents and business owners. Frederic Schilling (1909–1986) was a local character and radio announcer for WFOY (Fountain of Youth),

21

known to all as Pappy. Jane Schilling (1913–2003) was a pilot who ran her own real estate business for twelve years.[14] They bought the Vilano property when Pappy retired from the radio station, living in the two-story house that Shorty Rees had built for himself until a bad fire around 1975 caused them to move into one of the cottages on Beachcomber Way.[15] Several of their children and grandchildren lived on the property, too, and ran the business for them, mostly renting cottages by the month to college students and offering a laundry service. The couple lived at the Pagoda until the early 1980s.[16]

The Schillings were in their sixties in 1977, when they sold the four cottages to the four women of Terpsichore and leased them the two-story building facing A1A. The couple became an important part of the Pagoda community for the first decade of the new women's community and cultural center. For the most part, Jane handled business matters, and Pappy was just a nice old man who was always friendly with the Pagoda women and would sometimes help them out with maintenance. In 1973, St. Augustine "knighted" him for his volunteer work in promoting the town, at a ceremony that was part of an Easter festival.[17] Jane was sometimes friendly but at other times created challenges for the Pagoda women. She not only was a successful businesswoman but had been breaking gender barriers for a long time. She flew small airplanes, worked as an electrician during World War II, and was associate editor of *Florida Sportsman* magazine.[18] For her era, Jane Schilling was a strong, independent woman, like the women who bought the motel property from her.

Strong women building community is the feature of the Pagoda community that links it to the women's land movement that was sweeping the United States in the 1970s. Fed by an outpouring of feminist theory published mostly in local pamphlets and newsletters and distributed widely through feminist networks, women began to grasp just how destructive and disempowering patriarchy was for all people, particularly through exploiting the earth and promoting constant warfare, but especially for women, symbolically associated with exploited and abused Nature.[19] Stories of the many lesbian land groups that began springing up all over the country in the 1970s are told in *Maize: A Lesbian Country Magazine*; *Shewolf's Directory of Wimmin's Lands and Lesbian Communities*; and Joyce Cheney's *Lesbian Land*.[20] The Pagoda appeared in all three of these publications, and Joyce Cheney and her editors actually stayed at the Pagoda while putting together the twenty-eight interviews gathered in *Lesbian Land*.

Women's land groups emerged out of feminism and feminist ideals and goals; in large part, they have been experiments in "living feminism." To quote a poem of that title:

> I went to the ends of the earth
> to live the sacred feminine
> to be the cultural worker
> who helped birth lesbian freedom
> who stood in solidarity with all oppressed peoples[21]

The residential community surrounding the Pagoda guesthouse and cultural center was an experiment in living feminism, but one with many different views of what that meant. The widely shared assumption in that time was that women-only space was both healing and strengthening, because patriarchy had made the world so demeaning and oppressive for women in general, and lesbians in particular. Coming out at work in the 1970s and 1980s could cost you your job, and many gays and lesbians of that era were estranged from their birth families. A women-only residential community created a chosen family and, for the Pagoda, also a source of income for some residents. Because their intention was for the residential community to be all lesbian, the Pagoda was "separatist," but not all residents viewed themselves as separatists, or defined the term in the same way: "women-only" and "separatist" are not the same thing. Most Pagoda residents had jobs in the larger community, where they were closeted. Many participated in mixed-gender political and social justice groups and viewed the choice to live among lesbians as a way to recharge their activist batteries, a way to get away from the everyday oppressions women learn to live with. Others engaged in mixed gender community and professional activities, recharging their batteries at the Pagoda, too. They all supported the "for, by, and about women-only" policy of the guesthouse and cultural center because they understood the healing power that comes from prioritizing women, but they might not agree about policies for mothers bringing their boy children to the property, or hiring men to do jobs they could not find a woman to do. Different attitudes and beliefs about separatism would create divisions within the community throughout its existence.

While the Pagoda residential community shared with women's land groups a commitment to women-only space, and appeared in those books about women's land groups, the community differed from those groups in many ways.[22] Self-identified "landykes"[23] often chose country living, isolated from urban or even suburban development. Country living was not what the Pagoda founders were seeking. Even in the 1970s, when the land around the Pagoda had not yet been heavily developed, the Pagoda was only a bridge away from St. Augustine. The founders were looking for theatre space, not a lesbian land collective, and grew into communal living by various turns of events. As Morgana put it in 1978, "It seemed to almost happen to us—a gift from the Goddess who wanted to see a seaside women's community."[24]

The Pagoda's affinity with the landyke movement arose from their strong links to two other Florida women's land communities, the North Forty (called Longleaf in *Lesbian Land*) about an hour away, near Gainesville, and Sugarloaf Women's Land Trust, 450 miles south, near the tip of the Florida Keys. Both communities are still active today. The North Forty began in 1972 as an offshoot of a lesbian consciousness-raising group in Gainesville that banded together to buy forty acres just outside the town of Melrose. Cofounder Kathleen "Corky" Culver says they bought the land as a way of creating chosen family: "we decided we could be one another's social security. . . . We wanted a place where we could grow old with supportive friends."[25] For over a decade, the North Forty was off the grid, with no running water or electricity, and the women spent years building a house using hand tools. Members of the North Forty included several lesbians knowledgeable about other women's land communities. They felt an affinity with what the Pagoda women were doing and became regular Pagoda visitors, supporters, and sometime residents. Corky Culver, Dore Rotundo, and Flash Silvermoon were all active at the North Forty and later at the Pagoda. Pagoda residents likewise participated in events organized by members of the North Forty and others, such as LEAP (Lesbians for Empowerment, Action, and Politics), an outdoor conference and festival held at the North Forty in fall 1984 and again in 1985.[26] The North Forty and Pagoda residents also had connections to Sugarloaf, especially around the peace activism they were doing in those years.[27]

The Sugarloaf women's community is very different from the North Forty, more like the Pagoda in not having begun as a separatist community, but evolving and expanding in that direction and offering housing for visitors.[28] When writer and internationally known peace activist Barbara Deming needed to move to a warmer climate for her health, she bought two modest houses and a guest cottage on Sugarloaf Key. She moved there in 1976 with her life partner, Jane Verlaine, and two friends, the lesbian-feminist antipornography activist Andrea Dworkin and her longtime companion John Stoltenberg, a gay man. Within a year, Dworkin and Stoltenberg had left, and it has been women's land ever since, expanding to include more houses, RV parking and hookups, and a campground. It is now a community land trust and has several full-time residents as well as a community house and other guest spaces for women only. Throughout the life of the Pagoda community, Pagoda women had a strong connection with the Sugarloaf women's community, often directing lesbians there, and vice versa. Soon after meeting Barbara Deming, Pagoda cofounder and resident Morgana MacVicar took the paid job of administrator for Deming's Money for Women Fund,[29] which still gives money to women writers and other artists.

The Pagoda residential community operated very differently from both the North Forty and Sugarloaf. At the Pagoda, both the cottages and the land they stand on were privately owned. At the North Forty and Sugarloaf, residents do not own the land; a community land trust owns the Sugarloaf land, and a private corporation owns the North Forty land. Residents serve on the board of the trust or are members of the corporation. At Sugarloaf, the trust also owns all the structures on the land and some of the furniture. Like the North Forty, the Pagoda-temple of Love was a corporation, but the Pagoda was a nonprofit, an incorporated Goddess church, and the corporation never owned the cottages or the land that they occupied. Like Sugarloaf, the Pagoda residential community expanded over time to fill a relatively small physical space (Pagoda expanded to 1.67 acres, and Sugarloaf to just over two acres), but Sugarloaf has no close neighbors and is well off the highway and the ocean. The Pagoda has a highway and the Intracoastal Waterway to the west, the ocean to the east, and (in later years) close neighbors to the north and south. For the first ten years, Pappy Schilling and Jane Schilling lived next door in the first strip of cottages (Lot 1 GG), as did their son.

Like many women's land groups, the Pagoda residents initially shared a lot of things, such as tools, air conditioners, utilities, and mortgages. The Center building was originally bought by a group of women who pooled their money for a down payment and operated for nearly two years as a collective. The collective model did not work well for Center ownership, as most of them were not living in the building, and they soon found expenses well beyond what they could manage as a group. Things worked much better after 1979, when the group donated the building to the Pagoda-temple of Love. While Morgana describes the Pagoda as a "collective" in her 1982 *Lesbian Land* interview,[30] collectivity affected them mainly in the shared mortgages and utilities, and in the feminist processing required to resolve interpersonal issues and to make business and policy decisions for the cultural center.

The crucial difference between the Pagoda and any other women's land community is the Pagoda's emphasis on developing a very active cultural center with a theatre and meeting room, as well as guest accommodations throughout. This emphasis on the arts was how the group started, and cultural activities, especially concerts, often first drew women to the Pagoda. Well-known performers like Ferron or Lucie Blue Tremblay played there, and Alix Dobkin came nearly every year. The Pagoda also had regular art exhibits, and in the early days they produced lots of feminist plays. As long as Morgana was there, the Pagoda also had dance performances and sometimes bellydancing classes. A Pagoda event, in fact, often had all of these: an art show, a musician, and Morgana dancing. Multifaceted art experiences constituted the cultural center that Pagoda women worked so hard to build and maintain.

The Pagoda experience for guests was very different from that of residents. Often vacationers were only dimly aware of what was going on among residents, if at all. Many wrote gleefully in the Center guest books, and one wrote the ecstatic "Coming Home to Mother Ocean" review, mentioned earlier, for an Orlando feminist newsletter. For vacationers it had very much the feel of a women's music festival, freeing and safe and joyous, especially if they were there on a concert weekend. For residents, the long-term experience was more sobering. They recall the excitement and fun of potlucks and beach parties and nonstop romance, but also the frustrations of communal living, the pain of romantic breakups, and the work involved in keeping that cultural center going.

Racial and ethnic diversity was a goal that the Pagoda women sought but never achieved. Only two women of color—Paulette Armstead, a Black attorney from Tampa, and Maria Dolores Diaz, a Honduran from California—ever owned a Pagoda cottage. Each woman was half of an interracial couple who owned Cottage A, the cottage closest to the highway and facing Beachcomber Way. Armstead bought Cottage A from the Schillings in 1988 as part of a group purchase, and treated it as a vacation home, visiting on weekends. She sold it to Diaz and her partner, Lois Bencangey, who lived in California and treated it as rental property, renting only to lesbians. Pagoda women did better at geographic diversity. Guest books include appreciations from women from across the United States and Canada as well as from western Europe. At least two residents came from foreign countries: Myriam Fougère from Canada and Gaby Penning from Germany.

This story of the Pagoda community draws on the memories of more than fifty residents, supporters, and guests, memories from thirty and forty years ago. The experience of being there back then—or having been there over many years—evokes details and memories quite different from the experience of a writer like me, who first set foot on the Pagoda land long after the cultural center was no more. Memories of events collapse into one another. Sometimes people forget what they witnessed and what they just heard about. A story told often enough becomes a memory of its own. Our minds automatically seek to close gaps, fill in whatever is necessary to complete the story. We may not even know that this is happening. A memory will ring true because it is logical that it happened that way, and then we find that someone else remembers it another way, or that documents tell another story.

Some of these collective memories may or may not be true, such as the story that has a resident burning the bookkeeping records on the beach. Many of the residents I interviewed alluded to this story in some way, though no one really wanted to talk about it. Maybe someone burned the books, but the resident named in the story is sure she did not do it, and Morgana's then partner, Fayann Schmidt, backs her up. Another frequently repeated story concerns the pyramid on the beach. In 2016 after Hurricane Matthew destroyed beach houses near the Pagoda, but left the Pagoda cottages and the beachfront houses virtually untouched, many people told a story about a ritual in which a resident psychic, Kay Mora, placed a "pyramid" on the beach to protect the Pagoda from hurricanes. Some thought it was buried, some that it was just set down in the dunes, some that it was not a pyramid but a sort of triangular structure used to direct the weather away from the Pagoda. Former resident Barbara Lieu still has the cardboard model that was used to make the pyramid, designed with precise specifications and, she recalls, built of plywood painted silver and placed in the dunes near Kay's beachfront property, pointing toward the ocean. It is not there today (or not visible), but Kay Mora's predictions about earth changes coming to the Pagoda environment have proved accurate. Beach erosion, a new bridge, and heavy development of nearby beach property have made the property today much less open and breezy than in the days when women could stroll to the beach across almost empty dunes.

The capacious dreams of the founders changed over time, too. As they grew older, some left the community never to return, others taking their place. As the land changed and the people changed, the visions changed, but they always shared the goal of creating safe space for women.

In writing about these women, I have chosen to use first names most of the time, rather than the common journalistic and academic practice of referring to men and women both by last names. Partly that is because they were mostly known by first names, and partly in rejection of the patriarchal custom of children taking their father's name and women taking their husband's name. To help readers keep up with the cast of characters, I have provided at the end a biographical glossary that includes cross-references to those who used different names at different times. To avoid confusion in the narrative, Morgana (born Julie Eaton) is always Morgana, and Sue Parker Williams is always Rainbow.

In structuring the chronological narrative of the Pagoda community, I have divided events into four distinctive phases of its development, plus an "afterstory." In each phase, the cast of characters shifts and reassembles, as different women take on leadership roles. "Founders: 1977–1980" (chapters 1–4) shows Pagoda women starting a feminist theatre and then expanding their vision to become a feminist cultural center, resort, and church. Rena Carney and Morgana MacVicar were there at the beginning, very soon joined by a couple named Barbara and Lavender Lieu. Morgana, Rena, Barbara, and Lavender became the primary leaders in those first years when they were figuring out what to do with the property that seemed to be falling into their laps. Ellen Spangler was also very important in these years, building the stage in the theatre and assisting with repairing and remodeling cottages. During this phase, the women advertised as a lesbian "resort," with nightly and weekly cottage rentals. But their chief interests were in establishing the cultural center and theatre and in setting up the Goddess church that was to sustain the cultural center through the rest of the twentieth century. These women poured energy into manifesting their dreams, as four cottages morphed into eight cottages and a duplex, plus the building where they built the theatre, Pagoda Playhouse.

"Builders: 1981–1987" (chapters 5–6) describes the shift to a residential community with no overnight cottage rentals. In this phase, the women began using the cultural center as a guesthouse for short-term stays, in addition to concerts, rituals, and other events. Morgana, Barbara and Lavender Lieu, Emily Greene, Edith George, Martha Strozier, and Dore Rotundo all were cottage owners prominent in managing or developing the cultural center from the beginning of this second period. They were soon joined by Elethia (who uses only one name) and then Rainbow Williams. Morgana was central to spiritual activities, and Barbara and Lavender were her trusted allies, running a discount natural food store and building a library, as well as producing concerts and taking care of many business and legal matters. Elethia took on many Pagoda jobs, including bookkeeper, Centerkeeper, and newsletter editor, and Rainbow often produced art shows, concerts, and other cultural events.

"Growers: 1988–1995" (chapters 7–8) covers the expansion of the community to include more cottages plus major renovations to the cultural center, with new leaders. Marilyn Murphy and Irene Weiss were the driving force behind buying the last four cottages on Lot 1 GG, as well as Lot 2 GG with the swimming pool, and two beachfront lots (Lots 1–2 ZZ). Together with two Pagoda women, Rainbow Williams and Nancy Breeze, and four others, they formed the North Pagoda Land Trust and started their own cottage association with its own rules to control the new property. The Pagoda was now at its maximum expansion of 1.67 acres, including the four beachfront lots (three of them vacant). Marilyn and Irene became very active in managing the cultural center and renovating the aging building. Three other couples who arrived in these years made important contributions: Garnett Harrison and Cindy Watson, Lin Daniels and Myriam Fougère, and Paula Arden and Dorothy Campbell.

"Reclaimers: 1996–1999" (chapter 9) tells the story of what happened when the Pagoda women ran into difficulties and many leaders moved away. They restructured the board, getting a lot more people actively involved, and began the Pagoda's final phase as an active residential and cultural enterprise. Cindy and Garnett became active board members, as did Rena and ten others, working hard to get things on a better financial footing. Residents Jennie Iacona and She Fay became active in running the cultural center and guesthouse. When the Pagoda-temple of Love, Inc., decided to sell the guesthouse and pool and move church activities out of state, a new lesbian-feminist, nonprofit organization, Fairy Godmothers, Inc. (FGI), bought the property.

"Transforming with Fairy Godmothers, Inc." (chapter 10) describes the afterstory of the Pagoda's existence as an entity recognizable as the Pagoda, now called Pagoda by the Sea. It began in 2000 with FGI, the corporation that four Pagoda supporters created for the purpose of preserving the cultural center and transforming it according to their own vision. Rena Carney, Rainbow Williams, Marie Squillace, and Liz Daneman were the four Fairy Godmothers. In a very few years, they realized that they could not sustain their dreams for the Pagoda without drawing heavily on their own personal finances to subsidize it, and spent more than a decade trying to find a suitable buyer. While the Pagoda as a community of supporters of a cultural center ended when the Pagoda-temple of Love sold the property in December 1999, Pagoda as a lesbian-identified residential community ended with the sale of that property in December 2016, although the cottages remain, many of them occupied by lesbians.

The final section, "Living in Community," considers the many ways that Pagoda women faced the challenges of living in a lesbian-feminist community closely linked to a Goddess church running a cultural center and guesthouse. It was a brave endeavor and a monumental achievement.

Founders
1977–1980

Morgana on the beach in 1978 wearing an azut, a bellydancing costume that
Barbara Deming had given her.

Photo by Emily Greene

Chapter 1
Founding the Pagoda Playhouse

"A W♀MAN'S THEATRE" proclaims the Pagoda's grand opening program, boldly announcing the founders' vision for a cultural center foregrounding art by, about, and for women. The Pagoda would soon become a lesbian resort and residential community, but it began as a feminist theatre for Terpsichore. The troupe's politics were made manifest in the giant vagina they often used as an entrance. Painted by Kathleen Clementson in the days before they bought the Pagoda cottages and encrusted with real pubic hairs spray-painted purple, that vagina symbolized their woman-centered, woman-celebrating vision. Kathleen moved on soon after opening night, but her vagina art would become a feature of the Pagoda, and she made more than one of these, including a peach satin vulva used for many years as an altarpiece.

In the beginning, Pagoda Playhouse was the focus. Terpsichore was looking for dance theatre space when Suzi Chance saw a newspaper ad for "seaside cottages for sale, $6000." Kathleen, Suzi, Morgana, and Rena drove over the river and met Jane and Pappy Schilling for the first time. It turned out that the Schillings were selling the property in parcels, and the women could not buy one cottage. They had to buy all four, but what they really wanted was the two-story house at the end of the row of cottages, and that was more than they could afford at that time. So they scraped up the down payment on the four cottages and closed on the deal on July 7, 1977, financing them on a mortgage held by the Schillings, and leasing the two-story building with an option to buy. Rena, Morgana, and Suzi moved into the big house, leaving the cottages with tenants, whose rent paid their mortgage.

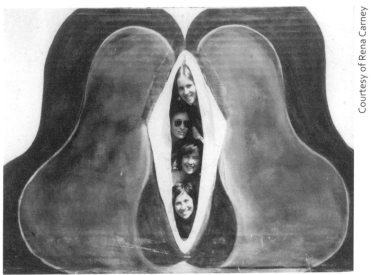

Pagoda founders in Kathleen's giant vagina backdrop. *Top to bottom:* Morgana, Suzi, Rena, Kathleen.

Courtesy of Rena Carney

They immediately started remodeling the downstairs garage as theatre space with a twenty-by-twelve-foot raised stage. They bought about fifty folding chairs from a local church that was closing and built stage lighting out of vegetable cans from the cafeteria at the school where Rena worked. Judy Miller's lesbian band JUICY had broken up and sold them a sound system, a light panel, and two Fresnels, specialized theatrical lights that can go from floodlighting to spotlighting. Suzi Chance went to a theatre supply house in Jacksonville and brought home colored gels for the lights. The control panel was at the back of the house, near the right rear garage door. The hot water heater was on the stage in the stage right upstage corner. The dressing room (formerly Shorty Rees's toolroom) was located behind the stage, where they set up a long board as the dressing table, with mirrors and lights to see to put on makeup. Costumes hung on a clothesline. Before long, they also used this little room as rented sleep space and called it the Cave.

Most of the carpentry work on the theatre was done by Ellen Spangler, who designed and built the stage, transforming Shorty Rees's old workshop into a much-loved and much-used performance space, one that endured for twenty-two years. Ellen had heard about the Pagoda from Suzi Chance, who had been her housemate in Jacksonville. At forty-three in 1977, older than the other Pagodans, Ellen was the recently divorced mother of four children, and had been a committed feminist activist since 1970, when she discovered the women's movement. She had learned carpentry from her father and from taking woodworking classes, and she also built musical instruments, including a harpsichord. A quiet person, once a church organist and choir director, she had completely bought into the feminine mystique until, in her words, "the women's movement came along, and for the first time I felt I had permission to discover who I was and what I wanted to do with my life." What she wanted to do with her life soon involved lesbians, which she also found through the women's movement. She met her first woman partner, Rose DeBernardo, at the Pagoda. Ellen not only built the Pagoda stage but spent weekends at the Pagoda for many years, often working on repairs to various cottages, and helping Rose build an addition to the cottage they shared, though they never lived there full-time.

The Pagoda Playhouse held its grand opening on the weekend of November 19–20, 1977, just four months after the women had closed on the cottages and leased the cultural center building. Morgana, Rena, and others tap-danced to "Women Loving Women" by Teresa Trull and performed a choreographed dance to "Leaping Lesbians" by Sue Fink and Joelyn Grippo. Most of the acts entered and exited through a backstage door framed by Kathleen Clementson's giant purple vagina, which covered the whole back wall. Except for the bellydancers, recorded music came from the brand-new album *Lesbian Concentrate*, produced by the new feminist record company Olivia, collecting songs by Meg Christian, Linda Tillery, Cris Williamson, and others. The album cover was a frozen orange juice can, a response to Anita Bryant's 1977 campaign in Florida against gay rights. Rena also performed a pantomime, and Morgana bellydanced with her friend Cassandra (Sandy Powers's bellydancing name) to Morgana's new dance piece "Matriarchal Images." The hit of the evening was Rena's impersonation of Anita Bryant. The evening ended with Flash Silvermoon and Pandora Lightmoon's band Medusa Music. After the performance, the band played on, and the crowd spilled out into the pool area. "That nobody drowned that night out of exuberance was a miracle!" Rena recalls.

Morgana remembers that "so many women came that night that we had to open the doors and find chairs out of houses to expand seating into the courtyard." A large crowd at that fifty-seat theatre might have been seventy women with the doors open, big for a small venue. The audience came from Jacksonville and Gainesville as well as from St. Augustine. Suzi was crowded into a back corner running the light panel. Rena entered through the audience impersonating Anita Bryant singing the Florida orange juice jingle, and delivering a bawdy script composed of "Authentic Quotes" from the homophobic singer's "Save Our Children" campaign (see script, below). The following afternoon, they had an open house with an exhibit of Kathleen's artwork, followed by a concert by the Berkeley Women's Music Collective, who had driven all the way from California to perform.

A WOMAN'S THEATRE

Saturday 9:00 PM
November 19, 1977

"Women Loving Women" - Tap Dance - music by Teresa Trull	Julie Morgana
	Sandy Powers
	Julia Juno
	Rena Carney
Slide Show	
Surprise Guest: Authentic Quotes.	Rena Carney
"Leaping Lesbians" - Dance - music by S. Fink & J. Grippo	Julie Morgana
	Sandy Powers
	Rena Carney
Pantomime	Rena Carney
The Beledi Dancers: Matriarchial Images	Morgana
Origins	Cassandra
Ritual	
Protection	
Celebration	
INTERMISSION: Refreshments	
Julia Juno	
Medusa Muzic . . . ? . . . . Pandora Lightmoon & Flash Silvermoon	

♀ ♀ ♀ ♀ ♀ ♀ ♀ ♀ ♀ ♀ ♀ ♀

Sound and Lights : Suzanne Chance

Special Thanks to Ellen Spangler for stage design and construction supervision, and to all the women who have helped us build our theatre.

✿ ✿ ✿ ✿ ✿ ✿ ✿ ✿ ✿ ✿ ✿ ✿

SUNDAY EVENTS:	
	OPEN HOUSE - 12:00 noon to 3:00 pm - Refreshments & Pagoda Crafts
	ART EXHIBIT - Faces and Flags by Kath Clementson
	BERKELEY WOMEN'S MUSIC COLLECTIVE - 3 P.M.

A program from opening night. Medusa Music had their own flyer promoting the event, showing the band performing three times during the evening instead of once, as here. Barbara Ester remembers the evening opening with a scene from a play. Everyone has a different memory of what they did that first night, and no photographs have survived.

Singer-songwriter Barbara Ester, who rode with friends over five hours from Miami to attend the grand opening, remembers it well, and would return ten years later to perform her own music. Barbara had heard about the Pagoda from her friend Mindy, who knew Medusa Music musicians Flash and Pandora and who had introduced Barbara to women's music. Mindy and Barbara teamed up with two other friends, Deanna and Mona, to share expenses for the trip. "We were in for a new adventure," Barbara writes, "a community outside of the butch and femmes, a new identity, and Pagoda would reveal another world."[1] She recalls Deanna's awe at Morgana's bellydancing: "She was not the typical dyke I knew. She embodied the Goddess. She was the Goddess!" Deanna said. "The next day," Barbara writes, "we mingled with the Lesbians filling the Center upstairs for a buffet. A room to the side was set up like an altar with colorful fabrics, carpets, candles and incense, photos and statues of the Goddess! . . . I knew then I was in a special place, in special company and felt transformed by the entire experience."

The Pagoda Playhouse grand opening featured primarily music and dance rather than theatre pieces, but in the next few years Rena's dream of her own playhouse for theatrical performances took flight as original plays by visiting lesbian playwrights filled that stage.[2] Rena was eager to get Morgana involved in plays as well as dance and variety shows, and she was always on the lookout for plays with good roles for women. In addition to feminist plays, Morgana and Rena performed Tennessee Williams's *Something Unspoken* and Alice Gerstenberger's *Overtones,* both serious dramas focused on complex women characters, strong women trapped in confining roles. They also performed Lorees Yerby's *Save Me a Place at Forest Lawn,* a dramedy with two old women sharing stories of their lives and looking into a future that holds little beyond death.

After Trudy Anderson moved to the Pagoda as resident playwright in December 1978, the emphasis on producing feminist plays accelerated. Trudy lived at the Pagoda until 1982, renting sleep space in the Center and elsewhere, and supporting herself with various paid Pagoda jobs since the residency was an unpaid position. At one time, she was making about $100 a month for maintenance and cleaning while living in the Center. From the time she arrived, Trudy's original plays were popular. In January 1979, just a month after she moved to the Pagoda, her one-act comedy *An Afternoon of Sophie and Myrtle* was produced, and that same month Rena and Morgana won a twenty-five dollar prize for performing it at "jam night" at a local Holiday Inn. That summer, the group produced it again,[3] along with two (maybe three) more of Trudy's plays.[4] Most of Trudy's one-acts are comedies with lots of physical humor and witty dialogue, often poking fun at serious topics with outrageous characters that the audience loved. In her time at the Pagoda, Trudy had several romantic relationships and tried to buy a cottage. When she left in 1982, Pagoda's regular productions of feminist theatre ended for a decade.

"Authentic Quotes"
from Anti-Gay Activist Anita Bryant

Rena Carney and Suzi Chance wrote the Anita Bryant monologue in 1977 from "authentic quotes" gathered from newspaper stories covering Bryant's antigay campaign. Bryant was well-known for publicizing Florida orange juice at that time. Rena performed the monologue at the grand opening of the Pagoda Playhouse and at venues in St. Augustine and Jacksonville.

[*Enter singing the Florida Citrus Commission jingle*]
Come to the Florida Sunshine Tree
Fresh Frozen Orange Juice Naturally
Orange juice with natural Vitamin C
From the Florida Sunshine tree.
Hi, I'm Anita Bryant
Da da da da [*to melody of song, as she throws oranges to audience*]
Seriously speaking, I suspect you are wondering why I decided to come here of all places. . . . It's because I feel I have been appointed by God as his personal messenger in the war on perverts. God drew a circle, and I stepped inside where he put fire in my heart. Tonight, Jesus Christ, the only man I can truly trust and give my love to, commanded me to come here and save you from life as a barnyard animal.

There is nothing gay about homosexuality. Homosexuals are extremely vicious with one another, plagued by drug addiction, alcoholism, venereal disease, suicide, and frigidity. NEVERTHELESS, lesbianism is painted as an irresistibly alluring and glamorous lifestyle to the young women budding and surging with sexual awareness. Let me heal you sister, be healed. [*Anita heals audience members.*]

Let's get down to it. Oral sex, even in marriage, is an abomination akin to cannibalism. Oral sex or cunnilingus is where the tongue is used to stimulate the female clitoris, producing an orgasm, and the discharge eaten is also a form of vampirism. Such degeneracy produces a taste and craving for the effects, as do liquor and narcotics. Let's face it, girls eating pussy is like eating heroin.

Well, if you don't believe me, there is scriptural proof from the book of Leviticus that there are two deterrents to the life of homosexuality—salvation through Christ, and the death penalty.

[*Exits singing.*] Glory! Glory! Hallelujah!

Glory! Glory! Hallelujah! Her truth is marching on.

[*Pie in face. Blackout*]

The excitement and energy of all that was going on at the Pagoda in 1978 and '79 shines through in a letter to the editor of the Orlando feminist newsletter *Changes* from two women who had just bought a Pagoda cottage:[5]

Dear Sisters,

Since we last wrote to thank you for your ad, which led us to find the Pagoda, everything has been happening so fast. Finding the Pagoda has really changed our lives, offering us an alternative—a Wimmin's Space. We bought our cottage, "Amelia," and now spend our free time in our space. It's been terrific—a really growing experience. The spirit there is so <u>free</u>. The atmosphere is totally free of males and it's beautiful to feel the freedom of the "Wimmin's Spirit," the freedom to breathe in the salt air in your own space. You can't escape the beautiful feelings—it's so unlike any space we've encountered.

The Cultural Center has been a continuing inspiration to us. In December we held a Winter Solstice Celebration including a play directed by Pagoda Theatre's new director, Trudy Anderson, and an entrancing program with dancing by Morgana and readings by Conni [Lavender] Lieu and Barbara Lieu. The evening really elevated the Wimmin Spirit in the group attending. We've also been lucky enough to attend an "Astrology Workshop" in December, and in January, a "Sexuality Workshop" by Martha Strozier, an original play "An Afternoon of S&M" by Trudy Anderson starring Pagoda Wimmin Rena Carney and Morgana, and a "Rock Revue" with Linda Wilson and Heather Vick. It has been incredible—all this done by wimmin, for wimmin.

In sisterhood ♀♀ Wiggy & Emily

Wiggy (Doris Wiegman, later called Nu) soon became the Pagoda bookkeeper, and Emily Greene an active volunteer and participant in many Pagoda activities for years to come.

By 1979, Pagoda women had formed Pagoda Productions, a group that managed their own budget for producing plays and other events in the Pagoda Playhouse. That summer, they produced several of Trudy Anderson's plays, plus *A Celebration of Women Artists*, a show consisting of monologues drawn from the writings of famous women, chosen by the actors. These actors and famous women varied, but Morgana always did Isadora Duncan and Rena did Virginia Woolf. A group of them were already performing *A Celebration* at the Pagoda when actor Pamela Shook first arrived there for an unpaid summer theatre acting gig in June 1979, and went on to perform it for a NOW-sponsored event at the St. Augustine Art Association, and in Nashville at a fund-raiser for a women's prison.

Pamela Shook had a fine arts degree with a minor in theatre and had moved from South Carolina to Atlanta to pursue an acting career when she saw an advertisement for a summer acting opportunity at the Pagoda. She phoned and spoke with Eloise Bruce, an actor with the touring company for Florida's Asolo Repertory Theatre, who was directing plays at Pagoda that summer. The summer of 1979 had an ambitious schedule, with plays every weekend in June, and the first two weekends of July and

August. Trudy Anderson's *The Weighting Room* and *An Afternoon of Sophie and Myrtle* were in June, followed by her play *Maraccas,* then Megan Terry's *The X Miss Copper Queen on a Set of Pills* the first two weekends of August. "Theatre was a grand experiment," Pamela Shook recalls, and "it's not an economically viable proposition," but she was willing to spend her summer supporting herself by cleaning Pagoda cottages rented to vacationers in order to be in all those plays and soak up the sun by the pool or at the beach.

That summer the women also opened the Backstage Bar in the Alcove that had initially been Morgana and Suzi's bedroom and later sleep space for Pagoda workers and guests. They sold wine, beer, and juice, and it was popular, but it was not profitable, and they soon opted for chem-free status in the Center.

It must have been after that big summer that someone, maybe Trudy Anderson, sent Rosemary Curb a description of the Pagoda Playhouse for a "Catalog of Feminist Theatre" published in *Chrysalis* in 1980.[6] It lists seven plays produced there in 1979. At least one of those seven plays, Arthur Kopit's *Chamber Music,* was never produced at the Pagoda, probably because that summer Ellen Spangler asked that Pagoda Productions "not do plays by men if it is at all possible to do a play by a womon."[7] There also may have been objections to the subject matter, which depicts women in an insane asylum.

Three original plays stand out in those early years: *Moonwomb, An Afternoon of Sophie and Myrtle,* and *Princess Cinderella.*

Rena and Morgana had collaborated on *Moonwomb* as a production for Terpsichore the year before they found the Pagoda, and Rena remembers it as the first play they performed in the Pagoda Playhouse: "We had a mind meld going on. [Morgana] danced, choreographed dances, talked about Persephone and spirituality and Tarot and the church. She gave me the words for that, and she taught me, and I taught her." They concocted the

story line together, Rena wrote the script, and Morgana choreographed it. Drawing on the myth of Persephone and Demeter,
the play allegorically traces the soul's journey to the underworld,
a sort of feminist Pilgrim's Progress, using poetry, dance, and
masks in the manner of ancient Greek theatre. Rena still has
the papier-mâché masks she designed and made for the characters: the Bird of Life and Death, Moon Goddess, and Rage. Suzi
wore the Bird mask and Kathleen the Rage mask—these were
mostly nonspeaking parts. Rena played the Moon Goddess and
Morgana danced the rape of Persephone by Hades in the underworld and her rebirth. As Persephone lies on the ground, the
Moon Goddess dances and chants to her:

Woman burning, soul alive
Fiery circle, soul alive
Blood to root, root to moon
Blood beats the truth into the womb

Left to right: Suzi in Bird mask, Rena in Moon Goddess mask, and Kathleen
in Rage mask pose in front of the giant purple vagina backdrop.

Then the cast chants to Persephone:

She will return, she will return
Blood to root, root to moon
Blood beats the truth into the womb. . . .

Terpsichore toured the show in Florida before Pagoda, and Kathleen did set design. One two-page *Moonwomb* script survives, opening with a speech that Rena can still recite from memory:

I am the moon [*I'm coming through the vagina*]
I am the Moon Goddess
Lover of all [*and I circle my arms*]
Mother of all [*I raise my arms*]
Creator of the universe
I have born the truth
My roots are deep
They grow, they are strong, they are life
Come [*I pat my gut*]
Eat!

Rena mimed and danced this passage wearing the Moon mask. Reflecting on her memories of *Moonwomb* more than forty years later, Rena wonders, "Why am I as a twenty-six or twenty-seven-year-old woman writing this? It was a birth of sorts. We were doing lunar calendars, worshipping life and love and song and creative energy. It was for me the birth of my lesbian woman self. And it was *fun* and poignant, and I think it was good." The connection of the moon to ocean tides and women's menstrual cycles was a continuing theme of Pagoda life and culture lived within easy sight and sound of the Atlantic, part of the magic of the place.

An Afternoon of Sophie and Myrtle, Trudy Anderson's one-act comedy, was outrageously funny and so well received that the Pagoda Playhouse produced it several times: the short version that Emily and Wiggy recalled in December 1978, a repeat in January; an expanded version that summer adding two characters, McFiddle and McFaddle, and a revival of the expanded version in the summer of 1980. The original two-character version starred Rena as Sophie and Morgana as Myrtle. In the 1980 revival, two summer visitors took the leading roles, Deanne Aime as Sophie and Brooke Triplett as Myrtle (Brooke stayed on and bought a cottage). Lavender had her one and only Pagoda acting role as McFaddle. Scripts for two versions of the play survive among Pagoda records, as do photographs of the two summer productions.

The Pagoda's fifteenth-birthday scrapbook describes the play as "the revised comedy about two 'Dolly Parton' type women fighting to get out of the closet." Sophie and Myrtle are bored housewives who are best friends. Sophie comes over to Myrtle's house to grill Myrtle about her recent encounter with Pete the Plumber, who had come to fix a toilet and in the process flirted with her. The slapstick humor is in the absurdity of the situations, and the pun on sadomasochism in the original title (*An Afternoon of S&M*) is carried out in stage business, as when Sophie hits Myrtle with a hairbrush and locks her in a closet. The closet is not only the heterosexual closet but, in this narrative, the confessional chamber when Sophie and Myrtle "Play Catholic." Sophie sits outside as the "priest" hearing Myrtle's confession and drinking communion wine to keep herself from interrupting. Sophie bemoans the fact that it was Myrtle, not she herself, who got hit on, and won't let Myrtle out of the closet. Then McFaddle and McFiddle enter, soliciting donations door to door for their "home for the wayward." The absurdity goes on as they counsel the wayward Myrtle, until Myrtle admits that she made up the story about kissing Pete the Plumber on the toilet to make Sophie jealous.

The short play makes fun of a host of topics that lesbians, then and now, take very seriously: religion, social work, sexual harassment, repressed lesbian desire, consensual sado-masochistic role playing. It must have been a relief to be able to laugh at these topics, some of which would become sources of major controversy in later years. Without the S&M in the title, that theme merges into simple slapstick comedy, and this is how it was received, simply as the absurdity of two comical women. No one missed the symbolism of Myrtle's being locked in the closet. The script has the feeling of a sitcom in which Sophie and Myrtle will return for more absurdity, à la Lucy and Ethel, but Pagoda Productions had no Sophie and Myrtle sequels.

The summer of 1980 brought another lesbian playwright to the Pagoda, Anna Rallo, who came from New Jersey.[8] Anna

Courtesy of Emily Greene

Morgana (left) as Myrtle and Rena as Sophie in *An Afternoon of Sophie and Myrtle,* performed at the Pagoda Playhouse in 1979.

worked differently from Trudy, creating her play *Princess Cinderella* from improvisations prompted by situations she set for the cast; after that, she would revise the script, adding songs that she wrote. It had a much bigger cast than the earlier plays, too, including Anna herself and her romantic partner Brooke Triplett (using the stage name Tamara Brooke), who also played Myrtle that summer. Anna cast Morgana as Cinderella (Cindy) and Rena as Prince Charming's sister Farah. Prince Charming was first-time actor Emily Greene. Emily has vivid memories of that show, because there was drama offstage as well as onstage:[9]

> I remember most Anna working with me to get in touch with the emotion of anger which for me at that time was difficult. She probably was one of the first to help me delve into how much I had suppressed the anger I had toward my father. It took a lot of private sessions with her before I could let it out onstage.
>
> It was a crazy situation. I was with Wiggy, who I had moved to Pagoda with in 1978. In 1980, she suggested we open our relationship—she would go out with Brooke and I would or could go out with Anna. Needless to say, Wiggy and I were having trouble with our relationship, and when I did go out with Anna, it led to my leaving Wiggy and moving to the Pink House next to Pagoda with Anna for about four months. This was during the time of rehearsals for *Princess Cinderella* and a tough challenging time for me. I was in no way an actress, but I gave it the best I had.

Emily's experience that summer was one of many, many romantic entanglements that Pagoda women experienced as they challenged all manner of restrictions in their lives, as well as onstage.

Photo courtesy of Rena Carney

Rena Carney as Prince Charming's sister Farah.
Rena found the dress at a thrift shop.

Princess Cinderella opened on July 4, 1980, and ran every Saturday night that month. The program describes it as "a unique feminist theatre experience—allegorically portraying the rebellions which rise from women's oppression—in a fairytale setting with words, music, mime and dance." The play depicts the sequel to the marriage of Prince Charming and Cinderella, with "Cindy" portrayed as a feminist activist who raises the consciousness of the women around her, even the prince's very, very pretty but empty-headed sister Farah. Cinderella's stepsisters oppose her activism and attempt to undermine her by tattling to the prince, hoping he will divorce Cindy and marry one of them. Farah has misgivings about the notion that women are equal to men until the court musician reveals "himself" to be a woman, and sings to her about it: "I must do what I must do . . . be who I have to be." In the final scene, the prince's adviser challenges them "to produce one woman who can do one thing as well as one man." The court musician dramatically reveals herself, and wins the contest.

Farah, the prince's sister, was Rena's last role at the Pagoda Playhouse. That fall Gainesville's regional theatre, the Hippodrome, recruited her to be part of its company, so she moved to Gainesville, where she also took a speech pathology job. This continued what would be a long acting career at the Hippodrome, which became a state theatre of Florida in 1981 and is now more than fifty years old. Rena's work at the Hippodrome has been closer to her vision for the Pagoda Playhouse, which had proved incompatible with the lesbian-separatist goals that began to emerge at the Pagoda.

The politics of feminist separatism as explored at the Pagoda led to clashes among the Pagoda women who founded it (and among later community members, as will be seen). Rena's dream of having her own theatre did not include limiting herself to plays by women. When she was told that she couldn't do scenes from Shakespeare, it was the last straw, and she found wider opportunities with the Hippodrome. Once Rena moved to Gainesville in 1980, theatre virtually disappeared from the Pagoda stage, except for the ritual theatre that was Morgana's main interest. The stage became more often the site of concerts and dance performances, and sometimes workshops or readings. In fact, the name "Pagoda Playhouse" rarely appears in Pagoda newsletters and meeting notes. Not until the 1990s did the group begin to produce plays again and, after Trudy Anderson and Anna Rallo left, there was never another playwright in residence.

During those first four tumultuous years of cultural activism with an emphasis on feminist theatre and dance, and including cultural activities of all kinds and lots of music, the Pagoda community was gradually coalescing: actors, dancers, writers, musicians—artists of all kinds—some of whom were cottage owners or tenants, performers or guests, locals who visited regularly, and guests who drove in from far and near. They were mostly white, young, educated, and economically privileged (some more so than others), with access to resources that allowed them to reach for their dreams when opportunities presented themselves. They aspired to create a lesbian-feminist community that was broader than their own youth and cultural privilege. They imagined a community that was empowering, freeing, spiritual, magical. For some, the mixture of art with feminist-separatist politics was problematic.

Morgana, Rena, and Kathleen were artists with varying commitments to becoming self-supporting as artists. Morgana's partner, Suzi, who had spotted the ad for the cottages, was neither a dancer nor an artist, but more of a technical assistant for Terpsichore. The grand opening program credits her for sound and lights. Kathleen Clementson was a visual artist, not a dancer or actor. For Terpsichore, she mostly worked on sets, and she exhibited her art at the grand opening. Kathleen's lasting legacy for the Pagoda was the artwork she created, the giant vaginas used as a stage entrance or backdrop and the fabric art vulva used as an altarpiece.

Kathleen and Suzi soon left the Pagoda. While Rena, Morgana, and Suzi moved into the two-story house they were leasing at the Pagoda, Kathleen stayed on in the St. Augustine house that she and Rena had bought downtown in Lincolnville, then a poor, predominantly Black neighborhood (now gentrified). Kathleen stayed connected to the group through opening night, but soon swapped her Pagoda cottage for Rena's share of the house in Lincolnville.[10] Suzi Chance sold her cottage in April 1978 and, like Kathleen, was no longer involved in theatre with Rena and Morgana. She was turned off by the feminist political analysis that became prominent after the group expanded to include the second strip of cottages, and she had never seen herself as a performer, the way Morgana and Rena did. Suzi says that she would have kept her cottage longer but had a financial crisis, solved by selling the cottage.

Rena and Morgana were passionately committed to the Pagoda project, but they had different underlying passions and visions. "All I wanted to do was sing and dance and act," Rena writes in an unpublished memoir of her Pagoda experience.[11] Although never a political activist herself, Rena did come from a political family. Her mother was very active in Democratic politics, serving as a delegate at more than one national convention. Her maternal grandfather had been in the state legislature before serving as sheriff of Jefferson County on the Florida Panhandle, in which role he was shot and killed in the 1930s, a family trauma that has informed Rena's art. For Rena, politics suggested ideas for plays, not activism. She had been performing skits all her life, often written by her mother. After two summer internships at the Asolo Repertory Theatre in Sarasota during high school, she was hooked for life, completing a BA in speech and theatre from the University of Florida in 1972. Rena was also serious about her professional life as a speech pathologist. She was finishing a master's degree in audiology and speech pathology at Florida State University when she moved to St. Augustine in 1975 (she would later earn a second master's, in instructional systems). As part of both her speech pathology work and her life as an artist she painted, wrote plays, did ASL interpretation for other performers, created masks for puppet theatre, and was a talented mime. Some of her theatre work was political, as in the monologue about Anita Bryant. Other times it combined theatre with dance, puppetry, and mythologizing, as in *Moonwomb*. Founding a feminist theatre at the Pagoda where she could create and perform was a dream come true.

Morgana was passionate about dance, politics, and feminism. Born Julie Eaton and raised in Miami, she came from a deeply political family. Her mother's father and grandfather were involved in politics in the early stages of the development of Miami. Her father's mother was the first woman elected to a state office in Florida. Her father, a state senator and then a federal judge, was considered a progressive in a conservative state. Morgana shifted from liberal to radical politics at Florida State University (FSU) when she joined and was president of Students for a Democratic Society, the radical student organization attempting to remake America through nonviolent activism, especially opposing the Vietnam War. She had studied dance all her life and chose FSU to continue it while earning a BS in social welfare in 1969. While Morgana later returned to FSU to pursue a master's in American studies and dance, radical politics took her to anarchism and eventually feminism. She helped start a Women's Center at the university and taught courses about the Goddess there along with Dorothy Allison. After cofounding the Pagoda, Morgana headed down a path that would dominate the rest of her life: pursuing her vision of lesbian-feminist spirituality and performing feminist bellydancing while living in a lesbian community.

Living together in community was not the Pagoda founders' original intention. Suzi Chance, interviewed more than four decades after leaving the Pagoda, is ambivalent about the experience. For her, "it always seems like there were two Pagodas, the one before it got all political, and then the one after." During the Pagoda's twenty-two-year history as a community with a cultural center run by a Goddess church based on emerging feminist principles, residents and supporters clashed over the political, social, personal, and communal meanings of their shared decisions, especially those involving separatism. For the first three years, Rena went along with decisions about separatism because she trusted Morgana and saw the importance of women's space. During those years, she devoted her free time to Pagoda Productions while holding a full-time job with the public school system. Suzi, too, was working full-time as a social worker and was not much interested in feminist politics. Morgana and two of the new cottage owners, Barbara and Lavender, were deeply committed feminists and had the resources to make the Pagoda itself the focus of their lives. That division of labor, and the fact that Rena and Suzi rarely attended business meetings, created friction among the founders, which led both Rena and Suzi to shift their energies elsewhere before the Pagoda became a full-time residential community in September 1981. Rena, Suzi, and Kathleen lived the rest of their professional lives outside the Pagoda community, although Rena kept her cottage and her connection to the community throughout its life and beyond. Of the original founders, only Morgana was all in for a lesbian-separatist community and cultural center.

Chapter 2
Creating a Lesbian
Community and Resort

In the summer of 1977, when the two lesbian couples in St. Augustine were discovering those beach cottages and the big house that would be perfect for their dance theatre, another lesbian couple were setting out from Charleston, South Carolina, on a cross-country road trip to find a new place to live. Barbara and Lavender Lieu were looking for warm weather, beach living, and lesbians. Starting in August, they drove a circuitous route to California, by way of Maine. By October, having found no place that captured their interest, they were back east at Pass-A-Grille Beach, a gay beach on the Gulf Coast near Tampa, when they saw a flyer advertising the grand opening of the Pagoda. They decided to check it out.

Barbara and Lavender arrived while Morgana, Rena, and others were rehearsing, tap-dancing to "Leaping Lesbians," and were "*bowled over*, swept away," Barbara recalls. By an eerily fortuitous coincidence, they arrived the weekend that the two heterosexual couples who owned the four cottages facing the Terpsichore cottages decided to sell their lot.[1] For sale were four cottages, plus a duplex next to the Center building, and a beach-front lot (vacant except for a rickety sundeck), the most valuable part of the property. The two wives went over to the leased

59

house where Terpsichore was rehearsing and asked if they knew anybody who might like to buy the property. Barbara and Lavender were immediately interested. Lavender had thought that she wanted more geographic distance from her old life in Charleston than north Florida, but Morgana did a Tarot reading that convinced Lavender that it would be a positive move. Here was the opportunity to bring in more lesbians and create what they would soon envision as a women's resort. In November, Morgana announced this new vision at the grand opening of Pagoda Playhouse, and very quickly the group had commitments from enough women to move on the purchase.

Drawing by Rainbow Williams

Drawing of cottages #5, 6, and 7 in the second strip of cottages, acquired in 1978. Rainbow Williams called the drawing "Dykestreet" and used it to illustrate a newsletter story titled "Pagoda: Paradise for a Pair of Dykes" (*Changes* Summer 1983). The story ends, "Ah, dykestreet. I could stay forever."

The women of Terpsichore had just met Barbara and Lavender, but Morgana says that the only question she asked them was whether they were Marxists, and was happy when Lavender replied, "No, I'm a Democrat." Morgana's experience with mostly male Marxist organizations in college and graduate school had put her off Marxism permanently. It was clear to her that "a wimmin's cultural and spiritual revolution was the answer to patriarchy," not a Marxist class analysis, and she found kindred spirits with Barbara and Lavender, who shared her privileged class background.

Barbara (left) and Lavender Lieu outside their Pagoda cottage in 1978.

Barbara Lieu (born Barbara Hering) had grown up on the campus of New York Military Academy, a residential prep school where her father taught and was later headmaster. She had majored in theatre (focused on production, not acting) at Emerson College in Boston and got into Democratic politics while married to a man and living in Connecticut. She found feminism through her local National Women's Political Caucus chapter. On a vacation with friends (after leaving her husband), she fell in love with Charleston, so much so that she moved to South Carolina.

Lavender Lieu was born Conni Ackerman and grew up in a wealthy Charleston family. After graduating from Smith College in Massachusetts, she came home and married a lawyer who joined her father's law firm. In 1974, she got her own law degree from the University of South Carolina and joined the family law firm. Then she met Barbara.

When Barbara moved to Charleston, she had inquired at an independent bookstore where to find feminist organizations in Charleston. The clerk directed her to Lavender, who was well-known locally for working through NOW and in liberal feminist channels as a spokesperson for the Equal Rights Amendment (ERA). When Phyllis Schlafly, the notorious antifeminist activist, came to town, Lavender was the one chosen to debate her, and she carried on frequent, spirited arguments with a columnist for the *Charleston Post and Courier*, who facetiously referred to her as Conni Ackerperson.[2] Barbara and Lavender came out to each other at a NOW conference. Neither had previously been lesbian-identified, and it took time to adjust, but nine months after that conference they took off on the cross-country trip that landed them at the Pagoda on the weekend that the second row of cottages came up for sale.

Most of the other women who came forward to share in buying Lot 4 were also strangers to Morgana and Rena. Three members of the Berkeley Women's Music Collective chipped in for one cottage.[3] Musicians Nancy Vogl, Suzanne Shanbaum, and Debbie Lempke had heard about the Pagoda by word of mouth and didn't know any of the Pagoda women before they drove there from northern California to play at the grand opening. The band had been together since 1975 (it would last until 1979) and was one of the first out lesbian bands. Nancy Vogl says that she was the band member "most passionate about the cottage" and borrowed her share of the down payment from her family. Suzanne and Debbie had some extra money at the time, and the fourth band member, Nancy Henderson, wasn't interested. They would name their cottage Helva (also the name of their van) after the name of the spaceship brain in an Anne McCaffrey novel, *The Ship Who Sang.*

Four women from Jacksonville—Vicki Wengrow and Pat Crouse, who were partners; Sherry Kliegman; and Beth Hodges— committed to buying two cottages and the duplex. Morgana and Rena barely knew them, but Suzi had been part of Ellen Spangler's housing collective, where Vicki, Pat, and Sherry lived. These four women each committed to a cottage (Sherry to the duplex downstairs and Beth to the upstairs duplex).

That's *nine* women who committed to a mortgage, plus another Jacksonville woman, Martha Strozier, who knew the other Jacksonville women and attended a 1978 meeting at which the group began making financial commitments and decisions. Since Martha was the only one of the Pagoda women with substantial financial resources, the plan was for Martha to pay cash for the beachfront lot, and the others to assume the mortgage for the cottages lot. It got complicated when the bank did not want to separate the cottages (Lot 4 GG) from the beachfront (Lot 4 ZZ), and Martha did not want to be part of a shared mortgage. Luckily, Martha had enough influence at the bank that she worked it out and the group closed on the property April 13, 1978.[4] The new cottage owners were already having meetings to set up their cottage association and decide how they were going to manage the property. Initially, only Barbara and Lavender were planning to live in their cottage. All the other cottages had tenants, including some men, and the new owners had to figure out how to shift that to women only.

While today it may seem surprising that nine women who did not all know one another would become partners in a real estate transaction involving a shared mortgage, it was a time when feminists relied on shared beliefs in the power of sisterhood. Something similar was happening on a larger scale in the creation of the Michigan Womyn's Music Festival in 1976, organized and funded by a few leaders and operated by a lot of women banding together as the We Want the Music Collective. Like the women who created that festival, the Pagoda women knew that they were not just investing in property: they were creating a women's world whose promise was limitless.

When those women banded together to buy Lot 4 in 1978,[5] the vision of creating a lesbian community with a cultural center expanded the original vision of theatre space with a few cottages to rent out. Morgana says of the original purchase, "We bought those cottages before we really knew what we were going to do with them. We just knew it was crazy not to take them. . . . It wasn't women's space, because we couldn't find women to rent them."[6]

Operating from feminist principles, and with a lot of good luck, they eventually achieved affordable housing in what would become a residential community for lesbians. They updated a "Cottage Association Agreement" that the Pagoda Playhouse founders had signed in 1977. From then on, the Association did its best to make sure those cottages remained affordable, and that they remained lesbian-owned. The two women most responsible for achieving that goal were Barbara and Lavender Lieu.

Barbara and Lavender soon seemed to have always lived there, though in fact they moved to the Pagoda about six months after Morgana and Rena did, initially renting Morgana's cottage while Morgana continued to live in the Center building. The couple were called Barbara and Conni Lieu when they came to the Pagoda, and most of the legal documents that Lavender prepared for the Pagoda are signed "Conni Lieu." The "Lieu" was a shared joke among their lesbian friends in South Carolina, who were taking the surnames Lou and Lu to signify lesbian. There were the Columbia Lus and the Charleston Lous, so Barbara and Lavender became the Florida Lieus. If all lesbian couples did that, Barbara said, when you moved to a new town you could easily find them in the phone book. Conni changed her first name to Lavender in 1979 or 1980, and then to Valentine around 1988. (For clarity, I have chosen to always call her Lavender.)

Both Lieus brought skills and experience that helped move the community to create a tax-exempt, nonprofit church that could be supported by monthly donations, by visitors who stayed overnight at the Center and in cottages, and by performers and artists who usually performed in exchange for a share of the gate and a week at the beach. Barbara and Lavender also developed a library inside the Center as well as a discount natural food store, where they also sold books, cassette tapes, Pagoda postcards, Pagoda T-shirts, pagan jewelry, and other items popular with lesbians. Often Lavender was the greeter for guests, who fondly remember her Southern accent, her engaging smile, and her Isis (thunderbird) swimsuit.

Lavender did the majority of legal work for the Pagoda, especially figuring out how to separate the cottages so that cottage owners had individual deeds. Barbara did bookkeeping for the Cottage Association until 1989 or 1990, and she took care of a multitude of business and financial matters for many years. They were hardworking, savvy women, and they also had a great sense of humor, as seen in the postcard a friend made of them posing as tourists on the beach wearing flippers and funny clothes.

The Pagoda women quickly moved forward to create their own special women's space that would attract women to fill those cottages. Meeting notes for April 7, 1978, show them voting to evict their male tenants by June 1 so that they could have only women in the cottages they owned. Then Morgana, Suzi, Barbara, and Lavender took off for New York City with Martha Strozier in Martha's motor home, leaving the rental property in the hands of a tenant, Ruth Lefevre, and her son, both of whom would be moving out. The New York trip was Morgana's annual visit for the board meeting of Barbara Deming's charity, Money for Women. The women used Morgana's travel stipend on gas for the motor home.

When they got back, they started advertising their "Lesbian Feminist Resort" and renting cottages and the duplex by the night and week to women only. Short-term cottage rentals was the first business model for the Pagoda, but it was part of a larger plan for what they hoped would become a lesbian residential community. The flyer they took to the Michigan Womyn's Music Festival that summer says they are doing short-term cottage rentals in the summer and looking for longer-term stays (a month or more) in the other seasons.

Since most rental income went to cottage owners, they needed a different plan to support the cultural center activities they envisioned. In meetings that spring, a group of cottage owners began to figure out how they could buy the big house that Morgana, Rena, and Suzi were leasing and that they all wanted to turn into a cultural center. In May, ten women agreed to meet Jane Schilling's price of $28,000 and to raise a $5000 down payment. Initially, they planned to limit ownership to ten women, but by the end of June, as the closing date loomed and Jane Schilling insisted on a $6000 down payment and a fifteen-year mortgage, they agreed to include more women in shared ownership. They were up to thirteen by November, but it was always a shifting number. Each woman would contribute $600 toward the down payment, with an extra $20 each for closing costs.[7] It was quite a financial risk they were taking, since they were also still figuring out how to manage the cottages they were renting. They were aware of the risks: the meeting notes read, "We are jumping into this purchase, as we did the cottages, without clearly knowing each other's views and perspectives." But they were full of enthusiasm and ideas for what they could do with that big house,[8] in addition to the theatre they had already built on the ground floor.

Their dream was "to convert the entire main house into a wimmin's cultural center, including a library and art gallery."[9] Amazingly, this is exactly what they did, advertising nationally, developing brochures, and networking through feminist newsletters. In those pre-internet days, feminists generally, and lesbians especially, were very skilled in working traditional social networks to find out who was doing what where, and there was enormous enthusiasm everywhere for what women could accomplish when they set their minds to it. Women's music festivals were getting started in these years, the National Women's Music Festival in Illinois in 1974 and the Michigan Womyn's Music Festival in 1976. Gainesville women had formed the first women's liberation group in the South, consciousness-raising groups (including what may be the first lesbian C-R group in the country), a Women's Center, a women's art festival, the Gainesville Women's Health Center, and a domestic violence program. These groups in Gainesville, all led by lesbians, very quickly learned about what was happening at the Pagoda.[10]

The first summer as a women's resort, the Pagoda women were renting everything on both lots except Barbara and Lavender's cottage. (Morgana and Rena were still living in the leased building they then called the Pagoda House.) It was a busy summer as they worked on publicity and started developing the store and library in the Center building. Nancy Vogl and Woody Simmons were there from the West Coast for concerts in May, and folk/bluegrass artist Jan Schim came from Tennessee. Medusa Music performed and played for dances, along with other Gainesville musicians like Abby Bogomolny and Linda "Rock Starr" Wilson.

Part of how the Pagoda kept the cottages affordable was through pooling rental income. In this economic model, nonresident cottage owners shared rental income equally, minus expenses for housekeeping, laundry, bookkeeping, etc. The rental pool allowed price controls through shared profits and losses, and removed competition among owners. During the resort period, this meant mostly nightly and weekly rentals. The accounting was complicated when cottage owners reserved a week or so for themselves, and when others chose not to be part of the rental pool. Shared utilities also complicated the bookkeeping. Gas and electric bills were not divided up by cottage for many years. There was no sewage bill. They had homemade septic tanks and in the early years bought water from Jane Schilling (she owned the well). Some people shared septic tanks and even water heaters. When they eventually got public water, they had only one meter for the Center and all of the cottages. The Pagoda women took all these variables in stride, convinced that they were on a path that would eventually lead to a residential community.

In addition to the financial issues, the cottage owners shared other challenges. That first summer, the Pagoda women cleaned up and decorated cottages that had been vacated by tenants. This often meant moving a lot of furniture and appliances. Sometimes the departing tenant owned the furniture, and Pagoda women had to find replacements before they could rent that cottage again. Two of the cottages on the new strip needed a new roof. Most of the window air conditioners needed repair, and they had to come to an arrangement with Jane Schilling about the water supply. They were also getting the property ready to host a conference in September, which included repairing the sundeck on Martha's lot and adding a screen room to it as a juice bar. They were filled with "We can do it!" spirit and dived into all manner of unaccustomed work with great enthusiasm.

After all that hard work, Rena, Morgana, Barbara, Lavender, and Martha headed for the Michigan Womyn's Music Festival in the first week of August. They went armed with the flyers promoting their new lesbian resort, describing the cottages and cultural center, the swimming pool, and Suzi's twenty-one-foot sailboat, which Morgana had named *The Matriark*, available for charter. It was Rena's first women's music festival, and she wrote a comedy sketch about the experience—the cold outdoor showers, menstrual sponges, nudity, mud baths. In her sketch, the initial festiegoers' reaction to their "resort" publicity is critical: "A cultural center, how middle class!"; "What kind of a community is it if you all live in separate cottages?"; "Sailboats? Think of all the women who don't have that kind of privilege!" As the Barbara and Lavender characters leave the stage crying, a critical festie runs over to her friends and says, "What are you doing after this concert? We can go to this place that has sailboats and cottages! It's called the Pagoda."

The Michfest publicity, together with national advertising, was paying off in recognition, but the high occupancy season was over, and by Labor Day the Pagoda women realized that they were financially overextended. Cottage owners could not count on breaking even with overnight cottage rentals to women only, even pooling rental income.[11] Because of their commitment to making the cottages affordable (both for rental and for purchase) and women-only, the cottages were not a profitable financial investment during the first ten years, only an investment in women's community. The women knew that they wanted to become a residential community with full-time residents occupying all or most of the cottages, but this would take years to achieve.

Not everyone could afford an investment that was going to lose money. Between June 23 and October 1 of that first year as a resort, 1978, there is a gap in Pagoda records. During that time, Vicki, Pat, and Sherry decided they wanted to sell their cottages and pull out of the project. Vicki and Pat also wanted back their $600 contributions to the Center. Pagoda women were discussing how to find buyers the weekend when Emily Greene and Wiggy (Doris Wiegman) visited and promptly offered to buy a cottage after learning how affordable they were, about $3000 down and $40 or $50 a month, Emily recalls.[12] By January, all three units had sold to lesbians who planned to live in them rather than rent them. The group refunded Pat and Vicki's shares in the Center, but there were hard feelings.[13] Vicki continued to visit the Pagoda, but Pat never came back. In a 1982 interview for *Lesbian Land,* Morgana put the disagreement like this: "What was more important, making a profit, or being a women-only space?" (p. 112).

Vicki Wengrow remembers it differently. She and the other Jacksonville women began with great enthusiasm, driving down together on weekends, usually with Vicki's ten-year-old daughter, and sleeping on the floor upstairs at the Center building. Vicki had just finished massage school and would give massages to guests and residents. She recalls the Pagoda as "a great environment for my daughter, because she had all these welcoming moms to go to."[14] But Vicki, Pat, and Sherry had joined the group with the idea of long-term rentals that would pay their share of the mortgage and expenses, maybe even bring in income, while building lesbian community. After the change to short-term rentals, absentee owner expenses came to $162 monthly. This included mortgage, taxes, and insurance, plus utilities, cleaning, laundry, and other short-term rental expenses. The figure is almost $750 in 2023 dollars.[15] That was a significant financial burden to these women, who identified as working class and did not have family money to draw on when they came up short. They shared the vision of women-only (preferably lesbian) space, and also, Vicki says, had "a parallel spiritual commitment to the Goddess and the female principle, and still do." But they had agreed on a gradual transition as women tenants came along. The change to a women-only lesbian resort doing short-term rentals that were not going to break even seemed to them a betrayal and an economic hardship. Since their work was in Jacksonville, and Vicki and Pat had just bought a house there, moving into their cottages was not an option. They had to have tenants. They went along with the new arrangement, and regularly attended many meetings that spring and summer of 1978, while they all tried to figure out how to run a resort and develop a cultural center.

The group's decision to evict male tenants became contentious when they decided to continue that policy past the summer. The original agreement was to see if they could make it financially renting only to women, and the Pagoda women expected to go back to the old way if they could not. After attending the Michigan Womyn's Music Festival, Lavender wrote to Morgana that she had completely changed her position: "I no longer feel that I can go backward at this point. . . . Somehow we must all pull together to make it through the winter."[16] Lavender's changed position may have shifted the balance among the decision makers at that time.

There were other sources of friction between the resident and nonresident cottage owners. Morgana, Rena, Barbara, and Lavender were living full-time in their cottages or in the Pagoda House. Sometimes the decision to share rental income and expenses led to conflict and misunderstandings. On their Pagoda weekends, nonresidents Vicki and Pat spent time improving their cottages, one weekend working hard on cleaning out a refrigerator. The next time they visited, they found that someone had moved that refrigerator to another cottage, and did not understand why Vicki and Pat objected. Vicki thought that the women living on the land believed that their wishes should have precedence over the wishes of cottage owners who were not living there. Residents met frequently about things that needed to be handled expeditiously, like maintenance issues, and other things also came up at the Thursday night meetings they called Group. Group became an important part of community building and interpersonal growth for the women living full-time at the Pagoda. Missing those Thursday night meetings put nonresidents at a disadvantage because they were not building the bonds of friendship and familiarity that the residents were.

As early as May 1978, meeting notes show the group directly addressing communication issues:

> We made a start at discussing visions, power relationships, personal feelings and concerns, politics, differing backgrounds, styles and perspectives—in short, real communication—among Pagoda cottage owners. Consensus seemed to be that, while most of our discussions to date have been of the nitty-gritty of Pagoda functioning, discussions of politics, visions, differing perspectives, etc., are equally important; and there is an interest, if not yet a commitment, on all our parts, to make time to discuss these concerns in relation to the Pagoda.[17]

If they made progress on these communication issues, it is not reported in meeting notes. The "nitty-gritty of Pagoda functioning" seems to have held sway, and separatism became increasingly important in decision-making. The Pagoda never rented to men again after evicting the male tenants in May/ June of 1978.

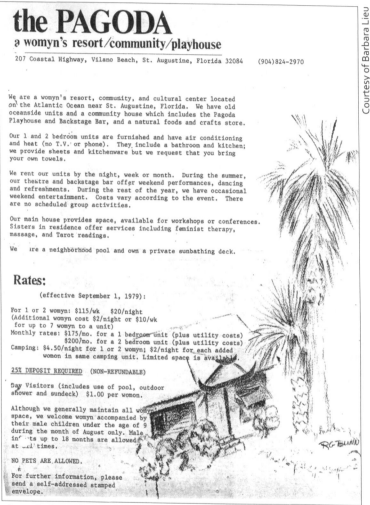

the PAGODA
a womyn's resort/community/playhouse

207 Coastal Highway, Vilano Beach, St. Augustine, Florida 32084　　(904)824-2970

We are a womyn's resort, community, and cultural center located on the Atlantic Ocean near St. Augustine, Florida. We have old oceanside units and a community house which includes the Pagoda Playhouse and Backstage Bar, and a natural foods and crafts store.

Our 1 and 2 bedroom units are furnished and have air conditioning and heat (no T.V. or phone). They include a bathroom and kitchen; we provide sheets and kitchenware but we request that you bring your own towels.

We rent our units by the night, week or month. During the summer, our theatre and backstage bar offer weekend performances, dancing and refreshments. During the rest of the year, we have occasional weekend entertainment. Costs vary according to the event. There are no scheduled group activities.

Our main house provides space, available for workshops or conferences. Sisters in residence offer services including feminist therapy, massage, and Tarot readings.

We are a neighborhood pool and own a private sunbathing deck.

Rates:

(effective September 1, 1979):

For 1 or 2 womyn: $115/wk　$20/night
(Additional womyn cost $2/night or $10/wk
  for up to 7 womyn to a unit)
Monthly rates: $175/mo. for a 1 bedroom unit (plus utility costs)
　　　　　　　$200/mo. for a 2 bedroom unit (plus utility costs)
Camping: $4.50/night for 1 or 2 womyn; $2/night for each added
　　　　　woman in same camping unit. Limited space is available.

<u>25% DEPOSIT REQUIRED</u>　(NON-REFUNDABLE)

Day Visitors (includes use of pool, outdoor shower and sundeck) $1.00 per womon.

Although we generally maintain all womyn space, we welcome womyn accompanied by their male children under the age of 9 during the month of August only. Male infants up to 18 months are allowed at all times.

NO PETS ARE ALLOWED.

For further information, please send a self-addressed stamped envelope.

RG BUNN

An early flyer advertising rates as of September 1, 1979. Note that the flyer foregrounds their "resort/community/playhouse," the combination that made the place unique among lesbian-feminist enterprises. They would later change "resort" to "wimmin's vacation spot" and then "retreat."

Forty years later, reflecting on what happened that year, Vicki writes: "We all had the dream of lesbian land and community, and I continued to support the Pagoda and attend events for years after this conflict. I wish these womyn hadn't convinced themselves that other womyn should be sacrificed so that they could have what they wanted, when they wanted it." She realizes now that "it was naïve of us to assume that if we had a similar feminist philosophy, we could automatically make it work. Since these womyn lived there, they could have more power over the process, and they used the power. . . . We still, all, as Mary Daly put it, had 'the pig in the head.' We just weren't coming from the same place on many other levels, and we weren't all ready to hear each other. That made it very difficult, and in the end, too difficult."[18]

Not only were the women not all coming from the same place, but the project that became the Pagoda was almost entirely serendipitous, a matter of seeing opportunities and following them enthusiastically. Moreover, women just seemed to appear at opportune times, as Barbara and Lavender did when Lot 4 came up for sale, and Emily and Wiggy did when the Jacksonville women wanted out. Seat-of-the-pants management and class differences may account for the big shakeup, with four cottages and the duplex changing hands in less than a year,[19] but these were feminists trying to overturn patriarchy and build a world they wanted to live in. They avoided rule-making at the beginning, not even writing bylaws. They did have a formal association agreement about their shared ownership of the cottages, setting out such matters as how to withdraw from that agreement,[20] but they valued consensus decision-making. Reading through their early meeting notes—sometimes two meetings in one day, one for cottages, one for the cultural center—one can see how a structure evolves. Collectively, they gradually moved toward decisions. They figured out that managing the cultural center was too much for one person, or two, until they landed on four people who were kept busy with correspondence (reservations and advertising), bookkeeping, greeting and taking care of guests, and maintenance and repair work—plus someone to clean the cottages and do the guests' laundry. Bookkeeping changed hands several times in those early years, and Center and cottage bookkeeping was combined.

After the cottage turnover that began in fall 1978, what with romantic breakups here and there, most of the cottages changed ownership with such frequency that by April 1979, the Cottage Association was maintaining a "Cottage Eligibility List" to control who could buy a cottage. This list is the only record of Pagoda supporters, those women who made a monthly donation entitling them to stay for free in a cottage (or, later, in the Center) and also securing their eligibility to buy a cottage. Being eligible for a cottage meant that you could buy a cottage once one came available, if everybody ahead of you in line passed on it.[21]

Buying a cottage meant assuming payments on that cottage's share of the mortgage, plus whatever additional amount that the Association deemed fair. For most of the years that the Association controlled cottage sales, this amount was the original selling price, minus the balance on the mortgage, plus an adjustment for inflation as calculated by the Consumer Price Index. It was a complicated calculation that Barbara Lieu managed scrupulously, with the intention that buying a Pagoda cottage was not a financial investment, but an investment in women's community. Lesbians were not to make money off other lesbians. It was a lesbian-feminist philosophy that not everyone shared, at least not when it meant losing money.

Barbara usually kept track of the Cottage Eligibility List, a complicated task as supporters were added, were "temporarily suspended" for nonpayment, or dropped out. Initially, most supporters were also cottage owners, but that soon changed as a growing number of women became monthly supporters.[22] The Cottage Eligibility Lists are the only record of the hundreds of women who came and went as Pagoda supporters, making regular donations. The list grew rapidly: for instance, in 1981, it doubled from 29 names in May (half of them residents or cottage owners) to 64 names in December. By 1986–1987, the list peaked at 150 names (not counting crossouts). I count 458 unique names in eleven versions of the list from 1978 to 1994, 458 women who at one time or another (sometimes off and on) contributed money to the Pagoda, not as guests but as "supporters."

Supporter status began to strongly link the community to the retreat and cultural center, implying that supporters were in fact part of that community and might want to be in line for a cottage. This implication continues throughout the resort period, when cottages were rented nightly for short-term stays, even though many (maybe most) supporters were primarily interested in the opportunity for beach time among lesbians in exchange for donations to a cultural center they greatly valued. Vacationers often knew little or nothing about the community around the guesthouse and cultural center where they were staying, or were not interested in owning a second home, or in moving into a tiny beach cottage in a tourist town, lesbian or not. For most of the resort period, the Pagoda women knew that they were moving toward becoming a residential community rather than building a resort, but they had not yet figured out how to make that happen. They needed to find more lesbians like themselves, women who wanted to live there and make community. One way they did that was by developing the cultural center.

Chapter 3
Developing the Cultural Center

In the fall of 1978, Margo George was an apprentice union carpenter and an active member of the Atlanta Lesbian Feminist Alliance, which hosted many lesbian organizations in an old house much like the Pagoda cultural center.[1] While visiting the Pagoda for the first and only time with her girlfriend Cathy Karrass and a group of friends, she bought a share in the Center.[2] Today, she remembers almost nothing about how that happened, and thinks it must have been a whim fueled by the lesbian-feminist enthusiasm that was creating a wave of activism and desire for women's space in the 1970s. That same wave of activism and desire was driving the Pagoda women.

Buoyed by the positive energy of attending Michfest, and knowing that they were taking a significant financial risk, the Pagoda women closed on buying the two-story house that would be their cultural center on August 9, 1978. Lavender signed the deed as trustee for what by November were thirteen co-owners: Rena Carney, Morgana MacVicar, Martha Strozier, Ellen Spangler, Pat Crouse, Suzanne Chance, Vicki Wengrow, Barbara and Lavender Lieu, Margo George, Alma Rose, Patty Johnson, and Darcey Ortolf.[3] The four who did not own a cottage at the time—Margo George, Alma Rose, Patty Johnson, and Darcey Ortolf—never in fact became cottage owners. Of those four, only Patty Johnson was actively involved with the cultural center, performing in several plays.

Lavender (right) talks to Laura Folk outside the cultural center. The sign on the building says Pagoda by the Sea Natural Foods. At the bottom of the steps is the Greeter sign. Guests were told to look for the Greeter sign, and whoever was in charge of greeting guests would place the sign outside her residence.

Alma Rose and Darcey Ortolf, who lived in Gainesville, were both trying to sell their shares by the following summer, Alma because of ambivalence about separatism.[4] Being a shareholder meant you had financial responsibility for maintaining the building and paying the mortgage, taxes, and insurance. This proved difficult as shareholders had entered into no official, legal obligation.[5] Several other women had bought shares, including Rainbow Williams and Ellen's partner Rose DeBernardo, by the time the group deeded the building to the Pagoda-temple of Love two years later, on August 25, 1980. Many of those original shareholders maintained a proprietary interest in the property long after they turned over the legal obligations to the church.

Again on feminist principles, the women did not run the cultural center as a profit-making business, keeping event prices low and just trying to break even. They also envisioned hosting conferences, and by June 1978 they had booked the Southeastern Regional Conference for Matriarchy for Labor Day weekend. At that point, they imagined using the building only occasionally as sleep space for "conference spillover." For the entire resort period, the women would rent rooms in the Center only on a monthly basis, usually to women working for the Pagoda as Centerkeeper or greeter.

The lines between Cottage Association business and Center business often get blurred in the Pagoda community's first decade, when they were building a community consisting of two rows of cottages, with the church-owned cultural center at the end of one row. In these early years, guests were renting the privately owned cottages (whose owners absorbed profits and losses from rentals), and also attending events or just hanging out at the cultural center. During the two years when a shifting number of women owned shares in the cultural center, meeting notes show them struggling to figure out how to keep up with expenses on a beach house that was over forty years old, and had had a fire upstairs before they bought it. For the entire time that these women and then the church owned the building, they had trouble keeping shingles on the roof (it had unrepaired fire damage). Nevertheless, these women were committed activists, many of them artists, with a dream and with sufficient education and privilege to figure out how to bring it to life.

When the collective owned it, they relied on monthly assessments from the shareholders, about twenty dollars each, which totaled not much more than the two-hundred-dollar mortgage payment when everyone paid her assessment (and often everyone did not). They had the first of many raffles and a yard sale, and they made some money renting the building for the matriarchy conference. Money from renting one or two rooms monthly covered the assessments that were not being paid, but they had many other expenses, such as advertising in national publications. Most of their guests were hearing about them through *Lesbian Connection, Ms.,* and *Gaia's Guide.* Their most reliable source of income to sustain the cultural center came from donations from people supporting their vision "to build an environment that will encourage and inspire all womyn to become a part of the growing women's culture."[6] After the Pagoda women officially donated the building to the church, those donations were tax-deductible.

During this early period, Pagoda Productions operated as a separate entity from the group that were managing cottage rentals and struggling to sustain the cultural center facilities. No one was paid for theatre productions, including professional actors like Rena Carney and Pamela Shook. The only performers paid anything were musicians. Records for 1979 show that Trudy Anderson, Kris Matson, Patty Johnson, Morgana, Rena, and several others had unpaid Pagoda Productions jobs. Patty Johnson was co-owner of *The Matriark* (with Suzi), and sometimes acted in plays. Kris Matson was an artist from Charleston who had the lead in Trudy's play *Maraccas*, and made many wooden signs for the Pagoda, including the Pagoda Playhouse sign.

At first, everything to do with the theatre belonged to Pagoda Productions, and they did their own bookkeeping, little of which has survived. Pagoda meeting notes show some conflict between the two groups as Pagoda Productions was not sending a representative to business meetings, leading Barbara Lieu to start attending their meetings to bring back needed information. Surviving Pagoda Productions records include mostly scripts, as well as flyers and other publicity. There are a few reservation lists showing concert attendees. For the month of January 1979, they have a side-by-side list of expenses and income, with expenses $249 and income $233 (plus a $100 carryover). The greatest expense is the percentage paid to entertainers ($81), followed by the cost of wine and beer for the Backstage Bar ($64.62).[7]

While Pagoda Productions concentrated on producing feminist theatre during those early years, concerts drew the biggest crowds. In the three years (1978 through 1981) before Pagoda Productions turned over the production business to the cultural center organization,[8] many popular area entertainers performed there, as well as touring musicians, including lesbian icons like Alix Dobkin and Kay Gardner. In 1979 alone, there were nineteen concerts and other musical events, and ten plays,[9] sometimes following a play with a concert. Some of these were dances with live music, but most were full-fledged concerts. The women started the year with local performers Heather Vick and Linda Wilson, followed by Medusa Music in March (replacing Alix Dobkin, who had been advertised); and Medusa Music performed four more times that year, including playing for a dance for the matriarchy conference. They closed that year with Holly

Near, who took time out from her antinuclear tour to perform at the Pagoda on Sunday night, December 2, waiving her fee. It was through musician and cottage owner Nancy Vogl that Holly came to the Pagoda, mostly to visit and relax, just that one time to perform.[10] Holly told them that the Pagoda was the only performance on her tour that was not to a mixed audience.[11]

Photo by Emily Greene

Alix Dobkin performing at the Pagoda in 1980.
The open door behind her leads to the Cave.

The summer of 1979 was a fabulous time for music and theatre, and Pagoda Productions had laid a solid foundation for the creative work that would be the hallmark of the Pagoda. The next two years were not nearly so busy, outside of theatre. In 1980, they had seven concerts, five of them by well-known performers: Kay Gardner, Alix Dobkin, Nancy Vogl, Teresa Trull, and Carole Etzler. California filmmaker Barbara Hammer came and showed her Goddess and lesbian films that September. That fall the Pagoda women decided to stop using the word "resort" in publicity and banned meat and alcohol in the Center, in line with emphasizing their role as a healing place. In 1981, Pagoda Productions again produced five concerts, with return engagements by Carole Etzler (now Carole and Bren, adding her cellist partner Brenda Chambers), Alix Dobkin, and Nancy Vogl, plus Sharon Riddell in August, and a group from Tampa called Fallopian Tubes in September. That year saw three January workshops, including a five-day Adrienne Rich poetry workshop, and Z Budapest visited for ten days in March and April. Z was visiting Florida for a month, staying with Pagoda cottage owner Dore Rotundo in Melrose, and came to the Pagoda to facilitate a circle.

The caliber of performers coming to the Pagoda says a lot about what their cultural center was coming to mean to lesbian culture generally. Outside of lesbian bars and women's music festivals, there were few places where lesbians could go where being a lesbian was not only the norm but was celebrated. For young women just coming out, finding that library of feminist books, or the feminist music and jewelry in the Pagoda store, was eye-opening, sometimes transformative. The Pagoda women had created a space for women's spirits to grow and soar, if only for a short time, a space to recharge their spirits to face the everyday oppressions of the outside world. Celebrities came there to support that and to recharge their own spirits.

In those fast-paced days, the lesbian grapevine was operating full steam, and the Pagoda was doing outreach of all kinds, including paid national advertising, as well as ads in feminist newsletters like *WomaNews* in Gainesville, *Changes* in Orlando, *Atalanta* in Atlanta, and even as far away as *The Lesbian Tide* in Los Angeles. Feminist newsletters often exchanged subscriptions, and reprinted interesting items and stories from other newsletters, expanding the web of information. In October 1978, *Changes* gave them the full-page ad that brought Emily and Wiggy there.

No one recalls how the New York–based Foundation for Matriarchy found out about the Pagoda, but founders Barbara Love and Elizabeth Shanklin chose the Pagoda for their matriarchy conference, held at the end of the Pagoda's very first summer as a resort. Their foundation's tabloid, *The Matriarchist*, published a full-page story promoting the conference at the beginning of the summer, headlined "St. Augustine: Our Place in the Sun," and a follow-up story that fall summarizing events at the conference.[12] Most of the first story describes the Pagoda, with a photo of Morgana seated in front of the giant vagina they used in the theatre. The story says they are looking forward to sailing on "The Pagoda's 21-foot Day Sailor called 'The Matriark.'"

The article includes extravagant descriptions of the swimming pool, "health bar and crafts store," juice bar, library, "body therapy clinic," theatre, and "dance studio which offers classes and workshops in feminist belly dancing, creative movement, theater improvisation, and karate." A registration form says women can sign up for all this for $30, including sleep space, a dance, and Saturday and Sunday dinner plus breakfasts. Judging from *The Matriarchist*'s follow-up story, the conference was a great success, and Pagoda women were a big part of it.

Southeastern Conference to Build MATRIARCHY

SEPT. 2, 3, & 4 *1978*
Registration: Sat. 9–11 a.m.
THE PAGODA – on Vilano Beach (A1A N.)
207 Coastal Hwy St. Augustine, Fla.

COST for the Weekend is $30 ($15 prepaid and $15 at registration) and includes:

SLEEPING SPACE in either cottages, tents, or main house

SAT. and SUN. DINNERS plus BREAKFASTS

SATURDAY NIGHT DANCE with MEDUSA MUZIC

SUNDAY NIGHT ENTERTAINMENT and CELEBRATION: Matriarchal Images

WORKSHOPS which include:
 Matriarchal Study Groups and Networks
 Planning for a National Convention
 The Politics of Wimmin's Spirituality
 Healing with Herbs
 Racism and Matriarchy
 Feminism and Anarchist Thoughts and Forms
 Tarot – Matriarchal Art of Divination
 Dream Workshop (bring your dream journals)
 Feminist Belly Dancing and Rituals
 Women's Karate and Self Defense
 Wimmin's Music and Percussion Jam
 Writing for the Matriarchist

(For those who wish private lodging in nearby motels, conference cost is $25.
Contact The Pagoda for information regarding room rates and details. For those
not attending the Conference who would just like to come to Sat. Night Wimmin's
Dance or Sun. Night Entertainment, Tickets are $3.00 at the door)
 SORRY – NO PETS

NAME _____

ADDRESS _____ STATE _____ ZIP _____

Preferred Lodging: Tent ( ) bring your own (small pup tents are best) Main House ( ) small groups
 Cabin Space ( ) send names of others with whom you would like to room Camper ( )

Publicity flyer for the matriarchy conference.

For the Pagoda women, "matriarchy" evoked the nurturing qualities associated with the divine feminine as well as the profound power associated with women's menstrual cycles, the phases of the moon, the power of giving birth. These ruling qualities were what they sought to honor at the same time that they worked to lift up women from patriarchal oppression by providing women-only space in a healing environment. Their interests were aligned with Shanklin and Love's definition of matriarchy: "By 'matriarchy' we mean a non-alienated society: a society in which women, those who produce the next generation, define motherhood, determine the conditions of motherhood, and determine the environment in which the next generation is reared."[13]

Closer to home, the Pagoda found a great source of outreach at Womonwrites, the Southeast Lesbian Writers Conference, which drew lesbians from all over the country.[14] At Womonwrites, Susan Robinson (then called Susan Wood-Thompson) recruited attendees for an Adrienne Rich workshop that she was organizing at the Pagoda in January 1981. "I'd never heard any major feminist or lesbian poet reading or leading a discussion in the South, where I had lived since 1974," Robinson recalls, and she wanted to provide that opportunity.[15] Robinson also advertised it in small Southern lesbian publications, hoping to attract "applicants who were from rural places, not connected to colleges or universities." The fifteen attendees used the Center building and four rental cottages; Rich stayed at a nearby motel.[16]

Like the Pagoda itself, the poetry workshop was flying under the radar, not seeking publicity. In fact, Robinson turned down a lesbian photographer's offer to photograph the event, assuming that "photography that would lead to publicity after the fact would undermine my aim," which was to create "simply a setting where work could get done." That aim was very much in line with the Pagoda philosophy of providing a place where lesbians could safely share their creative work and each other's company.

Chapter 4
Becoming Pagoda-temple of Love

"Every day there is a song, every night a gift of love, every moon a celebration." With those channeled words on their letterhead, the Pagoda community eagerly embraced the feminist spirituality of the ancient, matriarchal Goddess religion. Pagan and neo-pagan groups had been sweeping the United States since the 1960s,[1] and the feminist spirituality that grew from this movement developed at the same time as the women's liberation movement. Feminist spirituality and efforts to reclaim an ancient matriarchal culture that valued women[2] provided a counterforce to the misogyny inherent in many religions, whereby women were associated with Eve and the Fall of Man, and thus considered lesser beings, "Adam's rib." Tertullian, one of the early Catholic church fathers, called women "the devil's gateway," and this sort of view is found in other major religions, including Judaism and Islam.

The women's liberation movement of the 1960s and '70s challenged those beliefs, as some women worked within their church, temple, or mosque to raise the status of women while others sought spiritual sustenance in ancient earth-based religions. By the seventies, Zsuzsanna "Z" Budapest was being recognized as a founder of the feminist spirituality movement in the United States. In 1971, Z started the Susan B. Anthony Coven, usually regarded as the first women-only coven in the United States. She was reading Tarot cards at her small shop in Venice, California, in February 1975 when she was the subject of a police sting. She was arrested, tried, and convicted of fortune-telling. While she did not seek to be arrested, she did strenuously seek legal redress and got her conviction reversed nine years later by the California Supreme Court, on grounds of freedom of religion.[3] A first step in that direction occurred the same month as her arrest, when Z applied for official recognition of the "Sisterhood of Wicca" as a church. This became "the first incorporated feminist religion in 10,000 years."[4] The church that became Pagoda-temple of Love was the second.

Toni Head, a leader in the Florida chapter of NOW,[5] had been studying feminist spirituality and female deities when she and other NOW women decided to establish a church based on feminist principles. They incorporated the Mother Church in Florida in 1978, and Toni published an article about that experience, "Changing the Hymns to Hers." She wrote how her pursuit of feminism had repeatedly brought her "up against the stone wall of religious dogma . . . [which] functions to preserve patriarchal institutions and to prevent the establishment of equal rights and opportunities for women in the United States and other countries throughout the world."[6]

Lavender read "Changing the Hymns to Hers" and wrote to Toni that November 1978, asking whether the Pagoda might in some way become part of the Mother Church.[7] Luckily for the Pagoda, Toni had recently missed a deadline for filing for tax-exempt status and immediately proposed that the Pagoda women take over that chore. By March 1979, she had handed over the corporation itself. She had taken it as far as she wanted and believed that their commitment to feminist spirituality would take it much further.

Toni Head's Mother Church had its origins not in Wicca but in feminism and focused very much on one of the movement's chief goals of the 1970s, reproductive rights. Toni described reproductive rights as "the divine right of every child to be born to a mother who wants it, which in turn would assure every woman the right to control her own body and to bear children only when and if she wholeheartedly wants to do so."[8] This language was part of the official credo of the Mother Church, spelled out in its bylaws. Philosophically, she saw that the goals of the Mother Church could be met from different perspectives, including Wicca. She had published a Mother Church newsletter but realized that the church "needed some new direction" to stay alive.[9]

Meanwhile, the Pagoda women had been looking for a way to be tax-exempt and also women-only. Morgana's father, Joe Eaton, a federal judge, had advised her that forming a church was the best way to do that, and Lavender had come to the same conclusion. After Lavender's correspondence with Toni, things moved rapidly. On March 14, 1979, the transfer of the Mother Church to the Pagoda women was official. On June 6, Pagoda filed an annual report to the state of Florida giving their own officers; on November 9, they got their federal tax-exempt status; and on February 2, 1980, they filed to change the corporation's name to Pagoda-temple of Love.[10]

Morgana had been studying earth-based religions since she was in graduate school in Tallahassee. The first Goddess books were coming out then, including Z Budapest's *The Feminist Book of Lights and Shadows* (1975),[11] the founding book of modern Dianic witchcraft. Morgana and Dorothy Allison, who met while in graduate school, researched and taught about the Goddess in their classes at the FSU Women's Center, which they had helped to found. The Pagoda women didn't call themselves Wiccans, and Morgana never called herself a high priestess, but they did follow many Wiccan practices, while following their own inner guidance. Morgana had been doing Tarot readings and spiritual circles for years when Lavender discovered the Mother Church. When the Pagoda women took over the Mother Church, the bylaws remained much the same; the revisions mainly changed "Board of Trustees" to "Circle of Wise Womyn" and "Ministers" to "Priestesses," and set the annual meeting for the first new moon after Hallowmas.[12] The credo became much longer. Toni Head's brief credo had emphasized reproductive rights and the power of goodness, including "the intrinsic good of all expressions of love between humans." The new credo incorporates these beliefs, and emphasizes that "the Goddess, in her many names and representations, is our connection to the planet and this life cycle." When it comes to membership, the new wording is distinctly separatist. Like the Mother Church credo, it "welcomes all human beings to join without discrimination," but adds, "However, males who embrace our beliefs are required to develop their own rituals and to congregate in separate covenants." The first quotation is from the original Mother Church credo, and the rest is text added by the Pagoda-temple of Love.

Feminism, as it was being theorized in the 1970s and '80s, championed equal rights for all and thus saw itself embracing all social justice endeavors, not just women's rights. The feminism that guided the Pagoda women supported that view but differed from the liberal expressions of feminism usually associated with NOW women like Toni Head. Liberal feminism emphasized the ways that women and men are alike, while lesbian-feminism emphasized and valorized differences in women's lives as a result of being lesbians and woman-centric. Often, as at the Pagoda, lesbian-feminism sought to create women-only spaces to ensure and mobilize women's power and authority. Some feminists rejected beliefs that elevated women's difference and came to denigrate these beliefs as "essentialist"—i.e., having fixed properties that define it, or immutable essences. The Pagoda-temple of Love credo begins with a statement that many feminists would label essentialist: "The Mother Church believes that God, Creator of all, is female, and that everything in nature bears the touch of her divinity." This core belief guided the Pagoda women as they unabashedly celebrated women's monthly cycles at the full moon and made their stage entrances through that giant vagina. Formalizing these practices and beliefs in what became both a state and federally recognized church gave them legitimacy and no doubt contributed to the community's longevity. They were not just a bunch of crazy women howling at the moon on the beach. They were a tax-exempt church, and soon a property-owning tax-exempt church.

In August 1978, thirteen women had pooled resources to make a down payment on the house that became their cultural center, now the legal location of Pagoda-temple of Love. In August 1980, they signed paperwork to turn over that building to the church, becoming members of the Circle of Wise Womyn.[13] Now they no longer had to pay property taxes on the building[14] or file corporate income tax, and they could apply for bulk rate postage, a huge savings in those pre-internet years. Best of all, they were eligible to apply for many grants, and those monthly contributions became charitable donations that people could deduct from their income tax. From then on, anyone who bought a cottage was expected to contribute $600 to the Center and could join the Circle of Wise Womyn.[15] In this way, the community of women living in privately owned cottages was intimately linked to the cultural center that would be a hub of community activity for the next twenty years.

They were a formal church, but the Pagoda women were not strict about how they organized their rites and rituals. Morgana's copy of *The Feminist Book of Light and Shadows* was tattered from use, but she believed strongly in following inner guidance in spiritual matters. Barbara Lieu emphasizes that their circles "were very open, very eclectic" and that they began every circle by inviting women to feel free to contribute something. There was always a framework, but it was adaptable to individual needs. For many years, they cast the circle in age order from youngest to oldest, and the youngest would have certain duties. Sometimes a ritual would be developed into "participatory ritual theatre," Morgana's term for "reenacting Goddess stories with dance, narration, songs, and chants." While the holy day rituals would usually be held upstairs in the big room where they maintained an altar, ritual theatre would be performed in the theatre and might have a script. Morgana still has a script for a 1988 summer solstice ritual with lines for six priestesses, some of it taken from important Wiccan texts like Starhawk's *The Spiral Dance* and Z Budapest's *The Holy Book of Women's Mysteries*. "We usually had a program with words to the songs for all to sing," Morgana recalls. "Two priestesses would sit on the front seats on the aisle and pass out symbols to enable each person to participate in the ritual and to take them with them to place on their home altar." In these ways, dance, theatre, and feminist spirituality were intimately linked in the Pagoda's life as a community, and were part of what made it a healing place for so many women, a sanctuary from the world at large. The church-owned cultural center was what people came for, and it nurtured and sustained them in many ways.

Healing and sanctuary for lesbians were critical in those days when feminist consciousness-raising brought so many women to recognize not only the oppressions of patriarchy but their own longing and desire for the company of other women. Feminist activism gave them the courage to embrace new political ideas,

In the early Pagoda days, the women held scripted ritual downstairs in the theatre. In this rare photo from 1978 or 1979, Barbara Lieu reads from a script while Morgana MacVicar kneels before the altar.

including same-sex romantic love, but it was a harsh world they came out into. In the 1970s and '80s, coming out could mean losing your job, your family, even custody of your children. Psychologists classified homosexuality as a mental illness until 1973, and lesbians rightly feared being locked up in mental hospitals. With few or no role models in the media or among their acquaintances, women wondered if their forbidden feelings meant that they were insane, or that it was wrong to act on them. Emily Greene dropped out of college her senior year in serious emotional distress when her romantic partner told her she thought what they were doing was wrong. Barbara Lieu's parents received a hostile anonymous letter when Barbara and Lavender first became a couple. When Bonnie Netherton, a longtime Pagoda visitor, came out in Atlanta in the 1970s, her feminist divorce lawyer, who had considerable experience in the divorce courts, advised her to "never show my face in a courtroom if I wanted to have anything at all to do with my children." Finding a spiritual sanctuary that celebrated femaleness and welcomed women-loving women was a relief, even lifesaving, for some women.

In addition to the formal church, the Pagoda women explored many spiritual and psychic interests. Both Morgana and Rena had experienced psychic phenomena since childhood. Rena and Kathleen Clementson had regularly attended spiritual workshops and psychic readings at Cassadaga, a community of psychics and faith healers in central Florida. Two professional psychics, Kay Mora and Flash Silvermoon, had close associations with the Pagoda; Kay taught psychic awareness classes that enabled Ellen Spangler to learn channeling. When Barbara and Lavender moved to the Pagoda in 1978, they became friends with one of the tenants, Ruth LeFevre, who did automatic writing. Barbara still has pages of that automatic writing, including the one that produced the Pagoda motto, used on their stationery and in publicity: "Every day there is a song, every night a gift of love, every moon a celebration."

A group of about six Pagoda women had been meeting regularly to explore psychic awareness when Barbara Lieu learned about Kay's psychic work in St. Augustine and invited her to teach them. Kay and Pagoda resident Jean Adele became lovers and were a couple for twenty years, buying Martha Strozier's beachfront lot and building a beach house there, where they lived off and on for about ten years (1984–1993). The Pagoda leaders highly valued Kay's psychic skills and paid her to do readings.

every day there is a song,
every night a gift of love,
every moon a celebration

pagoda

temple of love

Art by Camille Saad

Pagoda logo with channeled motto, used on Pagoda letterhead.

For Morgana, feminist spirituality and ritual were closely tied to bellydancing. Mythological stories powerfully influenced her dance, especially the story of Persephone and Demeter as interpreted by feminist scholar Charlene Spretnak in *Lost Goddesses of Early Greece*.[16] During Morgana's years at the Pagoda, she developed a one-woman show telling the history of patriarchal colonization of women's bodies, using different goddesses: "Each dance with different masks and costumes expressed a different goddess dancing through the herstory of its origins (Gaia) to its subjugation (Hecate) to its rebirth (Kali Ma) and finally its liberation (Diana)." Her study of bellydancing's prepatriarchal origins as a dance of birth informed her practice. She writes of bellydancing:

It did not belong to the Middle East. Middle Eastern women saved it because they had birth tents that they didn't allow men to enter into for a very long time. Women gave birth inside those tents as their sisters danced in a circle to help with natural childbirth and to then celebrate the child at its birth. Every girl learned the dance and carried on the tradition for many centuries.[17]

Morgana also read Tarot cards and often consulted one or more decks, especially for important decisions like buying the Center building. She had learned to read the Tarot from Flash Silvermoon, using a traditional (and patriarchal) Rider deck, but switched to one of the first round decks, Daughters of the Moon by Ffiona Morgan, a Wiccan practitioner with whom she had done a workshop at a women's spirituality festival (Ffiona also did a Pagoda workshop about healing with crystals in March 1985).[18] Later Morgana began using the Goddess Tarot by Kris Waldherr, which includes male images, but returned to Daughters of the Moon because of its Dianic representations (all women).

Ellen Spangler had attended the first-ever women's spirituality conference, held in Boston in 1976, featuring lectures and workshops by many notable lesbians.[19] There were workshops by astrologers, healers, witches, and various kinds of Goddess worshippers. At the end, the conference organizers encouraged everyone to go home and start their own women's circles, and that's what Ellen did back in Jacksonville. By then, Ellen had already been instrumental in founding a domestic violence shelter and was also active in working to prevent the sexual abuse of children, giving workshops at the city's police academy, and combatting the view among some male psychologists that children were to blame for their fathers' sexual abuse of them. This was stressful work and when she learned about the Pagoda, she found it to be "safe and delightful . . , an ideal place for healing all sorts of things."[20] Healing work came naturally to her, and she would eventually become experienced in "inner child" work, believing that many difficulties between people stemmed from inner struggles that could be linked to childhood events that still affected them. Ellen's experience of tapping into a higher power, and letting go with meditation, was something that many Pagoda women regularly practiced, though Ellen and Kay were the only channelers.[21]

Elethia had just completed metaphysical studies with Mary Daly in 1980 when she learned about the Pagoda at the Michigan Womyn's Music Festival. She reserved cottage 1, stayed for six weeks, and would live and work at the Pagoda off and on until 1993. Her undergraduate degree was in theology and psychology, and she would later earn advanced degrees in prophetic ministry and quantum mysticism. She practiced feminist counseling and also pastored at small metaphysical churches.

Many of the musicians who came to the Pagoda also shared an interest in feminist spirituality. One of the earliest well-known lesbian musicians who performed at the Pagoda was Kay Gardner (1941–2001). A legend in lesbian feminist circles, Kay was a talented flutist and composer who often performed at women's music festivals. All of her music is spiritual, and her oratorio *Ouroboros: Seasons of Life* (1992–1994) celebrates the seasons of a woman's life through the Wiccan calendar, from birth (winter solstice) to death/rebirth (Samhain). Morgana had known Kay for many years, often dancing to Kay's flute at women's festivals, and touring with her at least once. Kay's performances at the Pagoda were memorable. She would plan to stay for a week or more and do a workshop on the concert weekend. "Women and Power in Music" was the title of her workshop in 1988.

Singer/songwriter Carole Eagleheart, who had been performing at the Pagoda since 1980 (as Carole Etzler), sometimes included a workshop. In 1988, she and her then partner, Brenda Chambers, offered "Womancircles, an Experience in Music, Art, and Spirituality." In later years, Carole would become a Unitarian Universalist minister of music, and she continues to do workshops at UU churches.

Among Pagoda residents, both Rainbow Williams and She Fay were strongly drawn to feminist spirituality in their music. She Fay and her ensemble Full Circle Round, who often performed at the Pagoda in the 1990s, sang only women-oriented, spiritual, and pagan songs. Rainbow's Amazing Almost All Girl String Band sang a variety of feminist and old-time music, some of it spiritual. The haunting melody of Rainbow's original song "I Am a Channel" accompanies lyrics adapted from a feminist author,[22] beginning

> I am a channel for healing and changing
> I and my sisters, we make new the world.

and ending

> My world is one with, one with the Goddess
> I can just let life ripen and fall.[23]

Flash Silvermoon (1950–2017) considered her band Medusa Music a sort of house band for the Pagoda in the early days, and she regularly performed there solo in later years. Unlike Kay Gardner and Carole Eagleheart, Flash wrote rock and blues, sometimes punk music, like her song "Take a Picture," whose refrain is "Take a picture, it lasts longer baby / dontcha look at me that way."[24] Flash also wrote music specifically for Morgana to dance to. Emily Greene videotaped Flash performing "Dancing with a Snake" while Morgana bellydanced.[25] Flash read Tarot cards (creating her own deck, the Wise Woman's Tarot, 2002), was an animal psychic (her weekly radio show was *What the Animals Tell Me*), and held regular moon circles at Moonhaven, her home in nearby Melrose. In 1990, she began producing a women's festival called Womanspirit Rising at Kanapaha Botanical Gardens in Gainesville. To call the directions, she brought in a "Jewitch Buddhist," a Native American, and a priestess from the Yoruba African community, as well as herself, representing the Wiccan tradition. The Rainbow Goddess Path was her name for this way of bringing together a diversity of spiritual traditions. For eight years in the 2000s, she produced the Wisewoman's Spirituality and Music Festival, which included a sweat lodge and priestesses from different traditions who played music.[26]

Courtesy of Barbara Lieu

Part of a Medusa Music concert flyer from 1979: Pandora Lightmoon on the left, Flash Silvermoon on the right. The flyer also advertised a one-act play the same night, *Save Me a Place at Forest Lawn*, and daytime workshops on astrology and Tarot that weekend.

Pagoda women regularly called on psychic energy to protect their little spot of lesbian community. Kay Mora's "pyramid" on the beach to ward off hurricanes was just one of many ways that the Pagoda women practiced magic. Barbara recalls that they "would always have a bubble of protection around the land," called forth in ritual and also established with crystals buried at the corners of the property. They needed that kind of protection from a world in which women, and especially lesbians, were not safe.

While not every Pagoda resident or guest was interested in feminist spirituality or attended rituals, the spiritual practices the women performed regularly in the cultural center and church, and the creative work they nourished, permeated the whole place. It was the ground they stood on, the air they breathed, whether they knew it or not. It was magic.

But a church-owned business also has bills to pay, and the resort business model was not working for them financially. In order for the cultural center that had become central to the community to survive, they needed to change.

Builders
1981–1987

Emily Greene's cottage, the Lily, being renovated in 1985. The bathroom was moved to the back of the second bedroom and the kitchen was expanded to fit a small stove and refrigerator. That meant hanging Sheetrock and changing windows. Martine Giguère is hanging a window on the right. On the left, Rose DeBernardo is using power tools.

Photo by Emily Greene

Chapter 5
Going Residential

What I have called the Builders period, from 1981 through 1987, marks a passage from founding a resort and cultural center to a focus on building the residential community surrounding the cultural center. The founders never had a formal business plan with budgets and details for making them balance. What they had was enthusiasm, vision, feminist ideals, and sufficient economic resources to obtain shared mortgages on property dedicated to creating an island of safety, celebration, and spiritual sustenance for women. The Builders built on the foundation that was established, gradually developing a new business model that worked better for both the cultural center and the residential community. Turning the Center into a guesthouse and switching to long-term cottage rentals allowed the women to build a thriving residential community surrounding a thriving community center. Three key founders were part of that work—Morgana, Barbara, and Lavender--joined by many more full-time residents.

The Pagoda came to these big changes through community burnout. By the spring of 1981, the business side of living there was encroaching on the women's personal lives and, for those actively involved in keeping it going, the work was becoming onerous. Emily Greene recalls that time:

We were having a steady stream of visitors and I was working full-time at a local nursing home. I can remember how we each had to take on jobs to keep the rental situation going—reservationist, greeter, cleaner of rental units—and often answer questions and talk with our visitors. Most of the time this was wonderful and interesting, but there were moments for each of us where we just didn't want to go up to the Center building to pick up our mail because we might run into a visitor.[1]

That spring, residents began meeting to explore new visions for what the Pagoda might be and how to manifest those visions. They had learned that managing nightly cottage rentals was no way to build a community. They needed more full-time residents in those cottages, but to sustain the cultural center, they needed to make space available to supporters who were sending in monthly donations. The community of residents and cottage owners came together to figure out what to do next to build their community.

About eight women were then living at the Pagoda. These were the women who charted the course of the next phase of community life at the Pagoda. Morgana, Emily, Barbara, and Lavender lived full-time at the Pagoda throughout this second phase of the community's development. Martha Strozier, a psychotherapist, had bought cottage 1 from Suzi Chance, and was soon joined by her life partner Dore (pronounced Dory) Rotundo, an architect; playwright Trudy Anderson was renting Rena's cottage; Meri Furnari (known as mica, which was intentionally lowercase) was living downstairs at the duplex. Martha and Dore were dividing their time between Melrose and the Pagoda. Laura Folk (then called Inca) was renting a room in the Center. Laura, at twenty-three, was the youngest; Martha and Dore, in their midforties, were the oldest.

Martha and Dore had been together almost two years at the time of the "going residential" meetings. Martha was from Savannah, and had inherited wealth that she controlled, the only Pagoda woman at that time who had substantial resources in her own hands. She had been married twice and was working in Jacksonville when she heard about the Pagoda opening night, attended, and immediately wanted to get involved. When Suzi needed to sell her cottage the following spring, Martha says, "I jumped on it. I didn't hesitate. . . . I was planning to move there, be there. That was my ticket to get in. . . . Well, I mean it convinced Dore that I was serious."

Dore grew up in Utica, New York, but her family had moved to Florida the year she graduated from high school, and she went to college at the University of Florida, becoming the second woman to graduate from its architecture program. When she met Martha in 1979, she had been living in Melrose, practicing architecture on the side while supporting herself teaching architectural drawing at Gainesville High School. In Melrose, Dore became friends with Corky Culver and other lesbian-feminist activists living at the Red House there.[2] These friendships led her to leave her husband and join the North Forty land group, teaching the others how to build a house with hand tools. After meeting Martha, Dore's life took a new direction. She began spending a lot of time at the Pagoda, renting space in the duplex and then the Center, attending business meetings, and even acting in *Princess Cinderella* in 1980. Earlier, Dore had contributed to the theatre by replacing an obstructive post on the stage with a box beam.

Martha regularly attended monthly business meetings once she got involved in buying Lot 4 (the second strip of cottages), often taking meeting notes. She took over correspondence from Lavender for a time, assisted in bookkeeping off and on, and gave workshops on sexuality, Gestalt therapy, and art therapy.

She hired Ellen Spangler and others to remodel cottage 1, and would soon buy cottage 2 for Dore, who needed more space for her work than Martha's cottage could hold. During this period, Martha and Dore treated those cottages mostly as vacation homes, and only sometimes as office space; they sold them in 1983. Martha and Dore would share their lives for the next forty years and maintained their Pagoda connections throughout the life of the community.

Courtesy of Emily Greene

Emily Greene on the doorstep of cottage 6, which she bought in 1982. She would live there, next door to Barbara and Lavender, until she moved into town in 1992.

Emily Greene had broken up with Wiggy (now called Nu) the previous summer. She had sold her share of cottage 8 to Nu and was hoping to buy her own cottage. Meanwhile, she was renting the upstairs of the duplex, shared with Gaby Penning, a German citizen who had been living at the Pagoda since about 1980 and would room with Emily until she returned to Germany in 1985.[3] Gaby had had a fling with Nu after the breakup but soon became good friends (never lovers) with Emily.

Laura Folk had heard about the Pagoda while attending Flagler College in St. Augustine, where she came out with her girlfriend. At that time, coming out was dangerous, and no one talked much about being gay or lesbian, except at the Pagoda, where she learned about the Goddess, feminism, and much more. She graduated from Flagler in 1979, moved to the Pagoda the next year, and worked various Pagoda jobs, such as greeter and reservationist, while renting space. She took a role in *Princess Cinderella* the summer of 1980, playing Prince Charming's wicked adviser. In 1981, she was working at the Clamshell, a restaurant across the highway from the Pagoda, and would soon be moving to New Mexico, where she lived for a year in a tepee at Arf, rugged women's land near Santa Fe.

mica had grown up in the South Bronx, married, and participated in starting two intentional communities with heterosexual couples before coming out in 1975 in Burlington, Vermont. In 1980, she was traveling with a feminist medicine show that unexpectedly disbanded when their bus broke down. Left stranded in New York City, with no job and no plans, she phoned her Burlington roommates, who suggested that she check out the separatist women's community they had heard about in Florida. So she took Amtrak to Jacksonville and caught a ride to St. Augustine, where she found a job in town, a cottage to share at the Pagoda, and a new girlfriend.

Playwright Trudy Anderson (sometimes known as Seaweed or Tinker) had moved to the Pagoda in December 1978 from Washington, D.C., and would live and work there in various capacities until 1982. The Pagoda had produced several of her plays in the summer of 1979, and produced her very popular one-act *An Afternoon of Sophie and Myrtle* several times. She rented various Pagoda cottages as well as Center space, and had various romantic partners.

Six of these women—all living and working at the Pagoda, but only three of them cottage owners—attended the first "going residential" meeting without Barbara, Lavender, and Morgana, and then reported to the larger group:

> We have no womyn willing or available to work the cottage rental jobs anymore. Most of us have taken our turn at this work and have burned out completely. The energy here at the Pagoda is so scattered, we want to use and focus our energies for our community and most especially to further develop the cultural center.[4]

They announced an all-day workshop for further discussion and solicited "your input in person or by letter." In true Pagoda fashion and synchronicity, Z Budapest spent ten days at the Pagoda that same month and facilitated a circle.

Photo by Emily Greene

"Going residential" meeting, April 17, 1981, upstairs at the cultural center. *Left to right*: mica (Meri Furnari), Barbara Lieu, Dore Rotundo (standing), Martha Strozier, Lavender Lieu, and Trudy Anderson. The geisha drawing in the upper right corner was done by Linda Mack in 1979 as a logo for Pagoda Productions.

On April 17, 1981, fifteen women attended the all-day workshop.[5] Barbara and Dore took notes with Magic Marker on big sheets of paper mounted on the wall of the big upstairs room at the Center. The brainstorming notes include hopes and dreams like "outdoor theatre," "more parties more fun," "more artwork," "adequate parking," "menless beach," "GARDEN," "more responsible workers with own vehicles." They discussed and approved a letter to supporters and "absentee cottage owners" that Lavender drafted, and set September 1 as the target date for switching to monthly rentals only. The letter to supporters explains just how burned out they are, but puts a positive spin on it:

> Dealing with a constant influx of new womyn takes a great deal of emotional energy, and we often find ourselves too drained to put on the kinds of events we want to have here. The business, as it is now, has burned us out. Making the rental part simpler and more manageable will give us time to pursue the creative endeavors we always envisioned the Pagoda having. We view this change in direction not as an end but as a new beginning.[6]

This new beginning for the residential community addressed more than burnout. They expected it to solve some financial problems, too. Their original business model connected management of the cultural center to management of cottage rentals, with 20 percent of cottage rental income going to management, and the rest of Center funding coming from supporter donations and fund-raisers like yard sales and raffles.[7] But management income from cottage rentals was not covering salaries (bookkeeper, reservationist, greeter, etc.). For example, the financial report for October 1980 shows management income at $257.75, and salaries for the same period at $399.50. At the November business meeting the women calculated that they "can't make it through the winter even if every cottage was rented nightly!"

This is an exaggeration, but they were certainly feeling the pinch and looking at cutting down staff or finding other sources of money. They didn't even consider raising their rates, which were $20 a night (for one or two people), $115 a week, $175 a month for a one-bedroom or $200 a month for a two-bedroom.[8] It was the feminist way as they saw it, and the Builders put heart and soul into trying to make it work.

Turning the cultural center into a guesthouse directly connected rental management expenses to other expenses of maintaining the building, but it was still hard to make ends meet. Handling short-stay rentals in the 1980s was a very different matter from today's internet-reliant reservation systems through VRBO, Airbnb, or even email, none of which existed then. It was labor intensive, relying on phone reservations and paper calendars. Someone had to answer that phone, take the reservations (and the changes to reservations), check the answering machine (when it was working), and make sure the messages got to the right place. Usually, that was several different people, since their budget never covered anyone full-time.

It was a recipe for burnout and staff turnover. That they persisted so long is a testament to the Pagoda women's commitment to their lesbian-feminist vision of providing safe space for women at affordable rates, while paying fair wages to workers. This practice nearly always guaranteed financial stress if not shortfall. In the early days, Morgana did most of the reservations, bookkeeping, and greeting, and she realized that she was earning about $1.00 an hour. After that, they began dividing up the work and attempting to pay an hourly rate above minimum wage, usually between $4.00 and $5.00, when the minimum wage was $2.90 to $3.80.[9] In May 1981, they divided the paid work of cottage rentals among six positions, reorganized to bring the total staff expenses down to $330 a month, plus housecleaning costs. They were already asking guests to bring their own sheets and towels or else pay extra for laundry. Often they exchanged skilled work for nights at the Center, and they were always looking for volunteers to help with renovations like fence building and cleanup. The only way they ever came out ahead on Center expenses was through supporter donations and fund-raisers. Fortunately, they were building a network of supporters who shared their desire for women's space and came through time and again when their feminist business model did not make ends meet.

The attic of the Center became the most sought-after sleep space because it had a wonderful ocean view. Rena had lived in the attic that first year when they were still leasing the two-story house. In September 1981, they started reserving the attic as supporter space, or temporary sleep space, as when Jean Adele moved to the Pagoda that fall before the cottage she was renting was ready. Performers could stay there, too. In December 1983, they started renovating the attic to extend sleep space under the eaves. By March they had room for eight in the attic, "with a possible 6 in the eaves, bring bedding." Considering that you had to climb a ladder to get to the attic from indoors (there were exterior steps, too), this was rustic sleep space, with no bathroom, but it was popular!

The Pagoda women went back and forth about allowing camping, especially vehicle camping with hookup to the Center. Mostly, they allowed it, and for tent camping there was a campground down the road. They also began working on Persephone's Pit as a place for day visitors to hang out. Dore got estimates for adding an outdoor shower and toilet there, which would be useful to campers, but that was too expensive. Instead they worked on beautification with plantings and a picnic table near the fire pit. Campers used a bathroom in the duplex, with an exterior door.

In the first two years after the switch to long-term cottage rentals, community membership frequently changed. By the fall of 1981, mica and her partner had moved to San Francisco, Laura and Trudy moved away in 1982, and Martha and Dore sold their cottages in 1983. But by the summer of 1983, most of the women living at the Pagoda would remain for a decade or more. Barbara and Lavender lived at the Pagoda well into the 1990s, with Emily their next-door neighbor from 1982 to 1992, when she bought a house in town. Morgana, too, was a long-term resident, renting her cottage off and on, and even expanding it in 1987 to allow her to visit while renting it in the summers. She spent winters at the Pagoda until 1997.

Several new women became permanent residents and important contributors to the community in these years of building community, notably Elethia and Edith George, who bought Martha and Dore's cottages in 1983; Rainbow Williams, who moved into the downstairs duplex in 1984; and Nancy Breeze, who rented from Rainbow and others from 1984 until 1988, when she bought her own cottage.

Elethia (born Bonnie Lee) lived in cottage 1 until 1993, working many Pagoda jobs during those years, including newsletter editor and cottages bookkeeper. Trained in both counseling and prophetic ministry, she was deeply interested in the spiritual work of the community and sometimes performed same-sex marriage ceremonies.

Rainbow Williams was a multidisciplinary artist who had been visiting from her home in Winter Park since 1978. In 1979 she made a $600 donation to the church in order to get on the Cottage Eligibility List.[10] She often published stories about the Pagoda in the feminist newsletter she edited, *Changes,* including reviews of performances and notices of upcoming events. In Winter Park (near Orlando), she had taught herself to play dulcimer and started a dulcimer band, the Amazing Almost All Girl String Band, "two artists and two lesbians who could sing or play some outrageous feminist materials." (She added "almost" to the band's name to make it sound interesting—it was always all-girl.) Rainbow bought the downstairs duplex in 1982 and moved there full-time in 1984. Once she moved into the duplex, she became an important part of the Pagoda community throughout its life.

Nancy Breeze had been weekending from Gainesville since the seventies, and her name came up often when residents were figuring out how to shift to long-term rentals. "What about Nancy Breeze?" they asked, wanting to make a way for her to continue her Pagoda weekends. Nancy Breeze's commitment to the Pagoda community prompted the Pagoda women to turn the cultural center into a guesthouse, creating more short-term sleep space for visitors. Nancy moved from Gainesville to St. Augustine in 1983 and spent most of the next ten years living full-time at the Pagoda, sometimes renting cottage 7, owned by the three members of the Berkeley Women's Music Collective, other times renting space in the duplex from Rainbow, before buying her own cottage.

Edith George, a Pagoda supporter since 1981, bought cottage 2 in February 1983. Edith had known Rainbow through NOW in Orlando and had attended the first performance of Rainbow's Almost All Girl String Band there in 1978.[11] She would live at the Pagoda until 1999, joined in 1986 by her life partner, Joycie Meyers. Before finding the Pagoda, Edith had spent twenty years in the army, retiring as a first sergeant, and then earned a computer science degree and managed a data processing department for a Florida municipality. She regularly attended Pagoda business meetings and often volunteered for work like having the pump house cleaned and repaired, or collecting cottage owners' share of the pest control contract and the shared water bill. She was practical, reliable, and assertive (she had been a drill sergeant). Edith was especially active in a project called Crones Nest.

Joycie Meyers was from north Georgia and had married while still in high school. By the time she found Edith and the Pagoda, she had been married four times, had a master's degree, and was working in St. Augustine as a licensed mental health counselor with a focus on substance abuse and alcoholism counseling.[12] She was a talented writer and participated in a Pagoda writers group that met in the Pagoda library. In a videotaped reading the writers group did on Christmas 1987 in the Pagoda theatre, Joycie read poetry and diary entries, often focused on observations of nature, with which she felt a strong connection. She remarked on how at writers group "we get high in the library," connecting that to research showing that intellectuals get the same phero- mone high that athletes experience, only from intellectual pur- suits.[13] Joycie did not attend many Pagoda business meetings or get involved in Pagoda business until the mid-1990s, but she did volunteer work like putting the Pagoda concert mailing list on her word processor. Edith and Joycie were a generation older than most of the Pagoda women—both were born in the 1930s— and their wise counsel was valued and often sought.

These long-term residents were the Builders, who devoted these years to building a lesbian culture in this community and especially in their cultural center.

Chapter 6
Building Lesbian Culture

During the 1980s, feminist Tarot cards, labrys earrings, and buttons that say "I Know You Know" became signals of lesbian culture. Until the 1970s, lesbians often felt isolated, with few places to meet one another outside of lesbian bars, if they even knew the bars—or other lesbians—existed.[1] Many lesbians felt as though they must be the only one and searched in vain for books with a positive view of lesbian life. That changed in the 1970s and '80s, when communal spaces like women's music festivals, women's centers, and feminist bookstores joined lesbian bars as places for women to be together, meet other lesbians, and learn what they were thinking and reading—places to build lesbian culture. The Pagoda was such a place. There women could experience lesbian identity as a positive thing, a move from outsider status, to finding their tribe.[2]

Like many women who established women-only communities, Pagoda women saw building lesbian culture communally as a form of living feminism—that is, practicing the ideals of feminist politics. At the Pagoda, that meant honoring and appreciating women as women, respecting individual needs for alcohol-free, drug-free, meat-free, men-free space, and making sure that space reflected their ideals. The ambience of the place was immediately recognizable as special, set off from the mainstream culture outside their gates. The Pagoda guesthouse and cultural center surrounded visitors with cultural artifacts in their wall hangings and bulletin board, their store and library. They often explored ways of honoring women of other cultures and generations, and they took a special interest in honoring aging. For them lesbian culture meant caring about women across generations and marking transitions in their lives. Above all, they built lesbian culture in their cultural events, celebrating women loving women in music, art, and theatre.

Cultural events at the Pagoda often included a blend of dance, theatre, visual arts, writing, and music—all mixed well with lesbian-feminist politics. Throughout the 1980s, Morgana danced regularly at Pagoda events and also painted pottery at her cottage, selling it at the Pagoda store and later at Mountain Mamas, a consignment shop for women artists that she and others started in Cloudland, Georgia. Artists of all kinds would come to the Pagoda to live, sometimes buying a cottage. Indeed, the Pagoda became a magnet for lesbian artists, despite the fact that the accommodations were rustic and the likelihood of selling much art on site was low. Making art was another story. Musicians wrote new songs while at the Pagoda, visual artists painted (sometimes directly on the walls of the Center), Morgana taught bellydancing and herself wrote a small book about the woman-centered roots of that misunderstood art form.[3]

The feminist theatre that had flourished with Trudy Anderson and Rena Carney in residence went into a decade-long lull after both moved away. Trudy's last play produced at the Pagoda was *A Rose Is a Rose Has Arose*. Performed in April 1982, with Elethia as Gertrude Stein and Dore Rotundo as Alice B. Toklas, the play is a comic celebration of the life of the famous lesbian couple. Elethia and Dore also performed it in Gainesville and in St. Augustine at Café Anastasia. It was Elethia's one and only acting role. When the July 1982 newsletter announced that Trudy was leaving permanently, the Pagoda Playhouse era was over.[4]

Music took center stage with concerts, dances, and sometimes open mic year round. The new women's music was an exciting expression of lesbian culture in the 1970s, '80s, and '90s. Many women musicians were finding their audience among women hungry for the affirmation pouring from their songs. Performers sang about lesbian romance and love as well as about important political issues, and it all appealed to lesbian-feminist audiences. The attraction was mutual: the audiences loved the music and the musicians loved the audience, especially at the Pagoda. Everyone noticed that there was something special strongly attracting women to the place.

The Berkeley Women's Music Collective (BWMC) experience shows just how extraordinary that pull was. The BWMC had just begun touring when they drove from California to Florida to play for the Pagoda grand opening. They had heard about the Pagoda through the women's music grapevine. Nancy Vogl remembers being impressed from the moment they arrived:

> When we drove up in the van, I felt like I was having some cosmic flashback or something because I was immediately transported back in time! St. Augustine felt exactly like the old beach cities in California during the fifties. I was enamored and just couldn't get enough of it. I fell madly in love with the cottages from the minute we pulled into the driveway. . . . We couldn't comprehend a bunch of lesbian feminists moving into St. Augustine, Florida, boldly proclaiming that they were feminists, buying a sizable property, and then creating a female/Goddess centered cultural center (a temple) that would bring in lesbians from all over the United States. It was truly mind-blowing. The bravery of these women cannot be overstated.

Nancy Vogl (right) with BWMC member Suzanne Shanbaum next to the band's van, Helva. The band also named their Pagoda cottage Helva. Vogl and Shanbaum continued to perform together after the BWMC disbanded in 1979.

It is amazing how many well-known musicians performed in that tiny theatre over the years. The roster of musicians who performed at the Pagoda reads like a Who's Who of women's music of the day: Alix Dobkin played there regularly, Kay Gardner several times, and June Millington came every chance she got, if only to visit. Holly Near, Lucie Blue Tremblay, Ferron, the Washington Sisters, Jamie Anderson, Karen Beth, Deidre Mc-Calla—all played at the Pagoda at least once.

Local and regional musicians came often, too. As mentioned earlier, Flash Silvermoon performed there often, sometimes splitting the evening with Rainbow Williams's Amazing Almost All Girl String Band. Flash played a mix of styles, from rock to jazz, all her own music, while Rainbow's band played old-time string band tunes, political songs like Malvina Reynolds's "We Don't Need the Men," and Rainbow's original songs, such as "Amelia," her tribute to Amelia Earhart. Both also played spiritual music like Flash's "Sacred Space" and Rainbow's "I Am a

Channel." Jane Yii and Cecily Paige, from the Gainesville area, performed together as Cecily Jane. The duo sang close harmony, mostly on songs that Jane wrote. A publicity flyer from 1994 describes them as "Florida's premier folk duo."[5] After they broke up, Jane performed solo at the Pagoda.

With tickets selling for as low as one or two dollars in the early days, and never more than fifteen dollars, no one was making much money on a Pagoda concert. Musicians came for other reasons: for the experience of being in women's space and playing for an appreciative audience unlike what they would find elsewhere. Performing at the Pagoda was never about the money, Jamie Anderson says: "I played there because of the women's community. I played there because I knew that I would have an audience of women who understood me, an audience of women who would enjoy my work. To me that was a much higher priority than putting a lot of money in my pocket. . . . At the Pagoda, they always cared. It was wonderful."

Musicians recall the energy they felt there, and often described the Pagoda as "safe space." June Millington spoke vividly:

> Pagoda was really a lodestar for me because it was private, set away, like a jewel or a gift. The fact that it was not so well-known was really fabulous because I could just be there, and every time I went there I felt like a seed had been planted in the ground, and I could just hang out and not only watch it grow but be a big part of its growth. . . . It was fantastic! I would go into this sacred space, really, within a sacred space, within the larger women's music world. This was like a deep, deep, deep inner place, and that's how I experienced it.
>
> It was like being in the center of a conch shell or something. And you could hear the echoes resounding from all

of time, really, if you just listened. You could hear it, you could feel it, you could read it. I mean it literally. When I say I felt like I was a seed who was replanted every time I went there and got to grow and was nourished, that's not a metaphor.

Part of the richness of the Pagoda experience was that it provided the rare commodity of lesbian-only or women-only space, much treasured at that time. Abby Bogomolny, a Gainesville musician from 1974 to 1984, who had moved to Florida from New York when Flash Silvermoon did (and would move permanently to California in 1984), recalls the Pagoda as "an island, a refuge, for you to do your primary work and feed yourself." She has a happy memory of connecting with Flash Silvermoon and June Millington while they were all staying at the Center. They stayed up all night playing, talking, and doing psychic readings:

> By the dawn, we all realized we had this profound connection, and we understood that we had known each other a very long time—as in previous lives. Flash and I and June and I, we had a stellar connection. . . . Our essences were connected deeply. And there were no drugs involved. . . . This was pure musical, psychic energy. A place like the Pagoda allowed this to happen. It allowed women's space. That safe space is a requirement for such life-changing journeys.

Elaine Townsend, a South Carolina musician who performed regularly at the Pagoda in the 1980s and later lived there, also remembers how supportive Pagoda audiences were, and that they would talk back:

Photo by Emily Greene

Elaine Townsend performing
at the Pagoda in May 1984.

The women sat and listened, sang along, chuckled if something was funny. But if someone took exception to something I said (that is, if I wasn't quite advanced enough in my evolution as a feminist), the person felt empowered to call me out on it. I learned about the give-and-take with an audience there. It can be literally a dialogue. I really think of Lavender when I recall this. It probably only happened once or twice, but it never happened anywhere else that I performed. I couldn't see the audience because of lighting, so out of the darkness would come a voice saying, "I have a problem with that." It was just a statement of truth, and some small discussion might ensue, and then the performance would continue. When I look back and think of that, it was really very dear. She didn't wait until after the performance to pull me aside and discuss it. It was right in the moment. I *loved* that about her! I learned so much from her.

Barbara and Lavender knew Elaine from South Carolina through their Columbia friends, the Columbia Lu's (Mary Bateman and Camille Saad), whom they had met at the same NOW conference where the Lieus came out to each other. Fifteen years younger, Elaine looked to them as mentors.

Lesbian-feminist activism was in the air at the Pagoda, and it often inspired artistic activity. Guest books include drawings and poetry. Nancy Vogl wrote four songs while staying at the Pagoda, including "Matanzas" and "Hagology." Elaine Townsend wrote "Song for Me" and "Fight Back," copying them into the guest book. "Song for Me" (1984) speaks to the importance of self-care, while "Fight Back" is more of an anthem about what to do with the strength regained by nourishing the spirit. Elaine recalls the audience joining her on the refrain: "Fight Back! Fight Back!"

Fight Back
By Elaine Townsend
July 19, 1985, from the attic guest book

Hold on to your anger
Don't let it fade.
Don't bury it in some feeble attempt
To create a Safe Space.
    There is no safety
    In this world of woman hate
    There is no promise of a better life
    If we don't work to lift the weight
    Their constant message of powerlessness
    Will keep us where we are
    If we don't Fight Back! Fight Back!

Cling to your Sadness, but don't let it cling to you
Take the very power it has and put it to use
    If we internalize
    The pain that they inflict
    It only takes us to that weaker space
    It only brings us down

Don't push away the very force
That gives us Energy to Fight Back! Fight Back!

There was the positive energy, the safe space, all of that, and also "it was *really* fun to do it," remembers Carole Eagleheart, who performed nearly every year at the Pagoda in the 1980s, and often in the 1990s. The title song on her album *Thirteen Ships* (1985) comes from the vision of a Pagoda resident in the eighties. "I always stopped in even if I wasn't doing a concert that year," Eagleheart recalls. "I never missed a chance to come to the Pagoda."

For performers, there was little incentive to become a Pagoda supporter, making monthly donations in exchange for beach time at the Center, because beach time at the Center was most of what performers got for playing the small theatre. Yet Alix Dobkin was a paying supporter from the start, since she connected so strongly with the underlying principle that becoming a supporter meant you had a share in the Pagoda. Here is how she put it in a guest book entry from November 1981:

> The idea that Center supporters who spend time here contribute their work, creativity, goods to the Center is extremely appealing! I love that we can share space (serial tenancy) and share responsibility for it. I love being in an environment created consciously and with care by other lesbians. When D[enslow] & I arrived, we were happy to throw out the dirty old rug up in the attic—to improve the environment. We feel like it's our space. It is. And it's yours, too.

Nancy Vogl's experience of owning a Pagoda cottage for ten years (1978–1988), even while living almost three thousand miles away in California, speaks to the power of the Pagoda's symbolism.

After all these years, I still remember what it felt like to be there because I like small spaces, and always have. There was something about being in that cottage by the ocean, in that protected space women had created, that allowed me to be more fully present with myself—what I was thinking, what I was doing. There was a solo/mindfulness that I experienced there that I still cherish to this day and honestly miss. It seemed impossible to re-create it here on the West Coast, but it's something I treasure and hold deeply as a part of myself—to be awakened in a way that I had not experienced before.

Visual artists, too, came from far and near to exhibit their work at the Pagoda. Myriam Fougère, a Quebecoise visual artist, had seen a Pagoda flyer at Bloodroot Vegetarian Restaurant & Bookstore in Bridgeport, Connecticut, advertising a free week at the beach in exchange for mounting an art show. Myriam became a supporter in 1984, and she and her then partner, Martine Giguère, stayed for two months when they came to exhibit Myriam's sculpture the following year.[6]

Artist, musician, and instrument maker Rainbow Williams began driving up from Winter Park on weekends after buying the downstairs of the duplex in 1982. Rainbow spearheaded most of the Pagoda art shows, often held at the same time as concerts. Her first big exhibit at the Pagoda was "Junk, Funk, and Xerox" (1985), a monthlong community show in which she and her then partner, Sarah Carawan, invited lesbians to create and post self-portraits. They had over thirty contributors, and the show was part of spring equinox celebrations. Rainbow would repeat it in 1988.

Most of the film showings at the Pagoda were videos from their extensive video library or slideshows by visiting artists, but several lesbian filmmakers and photographers visited Pagoda in this period. Experimental filmmaker Arian Sanz wanted to move to the Pagoda and still had a trailer parked there as late as 1982.[7] Although none of Arian's Pagoda films have so far surfaced (Arian Sanz died in Hawaii in 2016), Rena Carney recalls Arian filming her dancing with Morgana, and says that the resulting films were very abstract and artistic.

Sculptor Myriam Fougère turned to documentary film while living at the Pagoda, where she got her first movie camera and shot her first film, *Lesbian Art* (1989). She liked to stage artistic scenes with symbolic meaning, such as a woman sweeping sand into the ocean. She also made a sand sculpture: "a woman lying in the sand, and then I filmed it as the wave was coming, and the wave came between her legs, and the vulva-sand sculpture, too." Years later, she used parts of that short film in her widely viewed one-hour documentary *Lesbiana: A Parallel Revolution* (2012).

Legendary lesbian photographers also visited. Tee Corinne had an exhibit called "Tea to Tee at Two" in the theatre in February 1987. JEB (Joan E. Biren) visited in 1984 while giving slide-shows in Gainesville and Jacksonville, although no JEB events show up in Pagoda advertising. Not so well-known is the painter, photographer, flautist June Parlett Norsworthy, who drove up from Tampa with her "Sandwiched Woman Slide Show," which she had been touring for several years.[8] A sandwiched slide is created by putting two slides together, creating interesting effects. While showing the slides, June played her flute to recordings of Margie Adam's "My Best Friend Is the Unicorn" and "We Shall Go Forth."

Salons were another variety of culture building that the Pagoda explored in these years, beginning about 1982, the same year that a long-running lesbian salon began on the Gulf Coast of Florida, in St. Petersburg.[9] Salons were a cultural phenomenon of the time, harking back to the artistic and literary gatherings made famous in lesbian circles by the women of the Left Bank in Paris that Shari Benstock writes about[10]—Gertrude Stein, Alice B. Toklas, Natalie Barney, etc.— and long before that by eighteenth-century French and English intellectuals. Salons at the Pagoda often featured poetry readings, film, slideshows, dance, and sometimes music. Formality and variety seem to be the distinguishing feature between, say, the advertised poetry reading by Minnie Bruce Pratt (June 17, 1985), and the advertised Wimmin's Salon, when Gainesville residents Carol Aubin, Nancy Breeze, and Sandy Cosgrave "read poetry and writings," Gaby Penning read from Petra Kelly's new book *Fighting for Hope*, Rainbow played her dulcimer, and Morgana danced.[11] In December 1986, they had a discussion of Sarah Hoagland's "Some Thoughts on Power in Our Interactions," the first of monthly meetings of lesbians talking about something they read. The following January, they had a poetry/slideshow/jam session with Leslita Williams and Feral Woolsocks, from Atlanta. They advertised "Bring your harmonica, washtub, banjo, guitar or comb," and the February newsletter says they "performed their poetry to a packed Pagoda Playhouse."

Alongside this wealth of cultural events, mostly held downstairs in the theatre, the Pagoda women also maintained two important culture builders, the store and the library. One of the first things that Morgana and Rena had done when they leased the building was set up a store on the second floor. That area soon became Barbara and Lavender's pet project. They developed the cultural center by making the store a Discount Natural Food and Wimmin's Crafts store and collecting books for a library. Both of these ventures became favorites for guests and residents alike.

Always a tiny space, the store went through many manifestations. Barbara and Lavender cultivated a connection with a local natural food co-op in order for Pagoda residents to regularly order food at a discount. At the Pagoda, they sold snacks, cold drinks, and popsicles. Residents and guests have fond memories of a refrigerator well stocked with ice cream. In addition to food, they sold Pagoda memorabilia (T-shirts, postcards), as well as the feminist music, jewelry, books, and crafts that you might find at a women's music festival or in a feminist bookstore. Camille Saad, the artist who designed the logo used on Pagoda stationery, also designed a logo for the store, accepting as payment a stay with her girlfriend in a cottage over New Year's 1980–1981. In the Pagoda newsletter, the store advertised new products and new acquisitions to the library.[12] Barbara and Lavender ran both on the honor system, simply leaving a box on the counter labeled "Pay Here," and that worked most of the time.

It took longer to set up the library than the store. Morgana, Barbara, Lavender, and many others donated books. Barbara Deming and others donated money for shelving, and visiting playwright Trudy Anderson donated many scripts. Barbara and Lavender bought used books at thrift stores and yard sales, eventually adding videos to the collection. Barbara did the cataloging, though she had no previous library experience, and the borrowing was informal—"just take a book." Guests and performers who stayed in the Center recall the library admiringly. Here is June Millington: "They also had a great library, so I would read all of these books about women's lives: Marian Anderson, you name it, poets. . . . It was fantastic! . . . I'd get books from the library, and Ann [Hackler, June's partner] and I would drink coffee and hang out and just go off into bliss." Some residents and visitors credit the Pagoda library with raising their feminist consciousness. Shyne, who grew up in St. Augustine and began visiting the Pagoda in her teens, recalls that the feminist books she found there were "eye-opening and life changing. Writers like Audre Lorde, Barbara Deming, Rita Mae Brown, Gloria Steinem. Autobiographies and biographies. Whatever they had on Janis Joplin. . . . I read everything I could get my hands on. I was very fortunate that this happened to me at such a young age, before I stumbled into marriage and children."

In the spring of 1984, the Pagoda women added a couch so the library space could be rented as sleep space, too, and by the following spring they were out of shelf space for books. In 1988, Barbara and Lavender sold the store to Pagoda supporter Ski Kaye, who lived next door in the triplex that Pagoda women called the Tower. Ski wanted to concentrate on selling books, but the store had closed by 1989.[13] The library moved into the space that had been the store and lasted for the life of the cultural center, often doubling as office space for part-time guesthouse managers. The old library space became the Lavender Room, a sleep space with a double bed and an ocean view.

Photo by Emily Greene

Left to right: Gaby, Shyne, and Elethia about 1981.

As these reshufflings of furniture and books suggest, the space was funky and eccentric. The store and the library were adjacent to the meeting room, where both business meetings and rituals were held. The altar was there, and they also had meals and celebrations in that room. The proximity of these regular activities created the special ambience that was the Pagoda. Ann Hackler describes it like this in the attic guest book for December 1986:

> Lying in bed in THE ATTIC space, listening to the activity below: The debates over lesbian only circles, the "business" details, the store order being received and put away and all of it to the assuring sound of the ocean / always in the presence of the altar / wandering through the store—I feel like I'm in a lesbian novel—Daughters of the Coral Dawn or something[14]—but I'm here in this place that has been made with the hands of many women—I feel honored.

Being at the Pagoda *was* like being in a lesbian novel because the Pagoda women very consciously used the space to manifest the lesbian-feminist values that constitute lesbian culture. Respect for elder women and rejection of ageism were among these values. They draw on feminist spirituality and its valuing of the Divine Feminine and the maiden-mother-crone archetypes, which led to a nationwide trend toward "croning" women as they reached age fifty (or fifty-six in some circles). Z Budapest has been credited with starting the trend in California, and "crone" is one of the words that Mary Daly reclaims in *Gyn/Ecology*. Lesbians in Gainesville recall that Nancy Breeze was the first among them to be croned in a surprise ceremony planned for her fiftieth birthday by her friends, especially Flash Silvermoon, who may have been influenced by her friend Z Budapest. Nancy's croning was in February 1982 in Gainesville, and Nancy would participate in many more cronings both in Gainesville and at the Pagoda. She wrote a story about it for *Southern Breeze* magazine,[15] and the editors insisted that she provide photographs to prove it wasn't a hoax! She sent them photographs of the first croning at the Pagoda, held at the 1983 winter solstice, honoring Ellen Spangler and her then partner, Rose DeBernardo. Festive croning rituals became a tradition at the Pagoda. They were usually scheduled for pagan holy days with elaborate planning, decoration, and costuming. Rainbow had her croning in March 1984 (when she turned fifty), and for many years Pagodans offered croning ceremonies in association with Hallowmas. The Hallowmas croning in 1986 for Jean Adele, Joycie Myers, and a last-minute Canadian visitor known as Mountain had thirty-six attendees.[16]

Ellen Spangler and Rose DeBernardo were croned at the Pagoda at winter solstice 1983, the first of many Pagoda croning ceremonies. Rose turned fifty in October 1983, and Ellen in January 1984. *Left to right*: Nancy Breeze, Ellen Spangler, Rose DeBernardo, and behind her Edith George.

Photo by Emily Greene

As elaborate as any croning ritual were the efforts put into the Pagoda project they called Crones Nest,[17] an idea that goes back at the Pagoda at least as far as 1978, the year that the Matriarchy Conference was held there. *The Matriarchist* article promoting the conference quotes Lavender as saying, "We want to have a home for wimmin here—for older wimmin, for our mothers and ourselves one day, where women will be loved and respected and have the companionship and caring of other wimmin, where their talents can be utilized at any age."[18] The vision for "going residential" seems very similar to the vision that guided Crones Nest, a project that became the focus of a huge amount of community effort for at least the next four years.

Part of the vision for creating women-only space for aging women may have come from observing the women at the Sugarloaf women's community, where lesbians a generation or more older than most of the Pagoda women were "aging in place." During the time that Pagoda women were working on the Crones Nest project, Sugarloaf founder Barbara Deming died at her home on August 2, 1984. Deming and some of her friends had encouraged the Crones Nest project by donating funds to bring in grant writers to seek funding for it.[19] Later on, Morgana and her partner, Fayann Schmidt, made the cremation urn that holds the ashes of Deming and some of those friends. Living and dying together in community seems to have been attractive to those young Pagodans who would give so much time and energy to the Crones Nest project in the coming years.

Grantwriters Dean Brittingham and Sue Schein came in the fall of 1982, and Dean returned several times, applying for about a dozen grants in the early 1980s.[20] Dean was living in Vermont when she vacationed at the Pagoda and learned about the Crones Nest project. She had secured grant money for battered women's shelters and other feminist projects in Vermont, including a Ms. Foundation grant. She thought the Ms. Foundation would be interested in the Crones Nest project. The Pagoda's Ms. Foundation grant proposal did garner a site visit by Judy Sutphen on December 8–9, 1983, but the women faced stiff criticism. Sutphen told them that the name Crones Nest was not good for fund-raising, and that the goal of being interracial was not enough. They needed to change the name and involve women of color in the planning. Although the Crones Nest's vision was never limited to lesbians, Pagoda's bias in that direction was clear, and Sutphen warned them not to depend on straight women. A key part of their grant proposal was that the progressive, somewhat idealistic vision for aging women living in community that they were proposing would become a model that could be replicated elsewhere.

This replication issue is where they failed to convince the Ms. Foundation board, which rejected the proposal in January 1984 because "the experience of the Pagoda women in working to establish an alternative community for older women will be specific to the Pagoda constituency, and will not be replicable by other groups who want to start a similar project for aging women."[21] That summer, the Crones Nest committee issued a press release accusing the Ms. Foundation board of homophobia. Their reasoning was that the board's statement that "the project will be specific to the Pagoda constituency" was code for "lesbian." The committee continued to work hard on the project and in the winter of 1985 published *Cronicle,* a five-page newsletter full of stories about their vision and about attitudes toward aging and death.

The Crones Nest committee continued to work on the project another year or so, careful to make clear that their goal was "to create a residence for older women that welcomes all women who choose to live in community with women." Sadly, the most that the Pagoda women ever raised for Crones Nest through grants was a thousand dollars from the Eastman Fund to do a slideshow about elderly women. The slides, which they showed at several venues, still exist.[22] Although the Pagoda women never achieved their Crones Nest vision, the project demonstrates the ideological commitments of these lesbians and the breadth of their vision. While they could not translate the ideas into practice through a lack of capital, it shows the vibrancy of the culture they wanted to build.

Other pressing issues would draw energy away from Crones Nest, which they soon came to recognize as a project ahead of its time. One distraction was the fund-raising they had to do to cover legal expenses for fighting Jane Schilling's attempt to build a house in the narrow space between the Center and the swimming pool. After that died down, they began working on how to acquire the swimming pool and the last four Pagoda Motel cottages.

Running an active cultural center and guesthouse was stimulating, rewarding, and very hard work. At monthly business meetings, the leaders and workers constantly sought ways to keep expenses and prices low while dividing up the work of producing events fairly. They were a committed group, these women who were making a safe place for lesbian culture to grow and thrive, but they were getting worn out in the process. Fortunately, new women with new energies were on the way to develop the Pagoda into a new phase.

Growers
1988–1995

The Center building from the back, showing the balcony off the meeting room and the exterior steps to the attic. The Cave is beneath that balcony. The siding shingles are painted in three colors according to a design by Kathleen Clementson, intended to look like shadows.

Photo by Emily Greene

Chapter 7
Growth and Change

When Marilyn Murphy and Irene Weiss first pulled up to the Pagoda cultural center in their motor home in January 1984, they were there as guests of the Crones Nest project, their visit funded by Barbara Deming's Money for Women Fund. Marilyn was a writer, Irene had taken early retirement from a nursing career, and they were on a cross-country tour from their home in California giving workshops on classism and racism. Although they were not actively seeking a new home in a lesbian community, as Barbara and Lavender Lieu had been when they first visited the Pagoda, Marilyn and Irene's visit had equally momentous effects. They became regular visitors, and in the spring of 1988 were part of a large group who succeeded in buying the remaining lots of what had been the Pagoda Motel, doubling the physical size of the Pagoda. The new so-called North Pagoda residents brought fresh energy and new vision, signaling a new phase in the life of the Pagoda community.

These women, "the Growers," some new to the Pagoda, others longtime residents, were developing and expanding what the Founders and Builders had put in place over the previous ten years: a cultural center that doubled as a guesthouse, a mailing list, a substantial number of paying supporters, a reputation among lesbians, and, most important, a residential community that valued and sustained this extraordinary cultural project. During the eight-year period of the Growers, from 1988 through 1995, the Pagoda grew in physical size and in number of full-time residents. This growth brought changes, including debt and some differences that proved to be more than the women could manage.

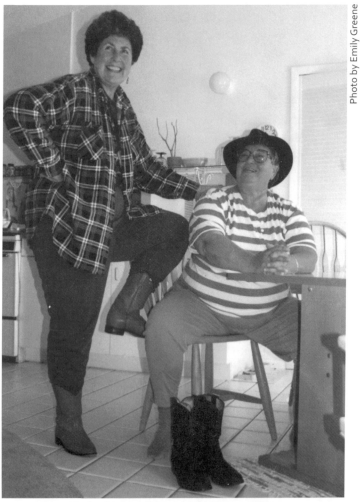

Photo by Emily Greene

Marilyn Murphy (left) and Irene Weiss, 1980s.

Pagoda residents and supporters had long dreamed of lesbians owning the swimming pool and the four remaining Pagoda cottages that lined the beach access road, Beachcomber Way, the northern border of the old Pagoda Motel. They were also well aware that the building that was their guesthouse and cultural center needed constant maintenance and repair, as well as significant remodeling to be more accessible; it was, after all, more than half a century old. All that began to become possible with the new energy, ideas, and resources that Marilyn and Irene brought to the Pagoda during the eight years that they lived there.

Marilyn and Irene brought "matriarchal magic"[1] to the Pagoda and, in many ways, became guiding lights for the Pagoda community. Their residence from 1988 to 1995 marked a major shift in the ways things were done. They picked up the reins that the Builders were ready to hand over, both relieved and hopeful about the changes that Marilyn and Irene were bringing. Writing about their new adventure for the Los Angeles *Lesbian News*, on the eve of closing on their new Pagoda cottage, Marilyn understood just what they had gotten themselves into:

> Participating in Pagoda's business process group these past months has seemed like re-living some of the best and the worst parts of my childhood in a houseful of sisters; of my years volunteering with my Catholic women friends in Sts Peter and Paul Women's Club, of my organized feminist activities with NOW, the National Women's Political Caucus, California Women in Higher Education, and the San Fernando Valley Rape Crisis Service and most of all, my almost ten years on the Califia Community Collective.
>
> There have been times . . . when we seriously thought of unhooking our house on wheels and leaving Lesbian conflicts behind us. Then some new and interesting Lesbi-

ans would arrive for their Lesbianland vacation, or a line of pelicans skim the roof of our RV, or we'd see a particularly beautiful sunrise or sunset, or we'd notice movement in the position of a previously immovable Pagodan, or the ocean would turn a shade of blue we hadn't seen before. And we'd remember that there is lots to see in living in a place where all the people you see putting out the garbage, sunning in the yards, walking down the road to the mail box, are Lesbians . . . even if you are mad at some of them![2]

Marilyn closes that story by encouraging readers to become Pagoda supporters "by pledging from 40 to 10 tax-exempt dollars a month," and asserts that even though it is "lesbian tacky," staying at the Center is free to supporters for up to three weeks, so "even when paying air fare, it's a bargain." Marilyn's enthusiasm, tempered by her own and Irene's long experience in "Lesbianland," would carry them through the eight years they owned Cottage B, and they left a lasting legacy.

In women's recollections of the Pagoda, Marilyn and Irene almost always figure as a power couple. They were both very strong and independent women, with firm opinions and a willingness to express them. Very knowledgeable about lesbian-feminist politics, they specialized in analyzing "classisms," especially characteristics of working class versus middle class cultures. They both identified as working class, though by the 1980s, they appeared to be comfortably situated financially. Irene's financial freedom came from investments in the California nursing homes that she had directed, and she used these resources to support Marilyn—and many other early lesbian-feminist women—in their movement work. While Marilyn's was the louder, more public voice, "Irene was the steadfast power in the background that made all of it possible," in the words of Irene's last partner.

Both Marilyn and Irene had grown up in the northeast and moved to California as adults. About coming out after a Catholic upbringing and marriage, Marilyn writes, "I feel as though I spent forty-three years being color blind, seeing the world as gradations of grey."[3] Irene grew up in a Jewish family in Pittsburgh, the daughter of Russian immigrants. She knew she was a lesbian from the age of fifteen and had her first lesbian relationship in nursing school.[4] Coming out to her family in her twenties, and being rejected, she moved first to New York City, and then to California, where she was introduced to feminism through Marilyn and the Califia Community Collective. "I never thought of myself as being like other women in any way," she says, "but I was. . . . I learned that at Califia and I learned that from Marilyn."[5]

Marilyn and others had been inspired to start the Califia Community Collective after attending Sagaris, a five-week feminist gathering in Vermont in the summer of 1975.[6] (Irene became important in Califia, but had not yet met Marilyn when it started.) Sagaris radicalized many of the 150 women who attended. It propelled Marilyn to leave a comfortable second marriage to embrace the lesbian-feminist consciousness that would dominate the rest of her life. It also left her longing for the stimulation of those women-only spaces for classes, discussion, and consciousness-raising. She and California friends formed the Califia Community Collective, whose mission was feminist education against sexism, classism, and racism.[7] They started organizing women-only retreats. The collective produced those retreats using consensus decision-making and applying feminist principles.[8] A retreat would have about 150 women and 25 children, and they averaged two to four weeklong conferences, or long weekends, each summer for over a decade, holding them at "forest camps" (Marilyn's words) in California where they hired cooks, childcare workers, ASL signers, and lifeguards.[9] Everything else was done by attendees. There were Wiccan rituals, nude swimming, and lots of sex. These retreats sound like women's music festivals without the music—or like the Pagoda.

These similarities to Califia, which ended for Marilyn and Irene in 1986, may have drawn them to the Pagoda, but there is a big difference between groups that gather three or four times a year (with planning meetings in between) and a residential community, some of whose residents are running a cultural center and guesthouse year round. Pagoda was not isolated in a park in the woods, not the summer camp for women and girls that Califia had been. Residents and visitors could not walk around topless on the beach or even anywhere outside the privacy fence around the swimming pool or, in the early days, the sundeck. When guests did (and they did), it caused problems for the women who lived there. Some residents might socialize with guests, especially on a weekend with a concert or other event, but more often guests would mainly interact with the Centerkeeper or greeter or whoever was involved in producing activities at the Center. According to Clark Pomerleau, in his history of Califia, the camps were "an unofficial lesbian space open to straight and questioning women,"[10] a description that might also apply to the Pagoda, except that to buy a Pagoda cottage, you had to be a lesbian, and the Pagoda sometimes scheduled lesbian-only concerts and rituals.

Perhaps Marilyn and Irene saw Pagoda as Califia with land, maybe even an evolved Califia. In fact, in the early days, a group of Califia women had formed a land collective and purchased twelve acres in Malibu as a permanent site for communal living.[11] Califia women, like many Pagoda women, were united in pursuit of feminist goals as well as bonding with other women and celebrating womanhood. But Califia was guided by a social justice mission.

No doubt, some women attended just for the fun of it (as did many Pagoda vacationers), but the Califia Community Collective had a clear-cut educational goal. The Pagoda was far more focused on feminist spirituality and performing arts. Also, Califia was run by a collective, while the Pagoda was a church-owned business, mostly run by women hired for the many jobs involved. The church that owned the cultural center had documents stating its purpose, which was primarily religious. Pagoda management— that is, the people running the cultural center—were volunteering or being paid for jobs like bookkeeping, taking reservations, and cleaning the building and pool. At monthly meetings, they were guided by feminist principles, but there was no mission statement posted on the wall or frequently reviewed to keep them on track. Pagoda women saw themselves as making a safe place for women to heal and grow, through theatre, concerts, art exhibits, workshops, Goddess rituals, and just being together around a private swimming pool on a beautiful beach. This was a big difference that may account for some of the difficulties the community faced in the years of rapid growth and change.

"Growing and Changing" was the title of a series of Pagoda newsletter stories leading up to the North Pagoda purchase. Rainbow Williams was part of the North Pagoda purchase and recalls those years as the Pagoda community's "Golden Age." This phase of Pagoda life had its physical manifestation in a complicated real estate deal involving not only Marilyn and Irene (who bought one cottage) and Rainbow, but also longtime Pagoda resident Nancy Breeze and four other Pagoda supporters.

Marilyn and Irene had been regular Pagoda RV visitors for four years when they saw a For Sale sign outside the last four cottages that Shorty Rees had built. For sale were two lots: Lot 1, with four cottages facing Beachcomber Way (1 GG), plus a vacant beachfront lot (1 ZZ), and Lot 2, with a swimming pool, vacant land between Lot 1 and Lot 3, and another vacant beach-front lot (Lot 2 ZZ). The Schilling family had been living in the cottages, but Pappy Schilling died in 1986 and Jane, now in her mid-seventies, wanted to move into town. The buyers, all lesbians, formed the North Pagoda Land Trust for the purpose of buying all of that with one mortgage held by Jane Schilling.

Rainbow's drawing of three North Pagoda cottages, with Marilyn Murphy and Irene Weiss walking down the sand road toward the beach. *Left to right:* Cottage B, Marilyn and Irene's; cottage C, with Nancy Breeze hanging out laundry on her rooftop deck; and cottage D, Rainbow's cottage, still wearing its horns from Pagoda Motel days.

After months of negotiation with Jane Schilling to set up the deal, the North Pagoda group met on January 1–2, 1988, and formed the North Pagoda Cottage Association, a cottage association separate from the Cottage Association that managed the cottages on Lots 3 and 4. North Pagoda asked the other cottage association to expand some things to include North Pagoda (insurance, maintenance fees, garbage collection, etc.) and planned to use the same bookkeeper. The group "expect to abide by most Pagoda guidelines" except about "male visitors, children, and pets." Their rules were stricter: no male visitors ever; chem-free outdoors; exceptions to be made one at a time.

They were very lucky to have a smart lesbian attorney will-ing to work with them to arrange for individual ownership of cottages and to untangle many a tricky legal issue involving easements and clouds on titles.[12] Three of the North Pagoda cottages would change hands during the fifteen-year mortgage: cottage A three times, B twice, C once. Rainbow held on to cottage D for twenty-five years. Exactly how the new regime affected the Cottage Eligibility List is unclear. Certainly, there was no re-quirement for North Pagoda cottage owners to contribute to the Center, although in years past several had already made the ex-pected $600 church donation.[13] There was no agreement about keeping the selling price low.

Those four cottages are different from the other Pagoda cot-tages in several ways. They are all bigger, 616 square feet instead of 440 square feet, and they are built on concrete slabs, rather than raised on piers. They are close to one another, but separat-ed from the other Pagoda cottages by a fifty-five-foot-wide lot that is vacant except for the swimming pool at the western end. Because North Pagoda cottages face a public road, they have a mailing address different from the address shared by all the oth-er Pagoda residences. Those original residences are all 2854 Coastal Highway, and the cottages are numbered. The North Pagoda cottages are lettered A–D, and are addressed 51-A, 51-B, 51-C, and 51-D Beachcomber Way. Marilyn and Irene shared cottage B, Nancy Breeze had cottage C, and Rainbow had cot-tage D. Paulette Armstead bought Cottage A, visited often from Tampa, and treated it as a vacation home.[14] Marilyn and Irene remodeled their cottage extensively, making the rooms much larger and more comfortable than most other Pagoda cottages. Not only were those four cottages the newest of the Pagoda cottages, but being on a city street greatly improved their access. The other eight cottages are accessed through sand roads, essentially driveways, and are now plagued by easement issues.

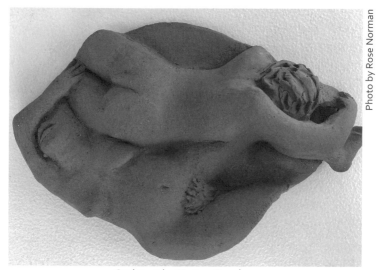

Sculpture by Myriam Fougère.

Photo by Rose Norman

Marilyn and Irene were not the only new couple who bought a cottage in 1988 and became active community members. Myriam Fougère had been a Pagoda supporter and regular visitor for several years when she brought her new partner, Lin Daniels, for her very first visit to the Pagoda at Thanksgiving 1987. As luck would have it, Nancy Vogl's cottage was for sale. Lin tells an interesting story about how they were able to buy that cottage. Myriam thought it would be impossible because so many people were ahead of her on the Cottage Eligibility List. As they sat on the Center porch one day looking at what Lin recalls as "that Pepto Bismol pink cottage," Myriam told Lin, "Don't even dream of it!" But Lin wanted to dream and consulted her friend Flash Silvermoon, a professional psychic, who said that they should approach the goddess Pele, give her an offering, and ask for it. So Lin and Myriam actually went to Hawaii, where the volcano Kilauea was erupting, and entreated Pele, who is the Hawaiian goddess of volcanoes. What happened when they got home was remarkable:

> We got back to California, and mind you, I hadn't been in touch with Nancy Vogl for a long time, since that first festival that I went to. We got back to our place, and we got a call from the Pagoda saying, "Nancy Vogl wants to call you. Can we give her your number?" . . . She called, and she said, "Well, I don't know if you're still interested, but I know your name was on the list."[15]

The sale of cottage 7 to Lin and Myriam closed in August 1988, and they paid the traditional $600 to the church.[16] Both Lin and Myriam traveled often, Lin as a producer of festivals and other events, Myriam as an artist and craftswoman. They also had a home in Brooklyn during these years, but for almost a decade Lin was very active in keeping the cultural center going, and she was especially close friends with Irene Weiss. When she first came to the Pagoda, Lin had mainly been diving into the women's music scene learning to do sound, helping to connect people through her magazine *Music Women*[17] and producing concerts. While active at the Pagoda (but also living in New York), Lin and Myriam produced the East Coast Lesbian Festival, which many Pagoda residents worked on.[18] Unlike Myriam, Lin became very involved in the business of the Pagoda. For a time, Lin was Centerkeeper, responsible for managing guest reservations and building maintenance, as well as producing concerts at the Pagoda.

The North Pagoda residents, as well as newer residents like Lin and Myriam, were full of energy and ideas for how the Pagoda could be improved, especially the somewhat shabby guest-house and cultural center. Fresh from their experience of producing Califia retreats, Marilyn and Irene became active in the business end of running the Pagoda. Mostly that involved renting sleep space in the Center, organizing events, and figuring out how to maintain the Center building and swimming pool. The Center building was old, and that fire in 1975 had led Jane Schilling to sell it; she thought it had a fire demon, and she may have been right.[19] The Pagoda women had quickly learned to be very careful with candles in that building.

Marilyn and Irene also worked to improve the diversity at the Pagoda. They drafted an antiracism statement published in the January 1988 newsletter ("The Pagoda is committed to eliminating racism in any form by peaceful means") and started an Affirmative Action Web to work on drawing more women of color to the property. The North Pagoda purchase brought in the first woman of color as a Pagoda cottage owner, Paulette Armstead, who had been a Pagoda supporter since 1984. While still in college, Paulette became the first Black female police officer in St. Petersburg, and went on to become an attorney. She came out as a lesbian after graduating law school in 1978, the year that the Florida Bar Association stopped disqualifying openly gay applicants. She had learned about the Pagoda from lesbian friends in Tampa, and thought that it was a good investment. "This was a win for me and a win for the lesbian community," she writes, saying that she and her partner, who was white, participated in regular maintenance of the Center and the common areas, but spent most of their time working on renovating cottage A. By 1990, her law practice had grown so rapidly that she could no longer spend time there, and she did not want to rent it, so the cottage association found a buyer, another interracial couple, Maria Dolores Diaz (from Honduras) and Lois Bencangey, who knew

Marilyn and Irene through Califia. Maria had been instrumental in Califia's outreach to women of color.[20] The couple, who lived in California, bought the cottage as a rental property.[21]

The Pagoda founders were all white women, as were all cottage owners until 1988. These women were serious about interrupting racism in their personal lives, and meeting notes do show them discussing how to attract lesbian women of color as cottage owners.[22] Women of color performers like June Millington, Deidre McCalla, and the Washington Sisters played Pagoda concerts, and stayed there as guests, but in the hundreds of Pagoda photographs, it is rare to see a woman of color who is not a performer. It is very rare to see more than one woman of color in a picture, and often those few cannot be identified. Paulette Armstead responded to a question about the absence of women of color from the Pagoda like this:

> I think there were so few women of color at the Pagoda because many women of color did not have extensive social interactions with white lesbians nor did many of them subscribe to lesbian publications like the *Lesbian Connection*, where the Pagoda regularly advertised. Consequently, they never heard about the Pagoda. I heard about the Pagoda because I read the *Lesbian Connection* and some other lesbian publications. In addition to that, I worked with white people, lived next door to whites, and dated some white women. My social interactions and personal experiences were quite unique.

It seems that the Pagoda's low profile worked against outreach to lesbians of color, but cultural invisibility worked both ways. Just as the Pagoda was invisible to lesbians of color who did not subscribe to publications like *Lesbian Connection*, so lesbians of color networks would be invisible to the white women.

White women, no matter how heartfelt their intentions, are hampered by their privilege and insularity, while women of color have a well-founded distrust of white women's intentions. These lesbians were living in the conservative South not too far removed from the days when civil rights activist Andrew Young was beaten by an angry mob during a peaceful protest in downtown St. Augustine. In a documentary film about this incident, Young says "I thought I could reason with them."[23] In their own time, a Confederate statue still stood in the downtown plaza where Young was attacked in 1964. Given the history of systemic racism in the United States, it is hardly surprising that the Pagoda never achieved the multicultural community they hoped for in the late twentieth century.

The Pagoda women had far more success with accessibility issues. In 1988, they began fund-raising to make the ground-floor bedroom (the Alcove) and bathroom wheelchair-accessible and managed to raise enough to build a ramp from the Center building to the swimming pool, using volunteer labor. The cost to remodel the downstairs bathroom, though, turned out to be far beyond the $500 they had earmarked: the whole bathroom needed to be torn out to make it accessible. The question of how to pay for renovations needed to upgrade the building was resolved in 1992 when Marilyn and Irene, plus several friends of theirs, loaned the Pagoda-temple of Love $25,000.[24] It was a substantial shot in the arm for not only accessibility renovations but for plenty of deferred maintenance on the building.

It could not have come at a better time. In 1991, chance, or synchronicity, or the will of the Goddess brought yet another couple to the Pagoda at Thanksgiving (known by then as Dykesgiving). Garnett Harrison was a lawyer who had been coming to the Pagoda for years with her older sister, Sallie Ann Harrison, staying with Sallie's then partner, Nancy Breeze. During that time, Garnett had a traumatic experience in her home state of Mississippi, where she had practiced family law for a decade. She left Mississippi disbarred, in fear of her life, and with a warrant for her arrest for civil contempt arising from a child custody case she was handling in which the mother (Garnett's client) took the child underground.[25] In 1987 and 1988, the Pagoda had been a sanctuary and healing place for Garnett, as for many others. By 1990, she had recovered, accepted a job in Vermont, and was about to drive her motor home to Vermont when she was injured bodysurfing at the Pagoda. Irene hired Elethia to drive the motor home north for Garnett, and flew Elethia back. That was the kind of community Garnett had experienced at the Pagoda. So when she decided to come back south with her new partner, Cindy Watson, to pull her life together and start over, her eyes turned to the Pagoda.

The couple had written to the Pagoda asking permission to park their motor home on the property in exchange for running the Center for a few months, doing whatever needed doing—reservations, greeting, housecleaning, laundry, etc. The women running the Pagoda agreed to the deal, making it clear that it was because they strongly supported Garnett's movement work, and that this arrangement was their contribution to that work.

The Pagoda became a sanctuary for Garnett's partner, Cindy Watson, too. Cindy was from South Carolina and had never been out in the South before. She had been married to a man for years before meeting Garnett and was just coming out as a lesbian at this time. What better place to be encouraged to grow into your lesbian identity than the Pagoda? They both brought exceptional skills to the community, as Cindy explains:

> We had a lot of energy. Garnett was very skilled with organizing and her legal thinking, and I had run a non-

profit for ten years. So I really understood boards of directors, and how you make things work in a women's community, because I had been the executive director of a women's center in a rural woman's community [in Vermont], a very progressive one. It wasn't lesbian-feminist, but it was feminist with plenty of lesbians.

From her work with nonprofits, Cindy was also an experienced grant writer and was able to win the Pagoda a $2500 grant from Lesbian Natural Resources to go toward the renovation project.

Cindy and Garnett came for three months and wound up staying nine months, until August 1992. In that time, not only did they run the Center but Cindy became project manager for the renovation of the Alcove, assisted by Irene. They hired an experienced carpenter from Jacksonville, a lesbian in her sixties named Shelby Mathis, who lived in the Cave during the week and knew how to do just about everything that needed doing. She didn't drive, so Cindy took her home to Jacksonville every weekend. For Shelby, too, the Pagoda became a sanctuary. She was a recovering alcoholic who had just gotten paroled from prison for DUI homicide. Shelby was "quite a character," in Cindy's recollection, and the Pagoda community was glad to be a part of her recovery.

Cindy Watson's project manager report describes her pleasure in the work: "I was on the worksite each day sweating with Shelby, the carpenter, and her assistants, coordinating volunteers, determining work schedules for various contractors, calling Dore [Rotundo], the architect, for consultations, and bringing supply lists and options for decisions to the Project Planning Committee."[26] Everyone involved felt great satisfaction in bringing the old building back to life and making that ground-floor bedroom and bathroom wheelchair-accessible. The Alcove renovation project, budgeted at $10,000, took $13,000 of their $25,000 loan, the rest going to painting the building, repairing the roof, putting in permanent stairs to the attic (no more built-in ladder), leveling the concrete floor in the theatre, repairing upstairs plumbing, and paying off the mortgage. The Alcove project was completed by June, but the work on the theatre and the upstairs kitchen and bathroom continued through the summer, with Marilyn stepping in as manager when Cindy got a job in Jacksonville and started commuting. The building had desperately needed repair and maintenance of all kinds, and the work done was important. That hard work toward a shared goal resulted in a bright and shiny new look for the building that they all loved and brought people together, giving them pride in what they had accomplished.

Another important new resident of the Pagoda in this period of expansion was Fayann Schmidt, Morgana's new romantic partner. Fayann had seen Morgana dance at a women's music festival, and recalls being "fascinated by spiritual dancing, anything spiritual. I had that connection all my life. I was curious to meet her and see what she did with her dance. So I made a point to see her when she was in Jacksonville performing." Fayann moved to the Pagoda to live with Morgana in 1987 and would partner with Morgana in many enterprises, including producing cultural events at the Center and making pottery for sale. She owned a recycling business in St. Augustine that kept her busy and never took any paying Pagoda jobs, although she did plenty of volunteer work, such as reclaiming Persephone's Pit as Persephone's Garden.[27]

This new constellation of Pagoda women renewed the community, as much as they did that old building that they put so much work into, as they continued to fill it with new cultural activities and events. Rainbow credits Marilyn and Irene with reviving an informal organization they call Culture Club, an umbrella term for groups organizing events in the Pagoda theatre.

Rainbow and her then partner, Sarah Carawan, produced a lively art show in March 1988, "Junk, Funk, and Xerox, Part II," a follow-up to the 1985 show inviting people to post self-portraits, ready to tack or hang. Gainesville supporter Beth Karbe had a photo exhibit, "Portraits of Lesbians," in the fall of 1990. Myriam Fougère exhibited her sculpture and showed slides at a free poetry reading by Jewelle Gomez in December 1988. Gomez returned in January to read more poetry from her book *Flamingos and Bears* and from the vampire novel she was writing that became *The Gilda Stories*. Concerts included Carole Eagleheart, Cecily Jane, and Lyn Thomas in 1994, Karen Beth in 1995. Emily Greene's video of Pagoda's sixteenth-birthday party (1993) includes several readings, as well as Morgana bellydancing by the swimming pool. Emily's video of the July 1995 eighteenth birthday captures more performances around the swimming pool, including Marilyn and Irene harmonizing on "I Want a Girl (Just Like the Girl Who Married Dear Old Dad)."[28]

Photo by Beth Karbe

Martine Giguère (left) and Myriam Fougère photograph from Beth Karbe's Lesbian Portraits exhibit at the Pagoda in 1990. To see more photography, follow @bethkarbe on Instagram.

Elaine Townsend performed at the Pagoda in the 1980s and then moved there after partnering with Karen J, a Pagoda resident. Elaine first came to the Pagoda at the beginning of her musical career, when she was leaving very conservative South Carolina. She was "very eager to make contact with lesbians and feminists and freethinkers, so to discover the Pagoda, especially within driving distance, filled my spirit."[29] When she came back to live with Karen, her horizons had expanded from living five years in California and touring with her music. Elaine and Karen had met and fallen in love at the Pagoda when Elaine was on a big tour from California. They shared the upstairs of the duplex from 1990 to 1993 or 1994. Elaine recalls:

> I was privileged to get to experience the Pagoda. I would see women pull up for their week there, and you could kind of see the outside world melt away. They realized they were in safe space, in women-only space. Whatever might be going on for me—teaching or whatever little mundane annoyance I might experience—watching those women arrive was always a reminder that I lived in a special place.[30]

Many different Pagoda women produced concerts, study groups, workshops, and other events during these years. Producing was always a volunteer activity, subject to frequent adjustments as to how to divide proceeds equitably among performer, publicity, and Pagoda (for utilities and room use). Sometimes they even allocated a small share for the producer's time. When you consider that they are dividing up, at most, $750 (if every attendee paid the top rate of $15 and all fifty seats were sold), and more often $250 or less, producing was generally a labor of love, and it is amazing that they were able to keep the stage filled so frequently.

For the two years 1988 and 1989, newsletters show considerable musical activity, with a few concerts by local musicians and eight by national performers: June Millington (twice), Carole and Bren (twice), Kay Gardner, Karen Beth, Alix Dobkin, and Martie van der Voort (singer-songwriter from Arizona). New age international composers October Browne (from London) and Evelyn Datl (from Toronto) performed on New Year's Eve 1988. For the six years from 1990 to 1995, records are spotty, but they do show seven concerts by national performers, most of them in 1994 and 1995: Lyn Thomas (twice), Kay Gardner, Carole Eagleheart (twice), Jamie Anderson, and Karen Beth. Those years also saw visits from two international performers, Anique from Australia and Jess Hawk Oakenstar from (at that time) New Zealand.

Kay Gardner playing her flute with Nurudafina Peli Abena (known as Nuru) on drums at the Pagoda Playhouse, 1994. The backdrop is a cutout depicting the St. Augustine skyline, created by Pagoda resident Sherry Tamburo.

Jamie Anderson, who is still touring as a professional musician, recalls that she appreciated the small Pagoda audiences: "That's the wonderful thing about playing for an audience like that. I can see them all, and I can connect with them, and see if somebody is so moved that they're crying. It's not always a bad thing [crying]. Sometimes it just means they're remembering an important thing that happened to them." Also, it did not take many people to make a full house. The Pagoda July 1995 newsletter described a performance that May by Anderson:

> Her concert packed the Theatre. Lesbians were sitting on pool chairs in the parking lot, on the stairs, in the cave! She was wild and so was the audience. Jamie is always good, but this concert was her best ever. Lesbians love to listen to the songs that reflect our lives, and that is what Jamie does best. We kept her on the stage for one encore after another. What a hot night!

Romances playing out among Pagoda residents and guests sometimes reached out to performers. Carole Eagleheart and Brenda Chambers had been playing the Pagoda most years since 1981 when in 1993 Brenda met someone else at the Pagoda and left in midtour to follow that woman to California. Ironically, that was the year that their album *You Are the One* came out. Thereafter, Eagleheart toured solo, and the Pagoda remained on her route for the rest of its life. Emily Greene's video of Eagleheart playing an April 1994 concert shows the joy of both performer and audience.

The feminist theatre that had been so important in the early years had been almost nonexistent at the Pagoda since Trudy Anderson moved away in 1982, but yet another lesbian couple who moved to the Pagoda changed that. Paula Arden and Dorothy Campbell had performed their skit comedy billed as Positively Revolting Hags at the Pagoda in the summer of 1991, and returned in December with Dorothy's play, *Same Ship, Different*

Day, inspired by Sonia Johnson's book about relationships, *The Ship That Sailed into the Living Room: Sexual Intimacy Reconsidered* (1991). The following February, Paula was suspended from her job teaching high school English in Smyrna, Georgia, when her lesbian identity became an issue. She had been teaching there four years and had developed an active theatre program, but when she came out as a lesbian, the Cobb County Commission acted swiftly to censor her. Paula recalls that they had "just made a resolution that the homosexual lifestyle didn't agree with the values of their community." The commission brought a notorious antigay activist, Nancy Schaefer, to Paula's school, and that led to Paula's suspension from the classroom.[31] That was when the couple moved to Florida, renting the North Pagoda cottage next door to Marilyn and Irene, cottage A. Dorothy soon moved into St. Augustine, concerned about her job security when she got a job teaching elementary school, but Paula became active as a Pagoda worker, especially taking care of the swimming pool. She took on several paid Pagoda jobs during her residence there, and for a time was Centerkeeper.[32] Paula is especially remembered for performing a staged reading of Carolyn Gage's one-woman show *The Second Coming of Joan of Arc* at the Pagoda in early 1993, and later at the East Coast Lesbian Festival and on tour.

Paula recalls becoming good friends with Marilyn and Irene, whom she greatly admired and viewed as role models. She describes herself before the Pagoda as "just a gay girl, drinking and dancing and having a good time with other gay girls, going to sporting events, and that kind of thing." She had never even attended a women's music festival before moving to the Pagoda, but once there began attending study groups with Marilyn and Irene, and reading everything she could get her hands on. Given the size of the Pagoda library, that was plenty.

In addition to formal concerts and exhibits at the Center, some events took place in private residences. Marilyn and Irene had informal study groups in their cottage that involved no producers or business transactions. Sometimes formal gatherings were held at Jean Adele and Kay Mora's beachfront house. For example, Old Lesbians Organizing for Change held a weeklong steering committee meeting at the Pagoda, April 21–26, 1992; they convened at Jean and Kay's, with attendees staying in cottages or the Center.[33] Jean and Kay's house was also the setting for two weekend workshops intended to heal some of the divisiveness that was brewing during these years of growth and change.

Chapter 8
Divisions and Challenges

When asked to think back to good times at the Pagoda, many residents and guests nostalgically remember the swimming pool, the site of many festive parties with live music and performances, as well as lazy, private, nude bathing. Phyllis Free, who visited from Atlanta as a performer and guest, captures some of this in her poem "The Pagoda Pool." The swimming pool "called us into its womb," with "the gentle sounds of surf nearby" until

> Drifting away into amniotic freedom
> Loving arms keeping me afloat
> I received the gift of her guiding hands
>
> My head at rest in the cradle of her palms
> She floated my body on the still healing water
> In choreographed patterns of magical swirls

The mystic, erotic, playful evocation of that beautiful swimming pool captures the healing power that so many women found at the Pagoda. Ironically, the swimming pool also became a symbol of the economic capital required to keep the community going, and of the inability of the Pagoda women to find an economically stable model to do that. Financial stresses, combined with the stresses of communal living, brought divisions and challenges to the Growers phase.

The long, complicated effort to buy the swimming pool illustrates a combination of personal and financial challenges. For the first decade or so, the Pagoda women paid Jane Schilling a monthly fee for using the swimming pool, always calculating how they could buy it outright. In 1982, they contemplated fund-raising for the $50,000 that Jane Schilling was then asking for Lot 2, which the Pagoda women envisioned as a "recreational complex."[1] That is when they started an escrow account for the Pagoda Aquatic Association, selling "lifetime membership" shares for $100 to $500, plus a "small yearly maintenance fee." Nothing much seemed to happen about that (and no one ever paid more than $100) until December 1985, when Jane Schilling threatened to sell the pump house and stop supplying water.[2] Between 1982 and 1989, the Pagoda recruited ninety-six women to buy $100 shares, making them lifetime members of the Aquatic Association.

Once the Aquatic Association assumed ownership, it attempted to maintain the swimming pool, but the lifetime-membership system didn't include a way to collect the "small yearly maintenance fee" originally envisioned. The women had meetings about it, built ramps to make it accessible, fences to make it private, and in the 1990s, worked on landscaping to make it beautiful. But it is always expensive to maintain a swimming pool, and they found these expenses averaged about $250 monthly, which was more than they could manage. Moreover, pool ownership was complicated. Legally, the Aquatic Association didn't own the pool. That property was part of the North Pagoda Land Trust, which acquired it along with the rest of the property bought on one mortgage. Mortgage sharer and Pagoda supporter Ann Harman was assigned Lot 2 GG, about one-third of which was the swimming pool. Not wanting responsibility and liability for the swimming pool, Ann quit-claimed just that portion of her lot to the Pagoda-temple of Love in 1989, leaving the church responsible for pool expenses, including a small mortgage payment.[3] Pool maintenance became a bone of contention that year, when liability insurance jumped to $1500.[4] Some supporters wanted to close the pool and redirect their resources, but were overruled.[5] The pool parties continued, and the swimming pool is still there today, much repaired and improved.

Acquiring the swimming pool, expanding the property, and upgrading the Center brought a glow of success to the Pagoda. But the financial challenges that came with the swimming pool signaled other challenges that gradually revealed fissures between the Builders and the Growers, interpersonal differences that when combined with financial and other challenges came to be irreconcilable. The divisions can be most easily characterized by the names North Pagoda and Old Pagoda, terms they began using after the North Pagoda Land Trust group formed the North Pagoda Cottage Association and began operating under different rules from the existing Pagoda Cottage Association.

These divisions manifest partly in the physical divide between the cottages, with the row of North Pagoda cottages separated from the two rows of Old Pagoda cottages by a vacant lot and the swimming pool (see aerial view, page 20). But it was not as simple as "old" and "new" residents. Nancy Breeze and Rainbow Williams had physically moved from residences in Old Pagoda cottages to North Pagoda cottages (C and D, respectively), but new residents Lin Daniels and Myriam Fougère had bought Nancy Vogl's Old Pagoda cottage, #7. All four were closely allied with Marilyn and Irene (cottage B), the most active North Pagoda leaders, although Myriam and Nancy tried hard to stay neutral as differences emerged.

Some of the new cottage association's different rules were relatively minor, but others bored deep into what had been standard Pagoda practice. On the minor side, the Old Pagoda way of notifying residents that a male worker would be on the land (for instance, to deliver an appliance) was to put a sign on the door of the Center. North Pagoda residents began to handle that with a few phone calls among themselves. North Pagoda also agreed to meet only when they needed to—something Rainbow considered a "RADICAL change." Perhaps more significant were the different rules North Pagoda adopted for cottage sales. Rainbow writes that she and Nancy Breeze wanted to ensure at least a 10 percent return on investment when selling their cottages, and all of the North Pagoda women wanted control over who could buy a cottage, without recourse to the Cottage Eligibility List. "I wanted to be able to choose my neighbors, and who I sold to," Rainbow Williams writes. "Choice is THE feminist issue."[6]

Different ways of analyzing and resolving patriarchal oppressions in their daily lives also came to be divisive. Feminists have long argued over analysis of complex issues. Early on, after Gainesville women complained of a cowgirl fabric sculpture wall hanging because it included a holstered gun, it was taken down (Morgana still has it in her home). Since 1983, Pagoda women had been celebrating Thanksgiving as a day to honor Native American women, calling it Native American Wimmin Day. Just before moving to the Pagoda, Marilyn wrote a Pagoda newsletter story explaining why that practice was colonizing, and thereafter they named it Dykesgiving. Previously, Marilyn had schooled them on the unintended racism of having a separate section of the library for books by women of color. The Pagoda women pushed back when they found that their Black friends did not view it that way.

Differing views on the politics of everyday life became a barrier in the relationship between some of the North Pagoda and Old Pagoda residents. Consciousness-raising around class was an especially prickly topic, one that Marilyn and Irene had studied and taught for many years. Their analysis of classism draws heavily on the Sagaris workshop Marilyn had attended in 1976. This approach to class was not a New Left critique of capitalism, but one that focused on cultural differences associated with family economic background and interpersonal dynamics.[7] Marilyn writes about her understanding of class differences in an essay titled "Did Your Mother Do Volunteer Work?" She defines three socioeconomic classes in terms of a set of standards whereby the middle class embodies and respects the standards, the working class emulates them, and poor people "neither respect nor obey the rules, nor teach them to their children."[8] (She mostly ignores the upper classes.) The "standards" referenced here are not explicitly set out but appear to concern ways that middle-class people speak and behave. Some Califia women who had thought of themselves as middle class came to see themselves as working class and were empowered by that, while many middle-class women involved in this training came to feel marginalized by their unearned privilege. More often than not in Marilyn's writings (including the essay in which she distinguishes the classes), poor and working-class women are lumped together.

At the Pagoda, residents from middle-class backgrounds and poorer backgrounds both chafed at these distinctions and the critiques they elicited. Elethia was one of the few Pagoda cottage owners who came from extreme poverty, and felt disadvantaged by her background among Pagoda women. By the time she moved to the Pagoda, Elethia had graduated from college and was a practicing therapist and a licensed minister. Yet when money or products were missing from the natural food store in the Center, she felt that she was always suspected because of her background. (Barbara Lieu says that this was not so, and that she did not know that Elethia felt that way.) Elethia's background taught her to deal with conflict directly and sometimes loudly, which offended her middle-class neighbors, taught to conceal strong emotion and not raise their voices.[9] "It seems that the higher you go in the class structure," she writes, "the more you are emotionally silenced."[10] What bothered her was not so much that they were different as "that the way I grew up with more direct expressions of emotion was seen as wrong and a bit uncivilized."

While some interpersonal difficulties and misunderstandings may have arisen from class differences, others arose from different attitudes to therapy, and even to spirituality. The Old Pagoda group were great believers in the benefits of counseling and therapy, believing that the longevity of the community owed a lot to their practice of meeting weekly to discuss and resolve interpersonal matters. They also had strong commitments to feminist spirituality and interest in psychic phenomena. Marilyn and Irene were skeptical about both therapy and religion, preferring weekly study groups and Sunday brunches akin to consciousness-raising groups. Morgana recalls that the remodeling of the Center included removing the altar they had maintained on the main floor upstairs for a decade and bringing in couches, making it more of a living room, unsuitable for rituals. Spiritual activities moved to the theatre, Persephone's Garden, or other outdoor spaces. Business meetings moved to the theatre as well.

In 1988 and again in 1993, these interpersonal differences became so great that the community hired a consultant for a weekend workshop, the first of them described as "for exploration and possible resolution of our 'knotty' intra-group issues."[11] That first weekend workshop happened the same month that the North Pagoda group closed on the new property in 1988. In 1993, they hired the second consultant for a weekend workshop focused on improving community relations, especially a dispute over bookkeeping irregularities and an accusation of stolen money.

Photo by Emily Greene

Elethia and her dog Sappho first visited the Pagoda in 1980, renting the cottage that she would later buy.

Both the bookkeeping irregularities and the missing money arose from cottage association bookkeeping. Both cottage associations paid Elethia to do the complicated bookkeeping for the various cottage mortgages, shared utilities, taxes, rental income, etc. Elethia had taken on bookkeeping tasks off and on since she moved to the Pagoda in 1981, and had held many paid and unpaid positions for the Pagoda. She had owned cottage 1 since 1983, although she often rented it out while spending months in her home state of New York. She was Center coordinator in January 1990, project manager for the Alcove renovation project in the summer of 1991 (before Cindy Watson took over), and signed the promissory notes for the $25,000 loan for renovation and remodeling in 1992.[12] Elethia was deeply committed to and involved in the community. Her strong spiritual beliefs and her decade of living and working at the Pagoda allied her with Old Pagoda, but she was good friends with Marilyn and Irene until about 1992. Then she became a magnet for strong disagreements around money and business practices, and that spring Marilyn and Irene took over her financial responsibilities. Elethia was accused of burning the books on the beach and mishandling funds, both of which she and others dispute. The disruption around this episode, and major differences of opinion about what happened, seriously divided the community, creating a tear in the fabric of community that the women struggled to repair.[13]

After each of the weekend intensive workshops came a time of relative harmony when community members seemed able to get along together better, but the disputes took a toll. Gradually, long-term residents began to move away. Emily and her partner moved into town and eventually sold their cottage to their tenant, Marie Squillace. Morgana dates her own discontent from 1987, when she began to have dreams of moving to the mountains. That was the year that her grandmother died and left her an inheritance that allowed her to add an extra bedroom and studio to her Pagoda cottage and also to go in with her mother on buying a cabin in the north Alabama mountains near Mentone. Morgana rented out her Pagoda cottage for the summer months starting in May 1988. The extra bedroom she had added allowed her to come back for short periods while still renting it out. From 1992 on, Morgana and her then partner, Fayann Schmidt, were spending summers at the mountain cabin, winters at the Pagoda, while they were searching and then negotiating for the land that became another women's residential community, Alapine.

Barbara and Lavender had been spending more time elsewhere, too, especially in Charleston with Lavender's family, who were having serious health problems. They had sold the natural food store about the time of the North Pagoda purchase, and spent over six months in South Carolina that year, when Lavender's brother was dying. They spent the summer of 1989 in South Carolina, and in 1990 their cottage was for rent June to December.

In "Pagoda, Temple of Love, 1994," Marilyn Murphy details numerous conflicts within the community during the years that she and Irene lived there.[14] Marilyn sees these conflicts arising from a combination of "serious ideological differences," probably alluding to her own disdain for therapy and Goddess worship, but also to different ideas about business practices, such as controlling cottage prices and sales through the Cottage Eligibility List. She also observes that "only about half, at the most, of the residents (and some dedicated local supporters) take any responsibility for its daily needs" and that "some renters and owners are here only because they can live at the beach inexpensively." She argues that this situation breeds conflict.

Marilyn does not write about her own decision to leave the Pagoda permanently in 1996 and to move with Irene to Superstition Mountain, a women's RV community in Apache Junction, Arizona. In a much later interview, Irene says that the women at the RV community were not radical in the way that the Pagoda women were, but that Marilyn thought she and Irene might change that.[15] Perhaps Marilyn and Irene were just tired of struggling with those "serious ideological issues." By the time they left, the Pagoda community had changed significantly. Lin and Myriam broke up and began taking turns at their Pagoda cottage. Jean and Kay had sold their beach house in 1993, the year that Elethia moved away permanently. By the end of 1995, three of the four full-time North Pagoda cottage owners had moved away, Nancy Breeze to live with a partner in town, and Marilyn and Irene to Arizona. Their young neighbor, Paula Arden, moved to Gainesville that year. Morgana, Fayann, and Barbara were already living in the mountains, and Lavender had moved to Atlanta.

They had come a long way from starting a cultural center and resort with property that seemed to fall into their lap. Women had worked hard to form and sustain a residential community and cultural center that by then was well-known and respected in lesbian circles. But growth and change had brought divisions and challenges that some stalwarts were no longer willing to face. It was still a lesbian community, with all of its twelve cottages and the duplex owned by lesbians, but it was a different community, with a new vibe and new challenges.

Reclaimers
1996–1999

Rainbow at the altar in Persephone's Garden.

Photo by Emily Greene

Chapter 9
Restructuring for Survival

Late one night in January 1996, a drunk driver crashed through the Pagoda front gate, hitting a parked car.[1] It was an ominous beginning for a new phase in the life of the Pagoda community, a phase marked by new and returning women, "the Reclaimers." When Marilyn and Irene came back to pack up their cottage for good early that year, few of the women they had actively worked with while living in their Pagoda cottage remained in residence.[2] Of the long-term residents, only Rainbow, Edith, and Joycie continued to live onsite full-time. In this phase (1996–1999), Rena Carney, Emily Greene, Garnett Harrison, and Cindy Watson returned to actively reclaim what was being lost, joined by several full-time residents.

Although Rena visited regularly and used her cottage for business, she had not been actively involved in Pagoda business for many years. Always working with few resources other than lesbian energy and enthusiasm, the women had achieved all and more than they could imagine back in 1977–1978; however, by 1996 community energy for working on the business was flagging, and the Center was not making monthly expenses. The December 1995 financial report showed an "available balance" of $20.74. Despite all these changes, in 1996, the Pagoda community made one last gallant attempt to reclaim and revitalize what so many had built.

Since the 1930s, Vilano Beach had been connected to St. Augustine and U.S. 1 by a drawbridge. When the bridge was raised for a vessel to pass, you had to wait, and when it was closed for repair, as was common, you had to drive all the way to Jacksonville to get on State Road A1A, the coastal highway. That changed in October 1995 when a grand new bridge soared over the Intracoastal Waterway (ICWW), dumping traffic onto A1A right at the entrance to the Pagoda. That bridge initiated significant development that changed the isolated hippie beach into an upscale area and created environmental and traffic problems for the Pagoda.

The old drawbridge had been a block south of the entrance to the Pagoda, at the west end of Vilano Road. By the 1990s, that bridge had become a thorn in the flesh of Vilano Beach community leaders, who had been lobbying for a new bridge high enough to allow boat traffic coming down the ICWW. Starting in 1993, Edith, Barbara, and Lavender engaged unsuccessfully in lengthy correspondence with the Florida Department of Transportation (FDOT) to relocate the new bridge away from the Pagoda front entrance, and, failing that, to provide safety barriers or a guardrail. Later Garnett Harrison corresponded with several project engineers about the matter, all to no avail. During construction, the horrendous noise was a constant reminder that their peaceful community was being invaded.

When the Usina Bridge opened in October 1995, the new traffic configuration placed a traffic signal directly in front of the Pagoda entrance. Traffic coming off the bridge is supposed to turn right or left onto Coastal Highway, but cars began smashing through the Pagoda front gate regularly, usually late at night, like the drunk driver in January 1996. One even drove all the way down the sand road between the Pagoda cottages to the beachfront lots before stalling. Within the first six months after the bridge opened, there were six accidents involving Pagoda property. This was exactly what the community had feared, and what Pagoda women had tried to prevent by proposing changes before the bridge was built. Luckily, no one was ever injured or killed, and sometimes the drivers had insurance to pay for whatever was damaged, but other times the drivers fled the scene. Pagoda women were advised to reroute their traffic via Beachcomber Way, but they could not erect a metal barrier to block the highway entrance because that entrance was needed for emergency vehicles. It was a very literal reminder of how alarmingly fragile their small enclave was, and how easily invaded.

After spending more than two thousand dollars of Center funds for a bridge study and fence repair, Morgana and Rena wrote letters to the county commission and finally got some concessions from the FDOT. The state installed a two-headed arrow sign near the Pagoda entrance, and set the traffic light to "rest" on red from 10:00 p.m. to 6:00 a.m. Both were recommendations of the traffic engineers whom the Pagoda had hired. That greatly reduced the car crashes, although a dump truck crashed into a parked car there as recently as 2021.

In 1996, the Pagoda Center faced a financial crisis precipitated by a declining number of monthly supporters making financial donations combined with increased reliance on guests paying nightly.[3] The guest price structure had never been adequate to sustain the Center. They asked supporters to consider adding $5 to their monthly contribution "during the lean months," and some did, but the request was a harbinger of things to come. Videos of well-attended Pagoda birthday concerts in 1995 and 1996 show the emcees asking for donations of money or goods or time.[4] They kept the admission prices low (throughout the 1990s, there was a $5–$15 sliding scale), and you could still rent a space at the Center for $15 a night (or only a pool fee if you were a paid-up supporter), but monthly Center expenses sometimes exceeded income by as much as $500.

Something had to change. The corporation (Pagoda-temple of Love) took the lead and proposed selling the Center and swimming pool to another lesbian group and moving the church to the mountains of Alabama. Morgana, Fayann, and Barbara were actively seeking financing for land they had found to start the new lesbian residential community that became Alapine.[5] The proposal needed community support. The community sprung into action at the prospect of moving the Pagoda hundreds of miles north, thereby losing the cultural treasure they had enjoyed for nearly twenty years.

Rena, Emily Greene, and Garnett and Cindy organized a February 1996 retreat to brainstorm alternatives.[6] None of them lived at the Pagoda, and only Emily lived and worked in St. Augustine, but they were committed to finding a way to continue the Pagoda as an active cultural center and guesthouse. At the daylong retreat, which had fourteen attendees, including Morgana,[7] they proposed several alternatives to selling the property, such as closing the guesthouse to nightly rentals except to supporters, or running it as a "dyke hostel" with no on-site greeting, and minimal housekeeping. They even pondered leasing it to a lesbian as a bed-and-breakfast for women. All the alternatives included keeping the theatre free for cultural and spiritual activities. No one wanted the life of the cultural center to end, nor did they want to sell the property. "We love supporting women-only space," they wrote to supporters, "we love creating women's culture. . . . Won't you join us in making changes at the Pagoda that help her to be the best spiritual, cultural, educational, healing lesbian community center that she can be."

To involve supporters in the changes they saw would be necessary, they sent a two-page survey to 240 women on their mailing list (cottage owners, supporters, and others), and got 40 replies, most from residents and cottage owners.[8] Almost all wanted to continue as it was. In the end, that is roughly what they attempted to do, with a restructured board. The idea was to have a working board, with board members heading committees and taking (unpaid) responsibility for the many different tasks involved in running the guesthouse and cultural center.

For many years, Pagoda-temple of Love had operated with a Circle of Wise Womyn, to which any paid-up supporter could be added. The number of supporters was constantly changing, but at times it had been over a hundred.[9] The official bylaws they had been operating under called for a board of from seven to thirty-three people. In practice, decisions were made by whoever showed up at the monthly business meetings, which were notorious for running too long because of the difficulties in reaching a consensus. They had struggled mightily to schedule those meetings at times when nonresidents might be able to attend, but most meetings for which we have records show from five to ten people present, all or nearly all Pagoda residents or locals.[10]

In restructuring the board and making a new start, the Pagoda community pulled together to find a way to sustain the sanctuary they had created and nurtured for so long. Of the longtime Pagoda women, Rena, Morgana, Fayann, Barbara, Emily, Jean, Edith, and Joycie all served on the new thirteen-member board. Garnett and Cindy took a strong role on the board, too, Cindy as membership chair and Garnett handling meeting minutes (eventually, she was made secretary of the corporation).[11] Under the new order, only board members would attend meetings and make decisions. Most of the thirteen board members would serve on one of eleven standing committees. The committees would handle decisions about day-to-day activities, and the board would meet less often.[12]

Things got off to a shaky start. With only seven board members living in St. Augustine, and only Edith and Joycie living full-time at the Pagoda, they had very few feet on the ground. (Rainbow still lived in her cottage but did not want to be on the board.) By April, Edith wanted to resign from the board, but agreed to continue doing bookkeeping.[13] Fayann, who lived almost five hundred miles away, was head of two committees, maintenance and building and grounds. During the winter months, when she lived at the Pagoda (until 1997), she was able to maintain the swimming pool and other tasks, but it was not enough. They hired residents to do reservations, pool maintenance, and housecleaning, but maintaining a building and grounds—especially a beach property—with overnight guests coming and going as well as events happening frequently, needed a manager who could give it daily attention. The part-time managers they hired for seventy hours a month didn't last, perhaps because Pagoda could not afford to pay for the number of hours really needed to do the job.

Then two full-time residents stepped up to hold things together, She Fay and Jennie Iacona (later known as Jennie Lin). Jennie was retired from the military and had bought Marilyn and Irene's cottage. Although a newcomer to the community, she soon took on responsibility for managing the Center, but often found herself at odds with long-standing community members when trying to enforce the rules. She relied on She Fay, who had known the residents longer and was better at interpersonal communication. She Fay had been cottage hopping at the Pagoda since 1982, and Jennie talked her into becoming more involved in Pagoda activities.

She Fay had been producing concerts at the Pagoda since 1992. Now she began taking on the thirty-hour-a-month job of cleaning the Center, and then handling reservations. A musician herself, she was on the Cultural Productions Committee and continued to produce many concerts, as well as performing with her band, SueShe, and her choral group, Full Circle Round.[14] During those years, her bands played at several fund-raisers for the Pagoda.

Full Circle Round ensemble. *Left to right:* Dorothy Campbell, She Fay, Susan Miller, and Amanda Ojay.

In 1998, She Fay bought the cottage she had been renting from Rose DeBernardo, but she was the only committee member who was not a board member. She and Jennie (also not a board member) often put in more hours than they were paid for. She Fay also worked in town as well as making and selling her art. They both did the Pagoda work out of commitment to the community and cultural center. It was worth it to live in a beach cottage surrounded by lesbians, only steps away from the ocean and with a private swimming pool.

But things were different. Decisions were no longer in the hands of whoever attended business meetings. The people charged with enforcing decisions—Jennie and She Fay—were shut out of the decision-making process. In fact, few full-time residents were involved in decision-making in these days, and without a newsletter, communication between the residential community and the wider community was sporadic.

In spite of the serious financial difficulties and organizational changes going on in those last four years, the Pagoda women, especially Lin Daniels and She Fay, did produce a substantial number of concerts by local and touring musicians: ten in 1996 and seven in 1997, although the number dropped to five in 1998 and four in 1999. Those numbers are comparable with the early 1980s. Pagoda had advertised only five concerts in 1981 and four in 1982. In fact, the women produced more concerts in 1996 than in all but three previous years. It also speaks of the Pagoda's symbolic power that the concerts in 1981–1982 and those in 1998–1999 included both Alix Dobkin and Kay Gardner.[15]

The Pagoda's spiritual activities continued during this period as well, although much more difficult to track now since there was no regular monthly newsletter during those years. Rena's 1997 calendar marks sacred circles for spring equinox, a white owl circle, summer solstice, and Lammas, and other sources show a Hallowmas celebration. That year, Rainbow published an occasional "Pagoda News" sheet, which shows a September full moon ritual with drumming and describes turtles being born on the beach. In December, a mailing advertising Inanna and the Five Directions has a note asking addressees for three dollars to stay on the mailing list. That same month, Jennie and Lin Daniels organized some community meetings and published a community newsletter just for residents, *Neighbor Wimmin*. There are no records of sacred circles in 1998, but for 1999 they had five, including a Hallowmas circle and croning.

In addition to concerts, in three of the last four years there is some kind of Pagoda birthday celebration in July. Rainbow's Amazing Almost All Girl String Band played for it in 1996, She Fay's band Squash Blossoms and her ensemble Full Circle Round performed for the twentieth-birthday celebration in 1997, and She Fay's groups Full Circle Round and SueShe performed in 1998.

That month of July 1998, wildfires turned Florida into a less desirable vacation spot for weeks on end. Pagoda women disagree about whether the wildfires were the tipping point in Pagoda finances, but they clearly had a negative impact on the Pagoda. Newspaper reports say that these were the worst wildfires in fifty years, with over two thousand separate conflagrations, seventy new ones starting daily.[16] Orlando, home of Disney World, had an almost 10 percent decline in out-of-state visitors that year.[17] The fires did not directly affect St. Johns County, but the smoke did. St. Augustine resident and Pagoda supporter Sandy Murphree described it in an April 1999 report to the board:

> As a result of the fires in Florida in the summer of 1998, the tourist industry in all of Florida was hurt. The Pagoda was not immune to this disaster. Women who had planned a trip to the Pagoda had to cancel their reservations because the major highways were closed for extended periods of time. Because the smoke was intense, some women came and left sooner than they originally would have. Supporters in the local area also did not come to the Pagoda for access to the pool or concerts. Publicity on the national news may also have contributed to fewer women planning to come to Florida on vacation. This had a critical impact on the income of the Pagoda during the second half of 1998.[18]

Income was down about 50 percent in both July and August 1998, just as the pricey liability insurance was coming due.

Correspondence between Jennie Lin and Barbara Lieu during 1998 and 1999 provides a window on how Jennie saw things. From having been praised in Rainbow's 1997 newsletter—"Jennie has the pool and grounds looking super and also keeps the guest rooms booked"—the Jennie in the correspondence of those last two years is beleaguered by problems with the facility, the neighbors, and the guests. The file includes Pagoda-temple of Love Supporter Agreements, and copies of emails and letters regarding various disputes that were going on. From the beginning, it is clear that Barbara is depending heavily on Jennie to keep the business running and to keep Barbara updated so that she (Barbara) can do the Center bookkeeping. During this time, Edith George, who had been handling many business details for the Pagoda cottage associations, suffered health issues leading to her death of cancer in February 1999. Barbara was turning over more and more business tasks to Jennie. Barbara herself was handling the new business of developing Alapine, as well as dealing with her mother's illness and death in New York.

Documents posted in the Center in January and February 1999 have an undertone of irritation probably arising from financial strains. There are disputes over "changes, repairs, donations or additions to the Center Pool and surrounding grounds" being made without Jennie's or She Fay's approval.[19] There is difficulty enforcing the requirement that only paying Pagoda supporters can use the pool and laundry room, and there is a testy note to residents saying that the Centerkeeper is not responsible for delivering their mail.

In this uneasy atmosphere, twelve Pagoda women met in February to discuss the financial situation and interpersonal issues.[20] This meeting included both residents and nonresidents (three board members attended), but She Fay and Jennie were unable to attend (perhaps they were purposely excluded). She Fay received a recording of the meeting that was incomplete. Rainbow's email to the Sugarloaf women's community about the meeting says that meeting attendees raised concerns about the deficit and the need for more paying supporters; ten more giving fifteen dollars a month would cure the deficit. Elethia (who attended the meeting, even though she was no longer a resident or cottage owner) wrote Barbara that she thinks the spiritual energy has left the Pagoda and that "I do strongly feel the temple belongs at Cloudland,"[21] the community near where Morgana, Fayann, and Barbara have started Alapine.

Spirituality was deeply embedded in the Pagoda community, in the crystals they buried at the corners, the pyramid on the beach, the music they played, the Goddess statues and pottery on lawns. Frequent visitor Martine Giguère recalls "the ambient spiritual sacredness and the Goddesses' faith."[22] It is typical of the Pagoda that during all of this upheaval, they celebrated Candlemas in February and spring equinox in March, the latter paired with a concert by Carole Eagleheart. But the divisions and challenges that had marked the Growers phase continued to trouble the waters of the Reclaimers phase.

Early in 1999, Morgana sent out a long, handwritten "Message from the President" announcing that the church was moving its operations to northeast Alabama, near Cloudland, Georgia. She words it tactfully: "we are beginning a new cycle of transition" since the restructuring in 1996.[23] On behalf of the board, she invites proposals by April 10, and says that the only way for the Florida community and cultural center to remain associated with the church is to form a chapter. It was a bombshell letter that left residents and supporters hurrying to find a way to save the day.

On May 1, Jennie wrote Barbara that she recommended selling everything and moving the church to Cloudland, saying that she had thought about buying it as a bed-and-breakfast, but now thinks "it is more trouble and money than I can afford."[24] Two months later, Jennie resigned, and Barbara turned to She Fay to carry on the work that Jennie had been doing. She Fay had been cutting back her hours, but now took on a major time commitment, thinking there was still hope of keeping the Pagoda going as it had been for so many years. Barbara's letter to She Fay lets her know that the business was in the red $4200 as of the end of June, insurance was coming due in September, and there was the water bill that all the cottages and the Center shared, and that Edith used to handle. The Pagoda was in dire straits.[25]

Jennie's resignation came a week after a Pagoda birthday letter that Morgana sent to the board, dated July 7, 1999, Pagoda's twenty-second birthday. With this letter, Morgana sent the board the proposals that had been received at the April 10 meeting, including a compromise proposal to continue the retreat and cultural center in Florida while also reviving the Crones Nest project by acquiring property in the Alabama mountains. The compromise requires raising $50,000 to $60,000 to renovate the building, eliminate the deficit, and have enough left for a down payment on property in Alabama for Crones Nest. They have to raise that much by October or "probably have to sell the building."

From this letter, it appears that the board was holding out what was little more than a forlorn hope in the proposal to raise the needed funds by October. Some hoped to continue as before. Back in April, She Fay and Jennie had submitted a proposal to promote the Pagoda and increase business with a website, which they offered to build. Businesses were in fact beginning to prosper through web advertising, but in 1999 websites were new, and the board didn't want to be that public. After submitting this proposal, She Fay and Jennie were told there would be another meeting, but that never happened. She Fay learned that the church had accepted an offer to buy the Center and pool when someone called her in October or November to tell her "Pagoda's closed." She had to cancel December bookings. The last advertised sacred circle under the auspices of Pagoda-temple of Love was the Hallowmas circle and croning on Sunday, October 31, 1999.

No one really wanted to sell the Pagoda Center and pool, but the Pagoda-temple of Love officers had moved and shifted their vision to the mountains. They made a business decision that made sense to the board. Morgana was making one last attempt to find a way around selling the property by proposing that Pagoda women raise $50,000 to $60,000 between July and October. Pagoda had never raised that kind of money except through mortgages, and the church was not interested in mortgaging the building, which probably would not have qualified for a mortgage anyway. Several groups were forming to try to raise funds, but not as a donation to Pagoda-temple of Love. All the fund-raising was focused on buying the building and swimming pool in order to keep the cultural center going under new management.

Fairy Godmothers, Inc., was the group that succeeded. For some, it was a sad ending, for others a brand-new beginning.

Afterstory
2000–2022

Path to the beach

Photo by Rose Norman

Chapter 10
Transforming with Fairy Godmothers, Inc.

It was a cold December night in St. Augustine when four women, giddy with excitement, purchased the property that had been the Pagoda-temple of Love guesthouse and cultural center. The new owners, known as Fairy Godmothers, Inc. (FGI), would call it Pagoda by the Sea and were filled with energy and optimism about this new adventure. It would never be the same, nor did they intend it to be. They were buying not a church but a building and pool that they envisioned as a women's guesthouse. For Rena Carney, it was a fresh start on the journey begun when she and the other members of Terpsichore first found those little beach cottages and began remodeling the garage of the big two-story house for their dance theatre. Rainbow Williams was excited about the opportunity to develop the cultural center for art exhibits and to celebrate pagan holy days there. Marie Squillace and Liz Daneman had less personal history with the Pagoda community, but all four Fairy Godmothers knew what it meant to people, residents and visitors alike. They were thrilled by the challenge of transforming the property and beginning a new phase of its herstory. These women had no idea what the future would bring. It was not what they expected.

Rena was the Fairy Godmother who had pulled it all together, motivated by her long history as a Pagoda founding mother and her commitment to sustaining the dream of preserving women's space in a cultural center. In the spring of 1999, when the Pagoda-temple of Love board had called for proposals, Rena had started recruiting friends to buy the property from the church. At one time, she had as many as eight people interested, including Morgana, as well as others closely associated with the Pagoda. In the end, four of them purchased the building and pool from the Pagoda-temple of Love. Rainbow had been at the Pagoda almost as long as Rena—in her case, since the early 1980s. Marie had been around since the late 1980s, and Liz, the youngest of them, had first come to the Pagoda during her freshman year in college, 1978–1979.

In the 1990s, Liz Daneman had taken what she calls a "midlife retirement" to figure out what she wanted to do with her life. Raised by two lesbian mothers on St. Simon's Island, Georgia, she had an idyllic childhood with lots of freedom to roam and sail and seek adventure. That spirit has guided her whole life, from training as a classical musician at Florida State to retraining as a merchant mariner in the oil fields off the Texas–Louisiana and Mexican coast, after she realized that teaching music was not going to pay her bills. During her "retirement" in the 1990s, she volunteered at the Okefenokee National Wildlife Refuge, played clarinet in the St. Augustine Symphony, built a sailboat in the river near Palatka, Florida, went back to college in the sciences—and bought the Pagoda Center as part of FGI. In those first years, Liz was project manager for major renovations to the house and pool, taking on as many renovation tasks as she could do herself. She also set up bookkeeping procedures, kept the books herself for several years, and prepared taxes with the accountant.

Fairy Godmothers Rena, Marie, and Liz taking care of some business.

Marie Squillace was the only Fairy Godmother raised outside the South. She grew up in Fall River, Massachusetts (the home of Lizzie Borden), went to Catholic schools, and at eighteen joined VISTA (Volunteers in Service to America), which got her out of Fall River and eventually to Vermont and New Hampshire, where she spent twenty years. She initially learned about the Pagoda through a book about travels for women, probably *Gaia's Guide*, and first visited in 1987, staying a week at the Center. She loved the town and the community so much that she subscribed to the *St. Augustine Record* from Brattleboro, Vermont, where she and her life partner were then running a used car business. When her partner died a few years later, Marie sold the business and moved to St. Augustine, first renting part of Kay Mora and Jean Adele's beach house, then buying the beachfront lot next door to it. After renting Emily Greene's cottage for several years, Marie sold the lot and bought Emily's cottage in 1992. Around 1995, she became the Centerkeeper, and really enjoyed the job: "I would touch up, clean, make beds, make introductions for where to go and what to do. I enjoyed that. That was the ambassador in me. I would often go out and have lunch with people. I saw an array of women for those years." She also met her next life partner at the Pagoda. Together, they adopted two baby girls. However, in the nearly thirty years she has lived in that cottage, she never shared it with a partner, reflecting that "this was always *my* safe space." Over the years, she would instead move in with the partner and rent her Pagoda cottage to lesbian weekenders, usually from the Gainesville area. It was after a breakup in 2001 that she moved back to her cottage permanently, and so had more time to devote to running the guesthouse for FGI.

Rainbow Williams was living on site, too, but was far less interested in running the guesthouse than in the cultural work. She had been an artist since childhood and focused her entire life on making art—especially assemblages made from found materials and crafts like weaving, batik, woodworking, and printmaking. Raised in Shreveport, Louisiana, by a single mother who encouraged her art, Rainbow was a generation older than the other Fairy Godmothers (born in 1934) and came of age before the modern women's movement was born. She had wanted to study architecture in college but found her way blocked at the University of Arkansas because of her sex. She studied fine art and married an architecture student: "Neither of us wanted to get married, but we wanted family (how gay is that?). We wanted to devote our lives to art, architecture, travel." They wound up in Winter Park, near Orlando, and adopted two children. She and a neighbor started a school for their children, naming it StoneSoup School.[1] Eventually, she fell in love with her neighbor, came out as a lesbian, found the women's movement, and divorced her gay husband. In 1977, she attended her first women's music festival, the National Women's Music Festival, where she learned about *Lesbian Con-*

nection, which in turn introduced her to a culture she heartily embraced. Rainbow and other Orlando NOW volunteers published the feminist newsletter *Changes* for eight years, from 1977 to 1985, and she hosted NOW and consciousness-raising groups at her Winter Park home. She called it the Wimmin's House and also hosted monthly full moon gatherings in the backyard, as well as "witchy weekends" that included Tarot readings. Through newsletter swaps, she learned about the Pagoda and started spending backpack weekends there in 1978, moving there permanently in 1984, the year she turned fifty.

Rena Carney was the Fairy Godmother who had been there the longest. Her decision to leave the Pagoda stage in 1980 did not mean that she left the Pagoda. Indeed, she considers her Pagoda cottage, now called Sea Turtle, her true home, and it has been her permanent address for more than four decades. She spent most of the 1980s and '90s living in what she calls her "work houses" in Gainesville, Melrose, and Tallahassee, while she built her career as a speech pathologist and continued her acting career at the Hippodrome Theatre. In the 1990s, her active role on the restructured Pagoda board had put her in a position to take on the challenge of buying the property. She credits Fairy Godmothers, Inc., with saving the property during the rapid explosion of development on Vilano Beach. The new bridge was just the beginning.

All four Fairy Godmothers knew that the condition of the Center building and swimming pool would not qualify the property for a mortgage. They each were able to offer $20,000 cash to meet the $80,000 asking price. The condition of the property made $80,000 "as is" a sensible price to both sellers and buyers, and the Pagoda women would not have dreamed of putting it on the open market. The church board was committed to selling at an affordable price to lesbians who understood the cultural work the Pagoda had been doing and wanted to carry it on.

The four buyers got expert advice from a lesbian attorney who specialized in probate law, and formed the corporation Fairy Godmothers, Inc. They proceeded to follow their attorney's advice that "if you want to be a corporation, you have to act like a corporation." That meant hiring attorneys to handle easements and other issues, rather than relying on pro bono work, and hiring licensed workers to repair the building and pool. This was a change that some old Pagodans, used to a more relaxed style, resented.

The Fairy Godmothers all wanted to provide women-only space at reasonable rates and to continue the cultural work of the Center. Rena, Rainbow, and Liz were artists and performers who treasured the performance space, and they all wanted to share it with lesbians. All but Liz owned a Pagoda cottage, and Liz's close friend Cindy Thompson had bought Morgana's cottage, so Liz always had a place to stay at the Pagoda. Rena was living in Melrose, Liz was living with Cindy in Macclenny (she also still owned a house in Melrose), and Marie was living with a partner in Micanopy—all towns over an hour's drive from the Pagoda. Only Rainbow was living full-time at her Pagoda cottage when FGI bought the property.

They held one of their first meetings as a corporation on February 13, 2000, at Liz's house in Melrose. There they decided that each of them would contribute $2000 for repairs. Three-quarters of that $8000 would go to repairing the swimming pool, which was full of rotten water and black mold. The rest went toward repairing the roof and painting and repairing the second floor and deck. It was the first of many monthly assessments as they made many repairs to the roof, plumbing, and flooring. They decide to rent the Alcove nightly for a year, then reassess, and that they would look for a second-floor tenant on a long-term lease. The theatre space would be kept available for events, but the attic would not be rented out because the stairs were not built to code and could create liability problems. At the April meeting they divided up tasks. Rena was named president and would focus on finances and corporate business; the vice president was Marie, who would handle reservations and investments; Liz became the treasurer and would manage renovations and handle bookkeeping; and the secretary was Rainbow, who would focus on trees and activities. They tabled discussion of the theatre and attic.

Since the early days of trying to run a lesbian resort, the women of the Pagoda had learned how much work was involved in providing space for short-term stays at the beach. Aside from bookkeeping and taking reservations, there was housekeeping and laundry, publicity, and dealing with issues like pets and parking and nudity. Initially, the four women had agreed to take turns running the operation, three months at a time. That would include managing tenants and guests. With only Rainbow, and then Marie, living on site, that soon became unworkable, and they struggled to find a fair way of dividing the work. Rena and Marie both had full-time jobs, and Rena's job soon took her to Tallahassee, over three hours away from the Pagoda.

In the beginning, Liz spent a lot of time on site managing renovations. There were, for example, major repairs to the pool, problems with the roof and flooring, and the upstairs plumbing had to be replaced. It seemed that every time they started a repair on the building, they discovered it was worse than they thought (as is often the case in old houses), and this property had had years of deferred maintenance. The roof had never been repaired properly after the fire when Jane Schilling owned the building. Roofers found that burned timbers had not been replaced and would not hold a shingle. That roof had leaked from the time the Pagoda first owned it.

Over time, FGI completely rebuilt three exterior walls damaged by the leaking roof.

Because of the condition of the building and pool, FGI focused on facilities during that first year or so. They had made a conscious decision not to acquire church status or to become a chapter of the Pagoda-temple of Love. As important as that church was in their lives (especially to Rena and Rainbow), their business plan called for a guesthouse with a theatre, and they needed to make the building fit to sustain that. They wanted tenants and guests, and they expected to produce events with low overhead, such as art exhibits, rather than concerts involving paid performers.

They also wanted to continue the rituals. Without Morgana's presence, the full moon circles and other spiritual events had already slowed down in the late 1990s, but the Fairy Godmothers intended to continue them. In that first year, 2000, Rainbow recalls meetings on her Pagoda porch to organize events, sometimes with as many as twelve women attending, including a combination of Pagoda cottage owners and St. Augustine friends.[2] Most of the work of facilitating circles fell to Rainbow. A flyer titled "Pagoda by the Sea 2000 Calendar" lists all eight pagan holidays, as well as Pagoda's birthday party, Fairy Godmothers' Birthday (November 11), Dykesgiving Day, and XXmas Potluck Feast. This seems to have been an aspirational calendar, and it is unclear which events happened. In a personal memoir of the Pagoda, Rainbow recalls a Lammas circle in August 2000 with thirteen attending, and says that she believes the last holy day celebrated under FGI management was a Hallowmas circle in the fall of 2000.[3] After they rented the ground floor to tenants, they no longer had the theatre space. Rainbow would organize events outdoors, on the beach or in Persephone's Garden,[4] which Pagoda-temple of Love (now relocated in Alabama) allowed them to use.

The vision of the Fairy Godmothers as a for-profit corporation running a guesthouse meant that they had to pay property taxes on the building and pool. While liability insurance cost less than if the building that had been the Pagoda Center were still owned by a church, it was a hefty sum. Rental income covered routine maintenance, but not the major repairs that came up over and over, nor the taxes, which skyrocketed during the real estate boom. Every year, the four Fairy Godmothers had to dig into their pockets to pay the property tax bill. In the first year, the taxes more than tripled, from $197 to $716; they would continue to rise rapidly, reaching $13,304 annually by 2008.[5]

Adding to these costs were damages associated with the new bridge over the ICWW, which continued to occasionally bring cars crashing through the front gate. Once, a car wreck took out the exterior stairs to the second floor. Because that was the only entrance to that floor, a firetruck had to be summoned to get the tenants out. The new bridge also brought major development of property in Vilano Beach. Real estate values ballooned in the years leading up to the global financial crash in 2008. In spite of a huge capitalization appreciation, FGI was not breaking even on expenses. Each Fairy Godmother personally owed $3326 in property tax that year, and $532.50 apiece for liability insurance.[6]

Plagued by financial worries and living in different towns, they struggled financially and with one another and tenants and neighbors, until they faced the fact that the property had become a burden. The building where so many lesbian artists performed, the symbol of the Pagoda community for over twenty years, where so many women enjoyed lesbian-only or women-only space, had to transform itself once again. They had agreed from the start to give it five years and then sell if they couldn't make it. It was time to sell.

The Fairy Godmothers first decided to sell in 2005, when property taxes reached $7822. That year, FGI and the owners of cottages 1–4 also spent $11,000 successfully defending their easement to the beach, a path now running between two new houses (where before had been vacant lots). Other inherited easement and zoning issues, as well as their desire to sell to lesbians, delayed any sale. Then the market crashed in 2008. When the market value plummeted, so did the appraised value and their property tax.

The property remained on the market for a total of eleven years. During these years, FGI shifted to long-term rentals to lesbians, renting parts of the building; nevertheless, they could not find enough tenants. In the end, they found that renting the whole building to one tenant was the only way to break even, and that they could not sustain the women-only policy.[7]

The property was still zoned commercial, so there was real concern that it not be sold to a developer who would open a gas station or convenience store so close to the cottages. Rena worked closely with a realtor who gave them years of free advice about pricing, zoning, and easements. These complicated matters required thousands in lawyer's fees on the way to a favorable resolution. Rena wrote many letters to former Pagoda supporters trying to interest them in buying the property, and attended many county commission meetings in pursuit of zoning changes. After much work of this kind, she succeeded in getting the space zoned residential, and they sold the property at the end of 2016 to Dustin Heath, an "old surfer hippie" (in Rainbow's words), who owned many local properties and who they thought planned to live there. In the end, he remodeled it extensively and listed it for short-term vacation rentals. Soon, the duplex sold to another man, who also rented it to vacationers, and a new era of unrest began among cottage residents, as a trail of tourists began walking down the little sand road between their cottages on the way to the beach. As long as FGI owned it, much as some of the neighbors resented the changes, at least it was lesbian property, but when it sold, the Pagoda was truly gone.

The community of cottages remains, mostly lesbian-owned and occupied on Lots 3 and 4, and now all legally zoned residential, a benefit gained when FGI got the Center building rezoned. That was an important change for cottages 1–5, which had been zoned commercial until then. FGI had also taken care of easement issues affecting the cottages on Lot 3.[8] In 2011, when she wanted to enclose her screen porch as a living room, Rena spent more than $10,000 of her own money on legal fees, finally obtaining a legal permit for the addition. Until that point, the county had refused to issue building permits on the Pagoda properties (cottages 1–8) due to nonconforming lot sizes.

Fairy Godmothers had been a grand experiment and a mighty effort to, in Rena's words, "keep the ol' girl afloat." FGI held on for sixteen years, paying huge taxes, keeping up with rapid coastal development, and enduring pushback from a community that found it hard to release expectations inherited from the Pagodatemple of Love days. FGI saved the building, ushered in masthead lighting, changed the zoning to residential, established the permitting processes for improvements, and, most important, established legal easements. Today, residents own their homes, and the property is a sound financial investment.

Although FGI was clear from the beginning that the church was gone (thus the old Pagoda was gone), it took longer for the residential community to internalize what that meant. No longer did two cottage associations govern a community. The cottages on Beachcomber Way became once more set off from the Old Pagoda cottages. Those eight Old Pagoda cottages are still there, mostly very well cared for, owned and occupied by women. They are still very close together, and parking remains difficult. Private ownership of the individual cottages has made a smoother transition than if they or the land had been collectively owned. Residents have benefited from community behaviors learned in Old Pagoda days. They still watch out for one another. The roots of the old Pagoda community run deep.

Chapter 11
Living in Community

"Lesbiana . . . it became my country, a space where I belonged. A territory beyond borders, made up of islands linked to each other by love, ideas, and political affinities." In these opening lines from her film *Lesbiana: A Parallel Revolution* (2012), longtime Pagoda cottage owner and sometime resident Myriam Fougère describes the alternative world that lesbian-feminists sought to create in the last three decades of the twentieth century. Through women's music festivals and women's residential land groups, lesbians attempted, in Myriam's words, "to break free from patriarchy and live beyond its narrow definition of 'woman'" by creating physical space in which to "grow individually as well as collectively, laying the foundation for this different world we envisioned," the world she names "Lesbiana." The Pagoda was one of those "islands," unique in combining the music, art, and social engagement of a women's festival with a residential community supporting a cultural center. It was a remarkable achievement. For two decades, the residential community surrounding the Goddess-church-owned cultural center strived mightily to sustain the Center and to build good relations among residents. But, as Irene Weiss remarks in *Lesbiana*, "We don't know how to live in community." This chapter explores the ways that the Pagoda women faced the many challenges of living in community and balancing the needs of residents with the needs of the larger community of supporters.

Creating and protecting women-only space was important to all of them, residents and nonresident supporters alike, but it was radical. It was a new idea and a bodacious experiment that they would have to figure out as they went along. They were united in wanting to protect women's space, but it was not always clear to them how to achieve that. Marilyn Murphy once described Pagoda women as "strong-willed, opinionated women who agree with the community's women-only policy but little else."[1] Singer-songwriter Elaine Townsend (thirty years younger than Marilyn) saw Pagoda women as "empowered, almost larger-than-life people." Undoubtedly, these women were not afraid of a challenge.

Perhaps their greatest success was in creating the feeling of a healing environment. And it wasn't just temporary, a transient feeling evoked by music or chanting or dancing or magic spells. Elaine recalls, "I would see women pull up for their week there, and you could kind of see the outside world melt away," and Lin Daniels has "wonderful memories of that place being a miracle in the world at that time." For residents like Elaine and Lin, there was an everyday awareness that building community means taking care of one another. The Pagoda residents saw themselves as family, chosen family that looked out for each other. When mica (Meri Furnari) had knee surgery and was incapacitated for six months, the community took care of her, "visiting, bringing food, and cheering me up and rooting me on."[2] When Garnett Harrison visited after fleeing her home state of Mississippi in fear of her life, she found sanctuary, healing space. When resident Emily Greene experienced serious emotional problems arising from her work as director of nursing at a local nursing home, Pagoda women brought Emily's mother and sister from Massachusetts to visit and got Emily into professional therapy.

At first, Emily resented their intervention, but "once I was somewhat out of the deep ditch I'd crawled into, I was able to feel grateful to these women who cared enough to take those steps. . . . That experience saved my life, and I moved on to be a more confident person." For these women and many others, the Pagoda achieved its goal of providing space for healing and growth.

One way of building that close community was through the weekly gathering known as Group. For the first ten years or so, some residents gathered on Thursday nights for the purpose of resolving interpersonal issues associated with living in community. They always began the meeting by calling a Power of Protection, visualizing a bubble around the land and sending energy to absent friends. They had a timekeeper, a "vibes watcher," and three communication rules: "1. Speaking in the I. 2. Staying in the here and now. 3. Identifying one's feelings."[3] Residents were not required to attend Group, but they were expected to bring neighborhood conflicts to Group if they could not work them out on their own. Group was neither a business meeting nor a therapy group, though some criticized it on both counts. It evolved over time, as the women experimented with different ways of interacting that may have seemed like psychotherapy to others (some regular Group attendees were therapists). For women who attended regularly for many years (such as Barbara, Lavender, Morgana, Martha, Elethia, Emily, Jean), Group built deep friendships, as they came to know one another better, and became a support group. Others found Group unhealthy and stopped attending (for example, Rena and Rainbow). After trying it out, Marilyn and Irene objected to Group vehemently, finding it way too much like therapy, too focused on feelings.[4]

Women who did not resonate with Group built community in other ways. What appealed to Marilyn and Irene and many of their friends were the Sunday brunches they offered at their cottage, where women could enjoy meals and discuss ideas in a consciousness-raising format, sharing personal stories on a theme (e.g., grandmother stories, attitudes to money), and getting to know one another that way. "That was community building," Cindy Watson says of those Sunday brunches. "It helped us get through some of those hard business meetings. . . . It supported the culture and gave us opportunities to see what we had in common during that really hard time." That "hard time" was when there was disruption around bookkeeping and how money was handled. Cindy goes on, "The lesbian-centered culture was really embedded in everything, and that's why you can't just look at the business aspects of it, which were very hard, because it was always in the context of this affirming aspect of community that continued to bring us together."

The community had been flourishing for over a decade when the North Pagoda expansion brought in new ideas about how to live in community and about many other things. Marilyn and Irene were strict separatists, but not vegetarians or teetotalers: they served meat at those Sunday brunches. For some, those brunches were a nice break from the rigors of lesbian-feminist life. The discussions were interesting and intellectually stimulating, and women formed strong friendships there. Both Group and the Sunday brunches included nonresidents, an extended community, but the brunch group's focus on discussion of ideas attracted more nonresidents and also led to more workshops and study groups. Marilyn and Irene had brought from their Califia experience a strong focus on feminist education and political activism, especially around racism and classism. These interests began to overshadow the focus on feminist spirituality, the moon circles and celebrations of holy days.

This change was important because spirituality was a big part of what made the Pagoda a healing place for women. Forming a women's residential community and cultural center was a separatist act based on the belief that millennia of women's oppression could best be relieved through creating a woman's world, a place where women were cherished and honored for being women, and where women-loving women were the norm. This attitude had its highest expression in spiritual practices celebrating the Goddess, the Great Mother, "the soul of nature that gives life to the universe," in the words of the poem "The Charge of the Goddess."[5] Over and over, at concerts and sacred rituals, these beliefs created the magic bubble that made the Pagoda a sanctuary, safe space for women. During the period of growth and change (1988–1995), new leaders were much more committed to political and social change than to spiritual growth, as suggested by the removal of the altar from the upstairs meeting room, which became more of a living room for guests.

In addition to social methods of building community and settling differences, like Group and Sunday brunches, Pagoda residents also had written agreements. The first association agreement was signed and notarized on July 7, 1977, the day the women closed on the first four cottages. The agreement was necessary because the cottages were on one lot and were purchased on one mortgage. That first agreement specified who had a right to which cottage, what could be done to the exterior of the cottages, and how to get out of the agreement. Residents modified the agreement in 1980 to include the new strip of cottages; at that point the Pagoda began to function as a cottage association, so there were additional agreements about financial arrangements, utilities, and how to handle cottage rentals and turnover. The agreement was revised again in 1982 and 1983 to include new rules for cottage sale. Meanwhile, the Cottage Eligibility List also evolved, and in 1983 their formal agreement linked sale price of cottages to the Consumer Price Index.

Amendments were handled through standing decisions. It was very complicated, and some residents signed the documents but paid little attention to them.

With the North Pagoda purchase, things got even more complicated, as the North Pagoda buyers formed a separate cottage association and handled their business differently, especially as to sale of cottages. Having two cottage associations solved some problems but created community divisions when North Pagoda Cottage Association members were excluded from the other association's meetings about topics they thought affected them all.[6] Their chosen family had become two chosen families.

Neither patriarchal methods like notarized legal agreements nor feminist processing in Group or Sunday brunches prepared them for the challenges of dealing with their extended family, the larger group of Pagoda supporters. The symbol of this larger community was the cultural center, the place where they gathered for concerts, workshops, moon circles, cronings, as well as for business meetings, where they struggled with financial and policy issues. For residents, the cultural center building became a community center, the place where they got their mail, sometimes gathered for meals, and held community celebrations. The church that owned the building and swimming pool encouraged that, and also encouraged nonresident Pagoda supporters to take care of the Center as if it were their own. Alix Dobkin and Denslow Brown discarded a worn-out rug when they were visiting one time, and also bought the first guest book for the Center. A couple visiting from Switzerland, where they ran a lodge, saw that the Center kitchen had only aluminum pans. The next time they visited, they organized a gourmet vegetarian dinner, charged a fee to attend, and used those funds to buy a new set of stainless steel pots and pans. Many visitors were drawn to make that kind of spontaneous contribution of time and skills as they felt themselves part of the Pagoda family of women.

The Pagoda residents worked hard to create this broader sense of community beyond the bounds of physical residency on the land. They posted letters and advertising from supporters on the bulletin board in the Center, frequently solicited feedback through their newsletter, and encouraged supporters to attend monthly business meetings, making great efforts to schedule those meetings when nonresidents could attend. Through the newsletter and opinion surveys, the residents actively involved supporters in decision-making.

Photo by Beth Karbe

Left to right: Beckie Dale, Lynda Lou Simmons, and Judy Keathley, along with Ruth Segal (not in this picture) were frequent visitors and loyal Pagoda supporters from Gainesville, known as "The Gang of 4." When the Pagoda asked supporters to weigh in on controversial decisions, they were likely to write thoughtful and informed letters.

Even though they felt a strong connection to the community as healing space, and generally agreed about valuing women, Pagoda women sometimes found themselves creating feelings of unfairness and hurt around separatist issues involving gender and sexuality. The policy on whether and under what conditions boy children could be allowed on the property changed many times. By 1989, the policy was no males of any age in the Center at any time, but a misunderstanding about that led to a rift with a longtime supporter and her partner, who brought their new baby to the Pagoda in August, the month when they thought that boy children were allowed. When they arrived, they learned that he could not be in the Center, where they had planned to stay. The Pagoda accommodated them by providing cottage space for the couple and their baby, but that couple stopped their monthly donation to the Center and stopped coming. Even strong supporters like Garnett and Cindy found that they could not visit as often after they adopted Garnett's nephews.

Bisexuality became an issue when the Pagoda tried to have some lesbian-only events, which would exclude several longtime Pagoda supporters and performers who identified as bisexual. For a time, when a person advertised with a flyer posted on the Center bulletin board, the Pagoda women labeled the flyer to identify those who did not identify as lesbian (i.e., that they were bisexual or straight). Kathleen Hannan, a musician and massage therapist whose massage flyer was marked "bisexual," wrote to say that, yes, she did identify as bisexual, and she was okay with the labeling. But she did want "to make it clear . . . that my massage sessions are not sexual or political." The ban on bisexuals meant that Kathleen was not allowed to perform in the Pagoda theatre, even though audiences there were rarely lesbian-only. This policy was voted on specifically for her because she was at the time partnered with a man, and she says that it felt different from having her flyer labeled "bisexual" on the Center bulletin board. A personal friend was among those voting against her performing at the Pagoda. At the time, it hurt. She appreciated her friend telling her about it, and in later years Kathleen was again able to perform at the Pagoda, although her sexual identity had not changed. She still has mixed feelings about that episode. She met her life partner at the Pagoda in that era, and they have now been together over twenty years.

Bisexuality and boy children at women's events were issues being negotiated in lesbian spaces nationwide, and occasionally led to major protests. In the fall of 1989, just after that Pagoda supporter and her boy baby were turned away from the Center, there was a huge controversy about boy babies attending the first East Coast Lesbian Festival.[7] Pro-boy lesbian mothers and their supporters drafted a statement read from the stage and cheered by the audience. Then the well-known lesbian-feminist academic Julia Penelope gave a pro-lesbian-only, women-only space statement that provoked boos, hisses, and name-calling. The question of what constituted safe space for women had become deeply divisive within the movement.

At the Pagoda itself, one safe space policy that got national attention in lesbian publications concerned consensual sado-masochistic role playing, now known as BDSM (bondage, domi-nation/discipline, sadomasochism). That controversy came on the heels of a separate controversy about lesbian battering. In both instances, the Pagoda attempted to establish a policy to ensure safe space. For many years, the Pagoda's practice in ad-dressing important policy decisions was to solicit the opinions of supporters through the monthly newsletter, and then post these responses on the bulletin board in the Center. When a topic produced too much mail for the bulletin board, they col-lected it in a file available for reading at the Center, or they would offer to copy and mail it to supporters for a small fee. The folder of correspondence labeled "safe space" (about the lesbian bat-tering issue, 1988–1989) is 95 pages; the folder about consensual sadomasochism (1990) is 102 pages.

These files show how the Pagoda women dealt head-on with issues of the day and their deep commitment to processing them. These two issues were *extremely* divisive, causing a split between the residential community and the extended community of supporters. Many supporters (both residents and non-residents) weighed in at great length on these subjects. They also read and talked about articles from feminist publications—for example, an Audre Lorde interview in 1980 about sadomasochism[8] and Melanie Kaye/Kantrowitz's review of *Naming the Violence: Speaking Out about Lesbian Battering*, in which she pointed out the shortcomings of a view of battering that relies on research done from a heterosexual perspective.[9]

Lesbian battering first became a topic of discussion in July 1987, when two Canadian Pagoda regulars ran a two-week workshop on surviving childhood trauma. The workshop drew twenty-one women, each of whom was asked to identify as a victim, an abuser, or both. Many identified as both. About that time, a Pagoda resident accused a former partner of battering and rape. Six months later, several Pagoda women were proposing a safe space policy that would mean banning lesbians accused of battering. The proposed policy, printed in the January 1988 newsletter, raised the sticky question of how to support the battered lesbian while being fair to the accused lesbian batterer, who usually denied the accusation.

By the late 1980s, women's movement activists had been working hard to address domestic abuse for nearly two decades, founding women's shelters and seeking to educate police about how to protect women in dangerous situations with intimate partners.[10] Feminists popularized the terms "battering" and "domestic abuse" and determined that shelters were a first step toward getting women and children out of dangerous situations at home. Was the Pagoda to become such a shelter?

Was the first partner to accuse the other of battering the only one to be believed? The Pagoda never approved a lesbian battering policy, and because of that some nonresident supporters (both victims and the accused) ended their relationship with the Pagoda community. Residents eventually agreed among themselves to make accommodations for both sides, and not to ban any lesbians.

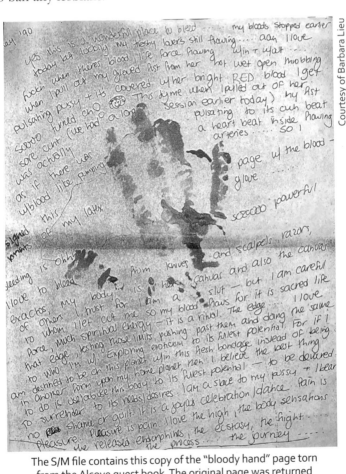

Courtesy of Barbara Lieu

The S/M file contains this copy of the "bloody hand" page torn from the Alcove guest book. The original page was returned during the controversy.

The S/M controversy, on the other hand, led to a proposed policy within days of the incident that started the controversy. Almost the entire Pagoda residential community rose up in protest in May 1990, when a lesbian left a bloody handprint in the guest book, surrounded by a heavily erotic description of consensual sadomasochistic sexual activity. The Centerkeeper removed the offending page immediately, and the incident might have ended there, but emotions around it were so powerful that it led to a community meeting, an anti-S/M policy, and a four-month period of meetings and comment, ending with final approval of the policy. The sign posting the new policy read:

The Pagoda Is Sadomasochism Free Space
Sadomasochistic practices and
displays are not permitted at the Pagoda.
This includes the Center, the Pool,
the Pool area and the Pagoda grounds.

Proponents of consensual S/M practices saw the policy as pure censorship, prurience, and denial of sexual freedom between consenting adults. The linkage of consensual S/M with violence against women infuriated women who understood the philosophy and practice of S/M role playing. The couple whose guest book entry led to the policy protested it vigorously, writing letters to local newsletters and to *Lesbian Connection,* as well as to the Pagoda. Here is the dyke whose blood made the handprint:

As you probably know, herstorically, blood prints are very powerful and highly symbolic of one's spirit essence. Menstrual blood is quite strong. I gave this gift of blood and spirit in perfect love and perfect trust. That blood print captured my passion and love of life.

To have it be in the hands of someone who does not respect my gift feels like rape to me. I feel deeply violated and vulnerable.

As that writer well knew, menstrual blood was indeed respected at the Pagoda, but in a completely different context. Most Pagoda residents were still bleeding monthly, often at the same time, as is common among women living together. They honored menstrual blood in ceremonies. They objected to the sadomasochistic context. The controversial guest book passage reads, in part:

I love fuckin when there's blood, life force flowing within and without . . . when I pull out my gloved fist from her hot wet open throbbing pulsating pussy & it's covered with her bright RED blood I get soooo turned on.

It is signed "a travelling slutty masochist from hell."

Friends who did not themselves practice S/M role playing wrote letters in support of the S/M dykes. For the most part, letters defending the practice are thoughtful and informed, as well as passionate. Those writing in support of the anti-S/M policy are also thoughtful and articulate in equating it with violence, plain and simple, consensual or not, and treating it as unquestionably wrong, case closed. Nipple rings and other uncommon piercings were also offensive to women who connected them with S/M practices. Pagoda resident Joycie Meyers wrote an autobiographical piece titled "I Choose Vanilla," connecting S/M to the horrors and brutality of the Holocaust, which she had learned about as a small Jewish child in America. Joycie's approach to the topic well expresses the incongruity of S/M role playing with what the Pagoda stood for. She recalls the empowerment she felt in coming into her lesbian identity late in life, exhilaration at her first experience of sex with a woman, and awe in gaining respect and admiration for being female, feelings wholly incompatible with S/M:

> We are the source of creativity and life itself, and having access to a woman's incredibly generous sexuality lifted me into a higher realm of existence. Frankly, putting rings and safety pins on the precious orifices that flow so freely with sweet juices; chaining bodies of women (who have traditionally spent too much of their energy serving others); and whipping women (whose greatest flaw probably is their desire to please others instead of themselves) seems, at best, to be a stupid exercise. . . . Surely we can find conquests more challenging and satisfying than dramatizing the patriarchal domination and denigration of women. Being forced to look at these imprints of subjugation upon the female body causes many of us to grieve, unless they are scars of unwilling abuse, which can be emblems of survivorship.[11]

Today, Morgana emphasizes that the Pagoda was a healing space, highly sensitive to the needs of women who had survived sexual abuse. The anti-S/M policy, she explains, was intended to respect those survivors and keep safe space, but did not ban any lesbian from coming to the Pagoda.

In some ways, the divisive energy of these controversies continues today in other controversies in lesbian communities, including discussions around gender identity. Twenty-first-century arguments for inclusiveness in support of gender identity choices echo the arguments supporting consensual S/M practices. In both, lesbians accuse one another of oppression and liken their methods of exclusion to patriarchal methods.[12]

While the Pagoda weathered these intense controversies, their reputation as a community suffered. Leather dykes and their allies, many of them Pagoda regulars, stopped coming to Pagoda events and dropped their monthly donations. Some supporters felt alienated; others felt they would be unwelcome. While the Pagoda women went on to work together to remodel the Center and continued to produce crowd-pleasing cultural events in the years that followed, their reputation for taking controversial positions persisted. Four years after the S/M episode, a colorful letter published in Gainesville's feminist newsletter *Mama Raga* terms the Pagoda temple "the Evil Church of Intrigues."[13]

The controversies around safe space came at a time when the Pagoda community had reached its greatest expansion, with all twelve cottages and the duplex owned by lesbians and the Center and the swimming pool owned by the church. As so many times before—when they bought the first strip of cottages, then the second strip, then the Center building—they just dove right in, driven by lesbian-feminist confidence that they could accomplish what they set their minds to if they worked together. Each expansion faced divisive challenges. The heated controversies around safe space and S/M resulted in more divisions, not so much divisions among residents as between residents and non-resident supporters. Rather than trying to come to consensus, as they had done with the safe space policy, the S/M issue came to a vote. Cottage owners each had one vote; nonresident supporters had one collective vote. That distinction between resident and non-resident voters shattered the illusion that the extended community of nonresident supporters were truly part of the Pagoda community. Even though a survey of all supporters showed strong approval for the policy among nonresidents, the damage was done.[14]

The distinction between cottage owners and nonresident supporters highlights the complicated relationship of the residential community to supporters and to the cultural center. At that time (1990), there were about sixty supporters paying to sustain the cultural center and sixteen cottage owners.[15] Nonresident donations were paying the lion's share of cultural center expenses, and some cottage owners were making no monthly donation to it. Yet residents had a proprietary interest in the Center whether they were sending monthly donations or not. They shared a water supply with the Center. The church owned and maintained the swimming pool they all used. What happened at the Center affected them. It was part of their psychic space, their home space.

For those running the cultural center, living in community meant bringing that residential community and the extended community of supporters into some kind of equilibrium, sometimes a treacherous task. Someone had to read the letters pouring in about the safe space policy, and decide whether some letters were too sensitive for posting. One resident assigned to that task wrote that the battering controversy was disrupting her own feeling of safety in the Pagoda community, that she felt "as though I am being torn apart."[16] She protested the community's willingness to "go out into a raging storm" swirling around the lesbian battering issue. The desire to avoid the "raging storm" expresses what many Pagoda residents and supporters felt about being encouraged to take sides in the various controversies. Most women came there for the beach and the magic and the affirmation that came from being with other lesbians. But that magic and affirmation came with a price. Some individuals are better able to flourish in a feminist community than others, particularly a community with houses so close together, sharing utilities, some of them even sharing water heaters or septic tanks. For Nancy Breeze, who lived at the Pagoda for over a decade, it was "like having a low-grade fever."[17]

Many overlapping reasons led some of those empowered, "larger-than-life" women to move away from the Pagoda, and impelled the church to ultimately sell the building and swimming pool to another lesbian group with a different vision. The Pagoda's ending began before the controversies and financial crises of the 1990s. As early as 1987, Morgana was thinking of the mountains of her childhood summers and drawing Tarot cards that directed her away from the Pagoda. She kept drawing the Tower card, which she always associated with the triplex overlooking the southern strip of cottages since 1980. Pagoda women called it the Tower, and felt that it was menacing in the same way as the new bridge; it invaded them.

When Morgana, Fayann, and Barbara moved to the mountains to start another lesbian residential community, they were guided by all that they had learned at the Pagoda. They bought 108 rural acres divided into two-acre lots. They no longer wanted to run a guesthouse and cultural center or have long meetings, but simply to write legally enforceable neighborhood covenants. Sheeba Mountain Properties, the corporation they formed to develop the property (as a for-profit corporation, not a nonprofit), sold nearly half of the lots to women who had been Pagoda supporters. In this new business model, the corporation could not make new rules beyond the established covenants, nor could a neighborhood association make new rules. Residents who wanted to do projects and socialize did form Alapine Community Association, a nonprofit that some residents joined and that now maintains a community house there.

Marilyn and Irene were deeply involved in the two controversies of 1988–1990, right at the beginning of their residence at the Pagoda. Their attitude toward both battering and S/M was as uncompromising as their views on separatism. Just as they saw no ambiguities in separatism and embraced it wholeheartedly, they equated S/M with battering and opposed compromise. After the controversies died down, they went on to do important work at the Pagoda, as mentioned earlier: they took the lead on remodeling and rescuing the Center and pool and instituted new business practices that improved the financial status of the cultural center. But ongoing disputes between the two cottage associations wore on these strong, empowered women, and they, too, found themselves ready to move on to another women's community far away and with less interest in lesbian-feminist politics.

By 1995, even Rainbow was proposing to lease the center "to a dyke who wants to run a B&B" in order to free residents "from the struggles of bizniz, able to interact socially as friendly neighbors."[18] She wanted to continue the cultural activities (e.g., concerts, art exhibits), and those activities did continue right through the controversies, testament to the community's commitment to and joy in the music and art that were so much a part of the place.

What made the Pagoda unique—that it was both a lesbian residential community and a cultural center—also made it divided. Beginning with a cultural center and rented cottages, the Pagoda Playhouse founders had a vision that continued alongside diverging visions for building lesbian community. Lesbian-feminist separatism in and of itself demanded rules that some found hard to live with (e.g., no boy babies or male relatives or friends allowed). Suzi Chance recalls it today as "two Pagodas," a place to have fun and a place with too many rules. Cindy Watson points out that it was their feminist values that led to decisions creating so many rules, and that the signs posted on the walls of the Center listed the rules, not the values. Other Pagoda women point to the divide between the resident artists and the "politicos," with Rena, Rainbow, Myriam, and others much more focused on art than politics, except as art is itself political. Living in community—even for a short time—can have profound effects. Given the strength of lesbian convictions and independence, there were probably as many Pagodas as lesbians living and visiting there.

THE DOGS OF THE PAGODA

Rita Mae   Sophie   Andy   Honker!

Courtesy of Emily Greene

A Pagoda guest sent this Dogs of the Pagoda postcard, identified on the back as part of "The Dykes Delight series 11 by J&J 1979." The caption on the back reads: "Each dog at the Pagoda, Vilano Beach, Fla., adds something special to the resort. Honker is a great watchdog, Andy, a beachmate especially, loves fetching shells, Sophie, the baby & very loving, and poor Rita Mae is dieting." Honker belonged to Morgana, Sophie to Rena.

The more I talked with women who lived at the Pagoda or visited there frequently, the more I came to see how much their stories resembled what was going on all over the United States during the second wave of feminism, both among lesbians and in the broader feminist community. These women felt their way toward women's community through expressing feminist ideals like nonhierarchical leadership, honoring the Goddess, and creating women-only space. To follow their stories is to view a microcosm of feminism in a cauldron of art, love, sex, politics, and power struggles. The challenges and conflicts live alongside the exciting possibilities of new ways of living and being in the world. While it lasted, what the Pagoda women built there was a powerful emblem of what life could be like when women's space is honored and protected. Singer-songwriter Carole Eagleheart remembers it this way:

> Even if all that stuff was roiling here, the Pagoda was still a symbol for us who lived in other places. It was a symbol of women who were able to come together and create their own community. Even if there was a lot of shit going on, it was still an important symbol for us nationally that this should even be able to happen. I think of it as a glowing beacon, even if things were going on underneath. . . . They were not publicity seekers, that's true. But they were certainly really, really important to people outside of it. This was something out of our ancient past that was being embodied here.

The question is not so much why it came to an end as how on earth it lasted as long as it did? One reason is that women really did have a lot of fun at the Pagoda—at dances, at concerts, at rituals. There was a playful energy alongside the feminist fervor, and a great joy in planning celebrations. They planned ten days of events for the tenth-birthday celebration. One highlight was a pet parade, with the neighborhood dogs wearing T-shirts, Barbara with a flea circus, Dore with a basket of squash, and Lavender with plastic flamingos from her yard. Joycie captured a grasshopper and paraded it on a leash made of twist ties. She set it free after the parade. When they weren't making policy or dealing with financial or emotional crises, the Pagoda women were having a really good time, and that was all about being with women and having a cultural center. For many years, that old building was an oasis in a world that did not provide many spaces where, as Ellen Spangler put it, "the whole spirit of women was really honored, spiritually, physically, emotionally." Women grew and healed there, found feminism and self-empowerment. The spiritual component bound up in the separatism made it safe for growth. Women came for the beach and the concerts; they stayed for the community.

It was always a delicate balance, maintaining women's community while running a business on feminist principles without any serious financial backing. Morgana remembers it as "a world of its own, that had a life force there already."[19] A poem by Pagoda regular and sometime resident Corky Culver captures some of what it meant to enter that world among women who valued women.

Ah, the Pagoda
By Kathleen "Corky" Culver

Ah, the spell of the Pagoda, to step into it is to step outside
patriarchy, into a women's space, Goddess space.
You are welcomed by the fence with folk art swirls
and hand-drawn lavender peace symbols,
alerted that the pool and sundeck are clothing optional and,
ah again, given the smell and taste of salt air,
the sound of mother ocean's primal surf rhythms.
The magic begins.

You might take a stroll down the sand street between
cottages mirroring the fiercely individualistic personalities of
their owners,
spiral staircases climbing to roof decks, porches
with hammocks or massage tables, cabins painted in a

festival of colors from muted gray to Caribbean
tropical flowers and cacti, gaily flaring pinks and purples.
You see home-made art and crafts everywhere,
figurines glued to an anchor, driftwood in fantastic shapes,
watercolors of water birds and mosaics of mermaids.

At the Pagoda when a visitor car appears, several women
will pop out of cottages to guide you; don't be
offended, parking is tight, and admittedly, curiosity is current.

In a tiny front yard, a roof-high philodendron rears up like a
                                       hippopotamus—
That could be a parking space! I don't care, Cindy defends,
I love her. Her name means love. Yep, that giant plant stays on
as a community member. It's hard to argue with those huge
                                       broad leaves.

Check out the Center, housing the feminist library, natural
                                       foods store
and the temple room. On the walls crayon colored mandalas,
a labrys, an Audre Lorde poster challenging us to brave activism,
a bulletin board that lets us know where and how.
Flyers announce women's art exhibits, support groups—
all giving a sense of being in the center of the women's movement.
When not in service of a ceremonial, the temple is a hangout room
with funky couches for happy slouching.

Step into the kitchen lured by the smell of popcorn to share,
                                  boiled peanuts, no meat.
You find your room. Maybe you're daring the attic ladder,
to the room with views of clouds and ocean,
a room legendary for inspired writing,
amazing dreams.

Or retreat into a little cabin bedroom
with your lover, a privacy enhanced somehow
by being surrounded by approving neighbors,
guarding you, shielding you.

Or choose the Cave, a room behind the stage,
with a wall to wall bed at one end
and a bar for hanging clothes at the other,
an amenity which you will share as the Cave
doubles as a dressing room on performance nights.

The women, oh the women. You'll want to meet them all.
She Fay and Sandi making music in Persephone's Pit.
Barbara Lieu with her flea circus, Rena's tap dancing with a cane
                                        and top hat,
Morgana's matriarchal belly dancing, Nancy Vogl's flat picking guitar,
Barbara Ester singing "Lesbian," Rainbow teaching dulcimer,
You get to know world class entertainers up close.
Myriam Fougère making an award-winning movie,
Kay Gardner teaching chanting, Ferron giving a guitar lesson
at the laundromat.
As far as clothes, the style is "anything goes."
Maybe a long skirt for a Lammas ritual, beads for Beltane.
Women in dresses, overalls, ripped t-shirts, boas—
glittered faces, Val in her tan.

Then after a rollicking night of theatre or music,
a moonlit walk to the beach
soothes and charms, whispers messages.

You leave the Pagoda with a soul full of intangible gifts,
after hugging and kissing and cavorting, lives

loosening, inviting new blessings, women becoming
themselves, flourishing, out of bounds,
brown-skinned and barefoot, a new kind of
community with consensus and camaraderie,
a community tingling with love, mutual respect,
magic to carry through the years.

Chapter 12
The Pagoda Today

Walking down the little sand road between the first two rows of cottages today, you still feel some of the ambience that Corky Culver evokes in "Ah, the Pagoda"—the spiral staircase, the roof decks, the festive colors, the sound of the ocean. That giant philodendron is still there in front of Cindy's cottage taking up a parking space. The tiny, closely spaced cottages are well maintained, and some Old Pagodans still live there—Rena, Marie, She Fay. The lesbian who bought Barbara and Lavender's cottage, Selket (#5), now lives in Ecuador and rents her cottage, mostly to friends or friends of friends. On the North Pagoda strip, Rainbow sold cottage D, Amelia, in 2013 to a straight woman who lives near Gainesville and has remodeled it so that part can be rented through Airbnb. Mostly it sits empty, and the vacant lot behind it (which she also owns) is roped off and marked No Parking. The other North Pagoda cottages are sealed off behind privacy fences and seem to be entirely vacation rentals, though lesbians still own Cottage A.

The Pagoda is no longer an exclusively lesbian community, and in summer you are likely to see tourists strolling down the sand road between the cottages to the beach. Some are staying at the expensively remodeled building that was the cultural center, now called the Beach Break, with rates starting at $370 a night.[1] Rates are more reasonable at the duplex next door, where Rainbow and Nancy Breeze used to live downstairs, and Elaine Townsend shared the upstairs with Karen J. Now advertised on VRBO as the dog-friendly Marvelous Mermaid, the upstairs rents for $219 nightly, downstairs $186. Until recently, parking for the duplex was across the street at Publix.

Of the Pagoda women profiled here, thirteen had died by the time this book went to press. Edith George died in 1999, the second of the Pagoda residents to die (Gaby was the first), and the only one to die while still living there, although she died in the hospital in Miami. Kay Mora died in 2003, Marilyn Murphy in 2004, and Lavender Lieu in 2005. Joycie Myers and Irene Weiss both died in 2016, before I was able to interview them, and Kathleen Clementson died in 2018, before I located her. Jean Adele and Nancy Breeze died in 2019. Ellen Spangler and Dore Rotundo died in 2021. Rainbow Williams died in 2022. Alapine women held memorials for many of these women and set aside a spot in the woods of their rural community as remembrance of them.

Lin Daniels still lives in California, and Myriam Fougère divides her time between Montreal and her partner Annalisa's home in Florence, Italy. Myriam followed *Lesbiana*, her 2012 film about women's land in the United States and Canada, with *Feminista* (2017), a documentary about feminists in Europe. At least once a year, Myriam and Annalisa visit the cottage that Myriam still owns with Lin. They rent it to lesbians only. Lin Daniels lives in the Bay Area and sits on the board of the Center for the Divine Feminine in Palo Alto. Before the pandemic, she regularly produced theatrical mountings of Eve Ensler's *The Vagina Monologues,* and she was working on a book and documentary film about Kay Gardner when I interviewed her.

Barbara Lieu lives at Alapine, and Morgana MacVicar lives on land bordering Alapine. Barbara continues to market Alapine lots to women interested in country living in a lesbian community, and they had a resurgence of interest during the pandemic. In 2022, Alapine had thirty-four residents. Neither Barbara nor Morgana has visited the Pagoda property since 1999, when the church sold the building and pool, and they think it would be painful to do so. Morgana has been dealing with serious health issues since a bad fall in 2001. She and Fayann Schmidt ended their thirty-year relationship in 2017.

Other Pagoda women living at Alapine are Laura Folk and Shyne. The lots that Martha Strozier and Dore Rotundo owned have been sold to another lesbian who remodeled their screen house into a home. Martha lives in Gainesville now. Rose DeBernardo owns an Alapine lot but lives in central Florida, near family; she is the oldest Pagoda woman still alive.

Most of the living Pagoda women have retired or are nearing retirement. Fayann Schmidt plans to retire soon from her work as a mail carrier, but continue as associate minister of a Unity church in Chattanooga; she divides her time between northeast Alabama and Jacksonville, Florida. Emily Greene moved from Alapine to Massachusetts in October 2013 after retiring from thirty-seven years as a nurse; she made this move to be closer to her blood family and has joined several groups working on racial and environmental justice. Liz Daneman describes herself as a "recently retired Environmental Scientist, Naturalist, USCG Master Mariner, sailor, and musician"; she lives in Melrose. Rena Carney retired from her speech pathology career in 2015, but continued actively consulting until 2020; she is now shifting her energies to creative work, painting and writing plays, and lives half-time at her Pagoda cottage, #4, once known as Sappha, now Sea Turtle. Before Suzi Chance retired, she was working as a certified master naturalist at a South Carolina resort, but returned to St. Augustine in 2000 to care for aging parents; she now lives in Athens, Georgia, and recently reconnected with Rena via Facebook. Elethia lives in Virginia and was retired and studying quantum mysticism when I interviewed her.

Marie Squillace and She Fay live full-time in their Pagoda cottages (Marie in #6, She Fay in #8) and hold jobs in St. Augustine. Paula Arden is living in her Georgia hometown and teaching high school English nearby. Garnett Harrison still practices family law in Georgia while living in Jacksonville, with Cindy Watson, who directs a nonprofit LGBT youth center there. For many years, Dorothy Campbell rented cottage 7, and worked nearby, but in recent years she married a woman and moved to Georgia.

Pagoda-temple of Love changed its name to Temple of the Great Mother on February 14, 2001, and still owns property adjoining Alapine. Although the church's Crones Nest vision did not come to fruition, Alapine's growth promises new life to the church. Several new residents are now working toward repairing the road into the church land bordering Alapine and resuming the ritual circles on the sacred knoll there. In that respect, the church still nourishes lesbian-feminist community.

Looking back from the twenty-first century, some Pagoda women regret that their dream of feminist community in St. Augustine did not withstand the challenges of economic and political change. Yet those eight cottages on Lots 3 and 4 remain women-owned, mostly lesbian-owned and -occupied, and the Next Door app has a "Pegoda [sic] Community" group. For many, there remains a Camelot-like memory of a time and a place, a community capable of sustaining many dreams for one brief shining moment.

Chronicles

Barbara Lieu (left) and Lavender posing as tourists on the beach in 1988. Graphics Ink, a lesbian-owned business, produced and sold this as a postcard in St. Augustine gift shops.

Photo by Nancy Hovater

Timeline of Key Pagoda Events

1934   Lucius "Shorty" Rees builds the two-story house that will become the Pagoda cultural center (in 1936, he begins building the cottages). He has bought five lots between the ocean and the coastal highway, the Surfside Subdivision Lots 1–5, GG and ZZ. He builds first on Lot 3, then Lot 4, then Lot 1. He never builds on Lots 2 and 5.

1970   Jane and Frederic "Pappy" Schilling buy Rees's Seashore Cottages and remodel it as the Pagoda Motel, adding a swimming pool on Lot 2. In 1976, they sell Lot 4 GG and ZZ to two heterosexual couples, the Lees and the Weingartners. That same year, they sell Lot 5 GG and ZZ to a local developer, Louie Dickinson (1929–2011), who later builds a three-story apartment building overlooking the Pagoda cottages, known to Pagoda women as the Tower, or the triplex (it was three apartments, one per floor).

Jane and Pappy Schilling at the Pagoda, 1970s.

Courtesy of Frank Halman

July 7, 1977   Morgana MacVicar, Rena Carney, Kathleen "Kathy" Clementson, and Suzanne "Suzi" Chance, who are the dance theatre group Terpsichore, close on the four Pagoda cottages on Lot 3 GG, with a lease on the two-story house at the west end of the lot, and an option to buy it. They draw straws for cottages: Suzi gets cottage 1, Rena, cottage 2, Morgana, cottage 3, Kathleen, cottage 4. The following year, Kathleen swaps her cottage for Rena's share of their house in town (February), Suzi sells her cottage to Martha Strozier (April), and Rena sells cottage 2 to Carolyn Levy (December). Like most Pagoda cottage sales, this is handled internally using quit-claims.

November 1977   Barbara and Lavender Lieu visit the Pagoda and see a rehearsal of the grand opening variety show. That same weekend, the wives of the two couples who own Lot 4, the strip of cottages across from Lot 3, come over and offer to sell it (four cottages, a duplex, and a vacant beachfront lot). Barbara and Lavender offer to buy one of the cottages if the women of the Pagoda can find other buyers for the rest.

November 19, 1977   Grand opening, Pagoda Playhouse: a production under the heading "A W♀man's Theatre." The Pagoda women announce a plan to buy the second lot and recruit lesbian buyers.

March 7, 1978   A group of Florida NOW women incorporate the Mother Church.

April 7, 1978   Pagoda cottage owners decide to evict male tenants by June 1. May 6 meeting notes say male tenants will be gone by May 7.

April 13, 1978   Closing on cottages 5–8 and the duplex; nine Pagoda women assume a mortgage. They are Barbara and Lavender Lieu (cottage 5), Pat Crouse (#6), three members of the Berkeley Women's Music Collective (#7), Vicki Wengrow (#8), Sherry Kliegman (duplex downstairs), and Beth Hodges (duplex upstairs). Only Barbara and Lavender occupy their cottage; the others are for rent. Barbara signs for Sherry. Martha Strozier pays cash for the beachfront lot (Lot 4 ZZ), which allows the sale to go forward.

August 9, 1978   Closing on the Pagoda Playhouse building; purchase price is $28,000. Lavender (Conni) Lieu is trustee for the twelve other women who put in $600 apiece: Alma Rose, Barbara Lieu, Beth Hodges, Darcy Ortolf, Ellen Spangler, Margo George, Martha Strozier, Morgana MacVicar, Pat Crouse, Patty Johnson, Rena Carney, Vicki Wengrow.

September 2–4, 1978   Southeastern Regional Conference for Matriarchy is held at the Pagoda.

September 20, 1978   Beth Hodges, who is moving to Boston, sells the upstairs duplex to Ellen Spangler.

November 3, 1978   Conni Lieu (Lavender) writes Toni Head expressing interest in Pagoda "becoming part of the Mother Church," a feminist church that had incorporated in Florida in March 1978.

November 8, 1978   Emily Greene and her then partner, Doris Wiegman, "Wiggy," both nurses, buy cottage 8 from Vicki Wengrow. They plan to move there from Orlando.

November 11, 1978   First mention in meeting notes of soliciting

Photo by Emily Greene

donations from supporters. Same meeting has an unresolved discussion of male children: Sherry Kliegman and her partner have a son. Sherry sells the downstairs duplex that month.

December 1978   Playwright Trudy Anderson moves to the Pagoda to write and direct plays, starting with her one-act *An Afternoon of S&M (Sophie and Myrtle)* on January 13, 1979. That year, the Pagoda

Laura Folk (known as Inca) lived in the attic of the cultural center while serving as the primary greeter, 1979–1980.

will produce nine plays, five of them written by Trudy, including an expanded version of *Sophie and Myrtle*. Trudy will take on various paying jobs at the Pagoda (writing and directing plays does not pay) and rent various Pagoda cottages and Center spaces until 1982.

January 31, 1979 Pat Crouse sells cottage 6 to Karen J and Leslie Eastman, who plan to live there. As of this date, four of the six units on strip 4 (the duplex counts as two) have changed hands since April 1978, and three of the buyers plan to live in their cottages. Now only half of the units on Lots 3 and 4 are available to rent, and the group are realizing that their vision of a residential community, instead of a resort, may be possible.

March 14, 1979 Toni Head turns over the incorporated Mother Church to the Pagoda women, who will rename it Pagoda-temple of Love and receive federal tax-exempt status by November.

August 25, 1980 Cultural center building deeded from Lavender (Conni Lieu), trustee for a private group, to Pagoda-temple of Love, Inc.

Fall 1980 Due to expanded separatist rules, Rena Carney moves to Gainesville to perform regularly at the Hippodrome Theatre and take a speech pathology job. The summer 1980 production of *Princess Cinderella* is her last show at the Pagoda Playhouse. She keeps her cottage.

November 1980 Elethia's first visit to the Pagoda, renting cottage 1 with her dog, Sappho. She will buy that cottage in 1983 (mostly renting space in the Center before that), move out in 1993, and sell it in 1999. By January 1981, she is maintenance coordinator and working on getting the electric company to separate the meters.

December 1980 Ban on meat and alcohol in the Center.

January 5–10, 1981   Southern Women's Poetry Writing Workshop led by Adrienne Rich, using the Center and four cottages for sixteen attendees. Rich sleeps off site.

April 17, 1981   "Going residential" meeting. Pagoda women agree to become a residential community by September 1 and begin figuring out how to accommodate frequent visitors like Nancy Breeze.

September 1981   Elethia takes over from Martha Strozier as bookkeeper.

September 5, 1981   Edith George becomes a Pagoda supporter. She will buy cottage 2 in 1983 and live there until her death, February 16, 1999.

October 1981   Jean Adele becomes a monthly tenant; she will buy cottage 8 from Wiggy/Nu in 1983. Jean will live in cottage 8 until June 1985.

Photo by Emily Greene

Kay Mora (left) and Jean Adele on the beach at the Pagoda.

April–May 1982   Sue Parker Williams, buys the downstairs of the duplex and rents it out until 1984, when she turns fifty; at that point, she changes her name to Rainbow, and moves there to live. In 1988, she sells her share of the duplex, participates in the North Pagoda purchase, and owns cottage D until November 2013.

Summer 1982   The Aquatic Association forms to raise money to buy the swimming pool by selling "lifetime memberships." At that time, Jane Schilling was selling the lot (Lot 2 GG, including the pool and vacant land) for $50,000.

October 1982   Dean Brittingham and Sue Schein visit the Pagoda to work on the Crones Nest project. Sue Schein has to leave soon, but Dean Brittingham lives at the Pagoda on and off until 1985.

February 19, 1983   First psychic workshop with Kay Mora, who will partner with Jean Adele.

March 1983   The newsletter reports that Edith George, Nancy Breeze, and Pamela Shook have moved to the Pagoda. Nancy Breeze will cottage-hop until she buys cottage C as part of the North Pagoda purchase in 1988. She will move into town with a partner and sell the cottage in 1995.

Winter Solstice 1983   The first croning ceremony at the Pagoda honors Rose DeBernardo and Ellen Spangler. The couple met at the matriarchy conference in 1978, and Rose bought cottage 8 from Jean Adele. They live in it off and on, more often renting it.

January 13, 1984   Marilyn Murphy and Irene Weiss arrive from California to give a workshop on classism and racism. They stay at the Pagoda in their motor home for a week as guests of Crones Nest, and will return many times before buying a cottage as part of the North Pagoda purchase in 1988.

February 1984   The Ms. Foundation rejects the Pagoda women's proposal for a $10,000 grant for Crones Nest. The Pagoda had been finalists, with a site visit in November 1983.

June 1985   Jean Adele and Kay Mora move into a beachfront house they have built across from cottage 5. Designed by architect Dore Rotundo, their beach house will often host Pagoda meetings and events.

January 1986   The newsletter announces, "We begin 1986 with 90 supporters." That year the newsletter regularly reports the number of new supporters, the number dropped, the number behind on their pledges, and sometimes the amount donated each month. January had the highest number of paying supporters, 69 (90 minus 21 late). Most months in 1986 had between 30 and 40 paying supporters.

January 23, 1986 Pappy Schilling dies, age seventy-six.

July 1986 Issues include lesbian-only circles and "labeling" publicity flyers of nonlesbians who advertise there to say if they identify as bisexual or straight.

October 1986 Joycie Meyers becomes a supporter and is croned at the Pagoda. She and her partner, Edith George, live in cottage 2 until Edith dies in 1999. In 2002, Joycie sells the cottage to Jennifer Pritchett and moves to Georgia to be near her children.

December 1986 Barbara and Lavender Lieu announce that they are selling the Pagoda store after running it for nine years.

January 1987 Discussion of lesbian-only events, especially celebration of pagan holy days. Future spring equinox and summer solstice rituals will be lesbian-only (this changes).

November 1987 The newsletter reports that one-third of the ninety supporters pay only when they stay in the Center, which makes budgeting hard. They discuss raising the rates. By December, "the Center is having a very difficult financial time."

December 25, 1987 Rainbow Williams videotapes a Pagoda Writers group event organized by Katy Wildsister. The writers reading that day include Pagoda residents Nancy Breeze, Marilyn Murphy, Joycie Meyers, Katy Wildsister, and Rainbow Williams, as well as nonresident Olivia Stryker. About twenty-five attend.

January 1988 Newsletter publishes a safe space story next to a reprint of a story about battered women. This generates controversy about how to deal with lesbian battering and whether to ban accused lesbians, following practices designed for battering by men.

March 13, 1988 "Ism's" group is established. Marilyn Murphy plans for this group to discuss racism and antisemitism.

March 27, 1988   Pagoda women hold a meeting to define "safe space" and work on developing a policy regarding lesbian battering.

April 4, 1988   Closing on North Pagoda cottages (Lot 1 GG, cottages A–D), to five women: Paulette Armstead, Nancy Breeze, Marilyn Murphy and Irene Weiss, and Rainbow Williams. The deal also includes the purchase of Lot 2 GG (swimming pool plus vacant land) to Ann Harman, and vacant beachfront lots to Earthstar (Lot 1 ZZ) and Dorothy French (Lot 2 ZZ).

April 23–24, 1988   Kay Hagan from Atlanta facilitates an intensive weekend workshop for Pagoda residents "for exploration and possible resolution of our 'knotty' intra-group issues."

July 1988   The swimming pool is now wheelchair-accessible, and Pagoda women begin fund-raising to make the Alcove toilet and shower accessible.

July 1, 1988   Myriam Fougère and Lin Daniels buy cottage 7 from Nancy Vogl (she has already bought out her two co-owners). Lin and Myriam still own cottage 7, although they are no longer a couple. They rent only to lesbians.

June 7, 1989   Quit-claim of the swimming pool portion of Lot 2 GG from Ann Harman to Pagoda-temple of Love.

June 17, 1989   Meeting to discuss financial issues associated with the swimming pool expenses (maintenance, repair, mortgage, and liability insurance).

January 1990   New supporter sliding scale of $15 to $40 is for the first time associated with a personal income scale.

May 1990   A bloody handprint in the attic guest book begins a lengthy controversy over Pagoda policy about "sadomasochistic practices and displays."

Summer 1990   Morgana starts spending summers at the mountain cabin she bought with her mother in 1987. She lives there while negotiating for the land that will become Alapine

Village, a new lesbian residential community begun with private funds. It will take years to clear the title on the property. The first Alapine residents, Ellen Spangler and Mary Alice Stout, move to the Alapine land in 1997, and build an earth-sheltered house there.

April 1991   The newsletter reports renovations, including new, permanent attic stairs, new fencing around the pool, and new decking that will make the pool wheelchair-accessible. Alcove accessibility plans are almost complete.

Summer 1991   The newsletter reports that accessibility architectural plans are final. They "radically change the layout of the downstairs" of the cultural center, providing "more space for the theatre and creating an accessible bedroom, bathroom and kitchenette." The plans also include a lightboard for the theatre and leveling the theatre floor. Retreat guest price is now $15 a night each (no couple rate).

July 27, 1991   Dorothy Campbell and Paula Arden, a "nontraditional musical theatre duo" from Atlanta, will do reader's theatre and monologues as Positively Revolting Hags (admission is $7 to $10). By September, Paula is a Pagoda supporter, and in 1992 the couple move to the Pagoda. Paula stays on, renting cottage A until September 1995. Dorothy moves to St. Augustine and continues her association with the Pagoda, sometimes renting space and occasionally performing.

Dykesgiving 1991 Cindy Watson and Garnett Harrison move to the Pagoda to live in their motor home in exchange for running the

Garnett Harrison (left) and Cindy Watson on the beach at the Pagoda in 1991, shortly after moving there.

Courtesy of Cindy Watson

Center. That spring, Cindy is project manager for the Center and pool renovation project, along with Irene Weiss. The couple stay until August 1992, then move to Jacksonville to resume their professional lives.

March 15, 1992   Pagoda-temple of Love borrows $25,000 to upgrade the Center and pool and make the downstairs bathroom wheelchair-accessible. At some point before May, there is a controversy over financial matters and Elethia resigns as bookkeeper. Win Frederick, who was Centerkeeper at that time, takes over bookkeeping. Irene takes over writing the checks.

May 1992   The newsletter reports changes in the board: president is Marilyn; secretary, Win; treasurer, Irene.

June 1992   Alcove accessibility renovations are complete, and Marilyn is coordinating upstairs renovations and theatre work.

August 1992   After spending about $25,000 on the Alcove renovation project, Pagoda women increase their insurance coverage to account for increased value of the building. Exterior painting is finished, and theatre has been painted and "looks like a new theatre."

September 17, 1992   With the remaining borrowed funds, the Pagoda women pay off the 1978 mortgage on the Center. They now owe $250 a month on the fifteen-year loan instead of the $197 a month on the old mortgage.

January 1993   The newsletter reports that Culture Club last fall produced five concerts, one play, a dance, a Hallowmas Celebration, and two potlucks. From all these, they made over $400.

February 19–21, 1993   Anne Rhodes, of Ithaca, New York, leads a conflict resolution workshop for Pagoda women. Nineteen attendees address interpersonal problems within the community.

April 1993   Kay and Jean's beach house is advertised for sale in *Sojourner*. It sells in May 1994 to the heterosexual couple who still live there.

July 1993   The newsletter reports that preliminary work on the new bridge has begun across the street, and that "the Pagoda is solvent, with a comfortable cushion for emergencies."

July 17, 1993   The Pagoda sixteenth-birthday pool party hosts over sixty lesbians. Paula provides music, and Marilyn emcees performance pieces, such as dramatic readings and bellydancing by Morgana and Sherry Tamburo.

January 1994   The Cottage Association for Lots 3 and 4 meets without members of the North Pagoda Cottage Association, leading to dissent about Center management and the Cottage Eligibility List.

March 17, 1994   Pagoda women decide that no new members are to be added to the Cottage Eligibility List as of March 27. This ends the association between monthly donations and eligibility to buy a cottage.

1995   Carole Eagleheart compiled a little booklet she called "Pagoda Notebook." It contains brief reflections on life at the Pagoda that year, as follows: "Emily and Karen do not live here any more. They live in town, but they still come to meetings"; "Barbara and Valentine no longer live together. Valentine is in Atlanta studying massage.[1] She now lives with a woman named Mary"; "Nancy [Breeze] is selling her cottage. This surprises many of the women, who thought she would never leave the Pagoda." In May, Nancy Breeze sold her cottage to a lesbian couple. Emily Greene also sold her cottage; she had been renting it to Marie Squillace, a lesbian who bought it in 1995 and still lives there.

March 1995   The "supporter rules" for the Pagoda-temple of Love include that new supporters can no longer pay retroactively the six months required to stay up to thirty nights without charge (exception: new girlfriend of old supporter).

March 1995   The newsletter reports a drop in income since 1994. An ad hoc committee will study this. Pagoda has 53 supporters and would like 75. Available balance is low.

April 14, 1995   Annual report of Pagoda-temple of Love to the state of Florida lists the following officers: president, Morgana MacVicar; vice president, Marilyn Murphy; treasurer, Irene Weiss; secretary, Edith George (replacing Nancy Gardner). In 1996, Morgana is still president, there is no vice president, Edith George is treasurer, and Garnett Harrison is secretary.

July 1995   The newsletter reports that Irene and Marilyn want to rent their cottage from October to April, furnished, for $500 a month. They will sell their cottage to Jennie Iacona in July 1996, although they continue their monthly donations as supporters.

July 6, 1995   The Pagoda eighteenth-birthday party is attended by over fifty women and videotaped by Emily Greene. Paula Arden emcees a talent show at the swimming pool, where Marilyn and Irene and many others sing, and they collect about $600 toward pool repair. That night in the Center, Rainbow's Amazing Almost All Girl String Band plays, followed by Flash Silvermoon on keyboard, and Morgana bellydancing to Flash's original music.

October 1995   The Francis and Mary Usina Bridge opens; it replaces the old drawbridge on SR A1A. This creates problems for the Pagoda because the bridge ends at their front gate, and cars are crashing through their fence.

January 1996   Last official Pagoda newsletter among Pagoda records.

February 3, 1996   All-day retreat to address Pagoda's financial situation. They are not breaking even on monthly expenses and there is "diminishing woman energy" to keep it going. They select a new managing board that day. The only full-time residents on the new thirteen-member board are Edith and Joycie. Board members Morgana, Fayann, and Barbara live in north Alabama (though not yet at Alapine), and Rena lives in Melrose.

April 1, 1997   Ellen Spangler and her partner, Mary Alice Stout, move to Alapine, the first of many Pagoda women to move to the new lesbian residential community that Morgana, Barbara, and Fayann have started in northeast Alabama. Morgana, Barbara, and Fayann have moved to the mountains but are not yet living on the land, which has no dwellings or utilities yet.

July 1997   "Pagoda News," Rainbow's substitute for a newsletter, mentions that "Jennie has the pool and grounds looking super and also keeps the guest rooms booked."

Edith, Joycie, Morgana, and Fayann at Alapine in about 1995, when Edith and Joycie bought their Alapine lot.

Courtesy of Morgana MacVicar

November 16, 1997   Jennie Iacona and Lin Daniels organize a community meeting attended by Edith, Jennie, Joycie, Lin, Rainbow, She Fay, and twelve more women.

December 1, 1997   Jennie Iacona and She Fay publish a one-page newsletter, *Neighbor Wimmin*, in which they call a meeting to discuss the future of the Pagoda. Jennie and She Fay have been running the Center operations but are not board members. From the newsletter: "We sometimes argued, many times agreed. But the one issue we never disagreed about was the issue of maintaining this Lesbian space for Lesbians only."

Summer 1998   Florida has its worst wildfires in fifty years, and tourism is down. Pagoda income for July and August is down about 50 percent.

April 10, 1999   Meeting at the Center to hear proposals for how to get the cultural center out of the hole. Proposals have been submitted by Rena, by Barbara Lieu, and by She Fay and Jennie.

November 22, 1999   Fairy Godmothers, Inc. (FGI), files articles of incorporation.

December 6, 1999   At the annual meeting of the Pagoda-temple of Love board, the board votes 8–0 to sell the building that has been the Center to FGI for $80,000; FGI would also assume the debt on the swimming pool, $1300. The church will retain ownership of Persephone's Garden.

December 13, 1999   Fairy Godmothers, Inc. (Rena Carney, Rainbow Williams, Marie Squillace, and Liz Daneman), close on purchase of the Center building and swimming pool.

April 10, 2000   FGI files articles of amendment with the state of Florida. They are an S corporation (small business filing taxes as individuals, rather than as a corporation).

June 22, 2000   For the first time, a Pagoda cottage, 51-B Beachcomber Way, is sold to a heterosexual couple. The question of to whom and for how much to sell a cottage had occasionally led to disagreements over the years, but everyone sees this sale as ending the dream of a lesbian community.

August 6, 2000   Rainbow's archives show that thirteen women attended a Lammas circle at the Pagoda. She thinks there may also have been a croning at Hallowmas that year.

February 14, 2001   Pagoda-temple of Love, Inc., files to change its name to Temple of the Great Mother, Inc. It is now based in northeast Alabama.

March 24, 2001   The minutes of the FGI annual meeting state that they agree to stop renting nightly. Each of the four Fairy Godmothers will have responsibility for the entire building for three months annually. Marie will handle reservations. They will sell annual pool memberships for $200.

September 22, 2001   FGI meeting notes show that taxes have doubled. They freeze spending and drop the monthly assessment to $200.

March 23, 2002   FGI annual meeting at Pagoda. They have a good tenant ($700 a month) but have sold no pool memberships.

January 29, 2005   After years of struggling financially, due to ballooning taxes and maintenance costs, they sign a contract to sell the property. Their realtor sets the price at $1,250,000. (The asking price plummets when the housing bubble bursts in 2008.)

September 14, 2007   The minutes of the FGI annual meeting say that upstairs and downstairs are renting month to month, the former to a heterosexual couple. FGI has paid taxes of $13,319 that year.

December 2016   FGI sells the Center building and swimming pool to Dustin Heath, who remodels it as a vacation rental. Karen J is the last Pagoda woman owner of the duplex. She sells it to Jim Sheils in January 2018 as a vacation rental. Seven cottages are still lesbian-owned. Six of them are on Lots 3 and 4: #3 (Cindy Thompson), #4 (Rena Carney), #5 (Sandi Macik), #6 (Marie Squillace), #7 (Lin Daniels and Myriam Fougère), and #8 (She Fay, who also owns the vacant lot next to her, Persephone's Garden). The seventh lesbian-owned cottage, #A on Lot 1, belongs to Jacqueline DiLeo, whose partner bought it in 1997 and transferred ownership to her; they were living in Massachusetts and bought it as a rental. Cottages B and C are vacation rentals. Rainbow sold Cottage D to a divorced straight woman, who also owns the vacant parts of Lot 2 GG and lives in Williston; she has set up a bedroom and kitchenette to Airbnb, but plans to retire to the cottage in the future.

Plays Produced at the Pagoda

Dates are from newsletters, publicity, and programs for Pagoda productions. Some 1977–1978 dates are from Rosemary Curb's national feminist theatre directory published in Chrysalis (1980).[1]

1977–1978   *Moonwomb*, by Rena Carney and Morgana MacVicar; first performed in 1976, and again at the Pagoda. Although no performance records survive, Rena still has the original script and papier maché masks, and there are several photographs from rehearsals.

1977–1978   *Overtones*, by Alice Gerstenberger; with Rena and Morgana.

1977–1978   *Something Unspoken*, by Tennessee Williams. Rena and Morgana may also have performed a scene from this during the grand opening weekend (November 19–20, 1977), but it is not listed in the programs that survive.

January 1979   *An Afternoon of S&M [Sophie and Myrtle]*, by Trudy Anderson; with Rena as Sophie and Morgana as Myrtle.

March 3 and 17, 1979   *Save Me a Place at Forest Lawn*, by Lorees Yerby; with Rena and Morgana.

May 24, 31, and June 15, 16, 22, 1979   *An Afternoon of S&M [Sophie and Myrtle]*, by Trudy Anderson; directed by Eloise Bruce of the Asolo Repertory Theatre. This production adds two new characters, McFiddle and McFaddle.

June 1, 2, 6, 9, 1979 *The Weighting Room,* by Trudy Anderson; cast includes Morgana and Patty Johnson.

Summer 1979 *A Celebration of Women Artists.* Selected readings performed at the Pagoda and other venues with a changing cast who choose their own artist to celebrate through readings.

July 6, 7, 13, 14, 1979 *Maraccas,* by Trudy Anderson; described as "a comedy with a sad ending, in three acts, dealing with the relationships between an immortal mother and her three daughters." Kris Matson has the lead, and cast includes Pamela Shook and Patty Johnson.

August 3–4, 1979 *The X Miss Copper Queen on a Set of Pills*, by Megan Terry.

August 31, 1979 *Animal*; a one-woman show.

September 2, 1979 *Crazy Ladies in a Junkyard,*[2] by Trudy Anderson.

1979 *Alleys,*[3] by Trudy Anderson.

May–July 4, 1980 Revival of *An Afternoon of Sophie and Myrtle*, by Trudy Anderson. With Tamara Brooke as Myrtle, Deanne Aime as Sophie, Anna Flower as McFiddle, and Lavender Lieu as McFaddle; Barbara Lieu, producer; Emily Greene, stage manager; Marty Youngblood, set design and construction; Trudy Anderson, director.

July 4, 5, 12, 19, 26, 1980 *Princess Cinderella*, by Anna Rallo. With Morgana as Princess Cinderella, Emily Greene as Prince Charming, Rena Carney as Prince Charming's sister Farah, Dore Rotundo and Brooke Triplett as Cinderella's stepsisters, Anna Rallo as the Musician, and Laura Folk as the prince's adviser. Rena's last Pagoda show.

April 16–18, 1982[4] *A Rose Is a Rose Has Arose,* by Trudy Anderson. With Elethia as Gertrude Stein and Dore Rotundo as Alice B. Toklas.

February 16, 1985 *I Wanna Live Don't Wanna Die.* A one-woman show featuring Yvonne Vogel, who was on tour from Switzerland.

January 23, 1988   *One Fool.* A one-woman show featuring Terry Baum, who was just back from a European tour.

Spring 1991   *Rites of Spring;* ritual theatre drawing on Charlene Spretnak, with Morgana as Persephone and Sherry Tamburo as Demeter.

July 1991   comedy sketches by Positively Revolting Hags, Dorothy Campbell and Paula Arden.

Photo by Emily Greene

Dorothy Campbell (left) and Paula Arden taking a bow after the 1993 Pagoda Playhouse staged reading of Carolyn Gage's *The Second Coming of Joan of Arc.*

December 1991   *Same Ship, Different Day,* by Dorothy Campbell. Described as "the return of the Positively Revolting Hags in their first full-length play"; Yemaya Productions.

October 31, 1992   Ritual dance performance for All Hallow's Eve, followed by a dance, fire, and drumming circle on the beach. Presented by Dorothy Campbell, Morgana, and Paula Arden; script and songs by Felicity Artemis Flower and Ruth Barrett; dance music by Krysten Gygi and Kathryn Warner.

January 9-10, 1993   staged reading of *The Second Coming of Joan of Arc,* by Carolyn Gage. With Paula Arden; directed by Dorothy Campbell.

February 26, 1994   Goddess Productions Traveling Feminist Theatre, Performance Art for Women's Empowerment and Community Building. The publicity flyer says, "Goddess Productions is a collective endeavor by a group of women in northwest Arkansas. It was originally conceived by Diana Rivers."

Pagoda Concerts

Entries are from Pagoda newsletters and flyers, Emily Greene's videos, and from publicity in the Jacksonville newsletter *COE* and the Orlando newsletter *Changes*. She Fay assisted in filling in 1990s concerts.

1977
November 19   Grand opening: Terpsichore, Medusa Music, Beledi Dancers, and more

November 20   Berkeley Women's Music Collective Sunday matinee

1978
May 6–7 and/or May 13–14   Woody Simmons and Nancy Vogl

May 27   Medusa Music

June 3   Open Stage: "Bring your creative talents to share. Plus Dancing"

June 10   Abby Bogomolny—singer, guitarist, lyricist

June 24   Jan Schim—singer, guitarist, lyricist

July 1   Gemini Dance with Medusa Music

July Fourth weekend   "Feminist theatre, dance, films, and music. To be announced."

July 29   Linda Wilson—bluegrass

September 2   Medusa Music plays for a dance for the Southeastern Regional Conference for Matriarchy.

October   *Changes* advertises "Saturday night shows at 9:00; $2 donation."

Photo by Emily Greene

The Berkeley Women's Music Collective performing at the Pagoda in 1979. *Left to right*: Suzanne Shanbaum, Debbie Lempke, Nancy Vogl, and Bonnie Lockhart, who joined the band after Nancy Henderson left.

1979

January	"Rock Revue" with Linda Wilson and Heather Vick
March 10	"Women's Dance" with Medusa Music
March 17	Medusa Music
April 21	Jan Schim—singer, guitarist
May 19	Blues/jazz review; with Linda Carol, Heather Vick, Doris Abood
May 26	Medusa Music
June 23–24	Linda Shear. The Pagoda's first nationally known performer
July 28	Music by Linda Carol
August	Nancy Vogl recalls that the last Berkeley Women's Music Collective concert at the Pagoda was after performing at Michfest in 1979. They disbanded that year.

August 10	Music by Androgyny (same night as the play *The X Miss Copper Queen on a Set of Pills*)
August 11	Pagoda Productions: "An evening of dance dance dance!"
August 19	Liz and Liz—from Charleston
September 1	Medusa Music
September 2	Ruth Segal—on guitar
September 15	Anima Rising—from Atlanta
November 2	Linda "Rock Starr" Wilson: "Florida's foremost outspoken dyke artist, singer songwriter and story teller . . . will perform her original feminist music. . . . Singalong welcome."
November 10	Cabaret/Pagoda second-birthday party: "A retrospective variety show" with a pianist in the Backstage Bar, Morgana and Rena singing and dancing. Rena's Anita Bryant monologue is the finale. (Future birthday celebrations are held in July, marking the anniversary of the closing on the first four cottages rather than the anniversary of opening night.)
November 24	Sharon Riddell—Nashville singer-songwriter
December 1	Medusa Music
December 2	Holly Near

1980

January 13	Linda Wilson and Heather Vick presenting "The Rock Star Revue." Plus "an original one act play by Trudy Anderson."
March 15	Kay Gardner
April 12–13	Alix Dobkin. Saturday's show (8:30 p.m.) is for lesbians only; all women are welcome at the Sunday matinee (3:00 p.m.)

May 3	Nancy Vogl
May 25	Teresa Trull
June 21	Summer Solstice Celebration: "Features originally choreographed dance works as well as original musical compositions written and performed by Pagoda womyn."
November 15	Carole Etzler [Eagleheart]—Atlanta singer-songwriter

1981

March 27	Carole and Bren
April 18	Alix Dobkin
June	Newsletter announces that Medusa Music has disbanded
August 22	Sharon Riddell. A benefit for St. Augustine Food Coop.
September 6	Going Residential Party with music by the Fallopian Tubes from Tampa
September 26	Nancy Vogl

1982

April 17	Kay Gardner
April 19	Karen Mackay
May 13 and 15	Cathy Cook, with signer Pamela Shook
October 5	Nancy Vogl and Suzanne Shanbaum

1983

April 1	Ferron
April 3	Sharon McCay
April 9	Gal—also known as Punk Mary
May 29	Sharon Ridell
October 29	Nancy Vogl
December 23	Debbie Fier

1984

April 13	Alix Dobkin
May 6	Elaine Townsend
June 16	Catherine Madsen
November 24	Kathleen Hannan

1985

February 2	Casse Culver. They record her song "Lydia" and get permission to use it in the Crones Nest slideshow in progress.
March 13	Elaine Townsend
July 28	Farewell potluck for Myriam and Martine, followed by music in Persephone's Pit by Rainbow, Sheila (She Fay), Sandi, Patty, and the Amasongs (neighborhood choral society)
October 5	Rene Russell—folk-rock musician from North Carolina[1]
November 2	Zoe Lewis—jazz-folk singer from England
November 23	Jess Hawk Oakenstar—singer-songwriter from New Zealand
November 28	Elaine Townsend—singer-songwriter from South Carolina (Thanksgiving)

1986

March 10	Elaine Townsend
March 29	Music Night: Dore and Rainbow producing; bring your instruments
May 14 (or 15?)	Karen Mackay
May 23	Carole Etzler and Brenda Chambers
July 19	Karen Beth
October	Karen Beth and Rainbow, Lucie Blue Tremblay[2]

November 13   Deidre McCalla

December 2   June Millington gave "a spontaneous,
                unannounced mini-concert for Pagoda wimmin"

1987

March 11   Karen Beth, Carole Etzler (guitar) and Bren
                Chambers (cello)

March 21   Kay Gardner. Concert and workshop

March 24   Kristan Aspen and Janna MacAuslan of Musica
                Femina—flute and guitar. On tour from
                Portland, Oregon; program of women composers
                from the 1600s to the present (including their own)

June 26   Karen Mackay

July 4   Flash Silvermoon

July 11   Morgana and Nancy Vogl: "An evening of
                music, dancing, and fireworks"

September?   Carol Prior. Prior
                was a supporter
                from England.

October 15   Washington Sisters
                and Melanie Monsur

November 14   Barbara Ester and
                Bairbre—music
                for Lesbians

December 13   Alix Dobkin

1988

January 2   June Millington—
                concert and dance

May 22   Carole and Bren

December 30   Kathleen Hannan

Courtesy of June Millington

June Millington performing in
the 1980s.

256

December 31   Particular Productions, International Lesbian
New Year's Extravaganza
9:00 p.m.—concert with New Age composers
October Browne from London, and Evelyn
Datl from Toronto
10:30 p.m.—New Year's Eve concert and dance,
with Flash Silvermoon

1989

January 21   Kay Gardner. Evening concert, with workshop
that afternoon
April 19   Carole and Bren
May 25 (or 5?) Karen Beth; performing with Mary Pantaleoni,
a fiddler
June 4   Kathleen Hannan
June 10   Martie van der Voort
November 17   Alix Dobkin
December 30   June Millington

1990

March   Cathy Winter
March 21   Carole and Bren
May   Jamie Anderson
August   Karen Mackay
September   Monica Grant
October   Kathleen Hannan
November   Deb Chris

1991

February 17   Alice Di Micelein: "This Southern Oregon
based singer/songwriter is on tour with
her third recording 'Too Controversial.'"

March 8	Cathy Winter
April 13	Elaine Townsend
April 23	Carole and Bren
May 10	Monica Grant
October 5	Rene Russell—folk-rock musician from North Carolina
November 2	Zoe Lewis—jazz-folk singer from England
November 23	Jess Hawk Oakenstar
November 28	Elaine Townsend: concert at 4:30 p.m. follows Thanksgiving potluck at one o'clock

1992

February 28	Monica Grant—comedian and singer-songwriter; "An Evening of Lesbian Music and Comedy"
March 27	Carole and Bren
April 18	The Rayne
May 8	Kate Messemer
June 27	Elaine Townsend
October 17	Jess Hawk Oakenstar
November 7	Cathy Winter
November or December	Cecily Jane (joined impromptu by Elaine Townsend)
December 4	Justina and Joyce
December 19	Ann Seale and Sasha Hedley

1993

March 13	Jamie Anderson
March 24	Carole Elle and Bren Chambers (same as Carole and Bren)
Spring or Fall	Cecily Jane
April 24	Deidre McCalla
July 17	Flash Silvermoon drums for bellydancing at Pagoda sixteenth-birthday party (videotaped by Emily Greene)

October 10   Monica Grant
October 23   Jess Hawk Oakenstar
November 20   Kathleen Hannan and Gale Kennig
December 31   New Year's Eve concert with Dayna Kurtz;
                followed by dance

1994

February 12   Lyn Thomas
March 12   Kay Gardner and Nurudafina Peli Abena
March 20   Spring Equinox Circle and Marsha Stevens
April 1   Carole Eagleheart (videotaped by Emily Greene)
April 23   Cecily Jane (videotaped by Emily Greene)
July 9   Barbara Ester and Kate Mesmer [sic] perform
                at Pagoda birthday pool party
September 17   Laura Chandler
September 24   Tracy Drach
October 22   Cecily Jane
December 10   Katie Larkin
December 31   Lyn Thomas
     (videotaped by Emily Greene)

Photo by Emily Greene

Carole Eagleheart performing
at the Pagoda April 1, 1994.

1995

January 28   Monica Grant
March 4   Cecily Jane
March 24   Laura Chandler
April 8   Carole Eagleheart
May 19   Jamie Anderson
June 3   Elaine Townsend
July 8   Pagoda eighteenth-birthday party, with Amazing
                Almost All Girl String Band, Flash Silvermoon,
                Morgana bellydancing (videotaped by Emily Greene)
August 19   Anique—"the premier Lesbian performer in
                Australia"

259

September	Elaine Townsend, with Susan Smith on drums
September 10	Monica Grant—comedian and songwriter
October 14	Karen Beth (videotaped by Emily Greene)
Late Fall	Kathleen Hannan (joined by She Fay and Sandi Macik on some tunes)
November 18	Cecily Jane
November 25	Jess Hawk Oakenstar

1996

January 27	Blue Heron (Deb Criss and Roberta Greenspan)
February 17	Kate Larkin—singer-songwriter; with special guest Rema Keen
March 9	Amy Carol Webb—singer-songwriter
March 30	Kid Sister—folk duo (Piper Kessler and Ruth Vienna) from North Carolina
April 20	Carole Eagleheart
May 11	Jane Yii—singer, songwriter, guitarist (formerly of Cecily Jane)
June 1	Kathleen Hannan: "Music That Makes Community"
July 6	Pagoda birthday party, with Amazing Almost All Girl String Band (videotaped by Emily Greene)
October 19	Karen Beth
November 2	Jane Yii

1997

March 22	Inside Out, Kathleen Hannan, Beth Schulman, Toddie Stewart
April 12	Jane Yii
April 26	Carole Eagleheart

June 7	Inanna and the Five Directions
July 5	Pagoda's twentieth-birthday party, with She Fay's band Squash Blossoms and her ensemble Full Circle Round
November 1	Jane Yii
November 15	Inanna (Carrie Gerstman)

1998

February 13	Alix Dobkin
March 14	Kay Gardner
March 21	Carole Eagleheart
July 11	Pagoda birthday party, with Full Circle Round and SueShe
November or December	Cecily Jane, with Elaine Townsend joining

1999

March 20	Carole Eagleheart. This concert is part of Spring Equinox Weekend (the concert attendance was thirty; revenue was $50)
April 30	Amy Carol Webb
May 22	Jamie Anderson
October 16	Big Blue Sky—acoustic duo (Sue Crago and Jill Apolinario)

Pagoda Women

In shaping the mass of material collected for this book, I have tried as much as possible to include the voices of the women who made the Pagoda a community, especially cottage owners and tenants actively involved in the life of the community. When possible, I quote from their recorded interview, mostly my own interviews with them, but in some cases interviews recorded for the Old Lesbians Oral Herstory Project, OLOHP.[1] Where I had no interviews with people who have died, I sought material from their partners, close friends, relatives, obituaries, or their own writings.

Many Pagoda women chose new names while at the Pagoda. Some of those were legally changed; others were just informal. Morgana and Ellen both took their mother's birth surnames as their legal surname, Jean took her mother's first name as her surname, and Barbara and Lavender chose a shared surname. So we have Morgana MacVicar, Ellen Spangler, Jean Adele, and Lavender and Barbara Lieu. Morgana and Lavender also changed their first names. Morgana was born Julie Eaton, named for her mother's aunt, and changed it to a form of her ex-husband's last name, Morgan, becoming Morgana. For a long time she went by one name only, until it became convenient to have a legal last name. Lavender changed her name several times in her lifetime. Born Constance Beth Ackerman, she became Conni Kaynard when she married, Conni Ackerman after her divorce, Conni Lieu during her first year with Barbara, Lavender Lieu (1980–1987), and then Valentine Lieu (1988 and after), sometimes Lavender Valentine. After her father's death in 1999, her mother asked her to go back to Ackerman, and Barbara has a driver's license in the name Valentine Ackerman. I chose to call her Lavender throughout.

Taking a new name was a radical feminist act, and it was fairly common in the 1970s and '80s among lesbian-separatists and landykes. At the Pagoda, the names were sometimes temporary: Tinker, Seaweed (both Trudy Anderson), Inca (Laura Folk), Flame (Deb Ennis). Many names lasted long enough that most of their friends knew the women by no other name: Barbara Lieu (Barbara Hering), Morgana, Elethia (Bonnie Lee in legal paperwork only), Kay Mora (born Kathleen Blaisdell), She Fay (born Sheila Fay Thompson), Flash Silvermoon (born Deborah Kotler), Nancy Breeze (who changed her name from McAdams to Breeze after her divorce), and mica (Meri Furnari). Occasionally, a resident preferred to be known by a pseudonym in meeting notes or newsletters for privacy, but this seems to be rare. Some Pagoda women whose names appear in the Pagoda newsletter and other archives asked that their names not appear in this book.

The list is alphabetical by first name and includes almost all cottage owners, as well as many others who were prominent in Pagoda herstory.

*   People interviewed for the Pagoda project

∞   Interviewed but not about their Pagoda experience

Ann Harman* (b. 1950) was a frequent Pagoda weekender when she lived in Tampa and became part of the North Pagoda

Land Trust that bought the Vilano Beach property in 1988. Her share was Lot 2 GG, including the swimming pool, which she quit-claimed to Pagoda-temple of Love in 1989. She found the Pagoda a healing place and at one time contemplated opening an osteopathic practice for women there. She appears in meeting records giving osteopathic workshops twice in 1986.

Barbara Lieu* (Barbara Hering; b. 1945) was a leader in the first decade of Pagoda's life and an officer in Pagoda-temple of Love, Inc. (now Temple of the Great Mother). Barbara did cottage bookkeeping off and on throughout the time that the church owned the Center and swimming pool and took care of a myriad of business matters. Her life partner was Lavender Lieu.

Beth Hodges* (Elizabeth L.; b. 1938) was part of the group that bought Lot 4 GG in April 1978; she sold her share (the upstairs of the duplex) to Ellen Spangler that September and moved to Boston. She rented several different cottages for most of 1992 and tried to heal some of the divisions she witnessed. Beth earned a PhD and taught college English at various universities. Later in life, she has been a successful artist, exhibiting as Elizabeth Barakah Hodges.

Bonnie Lee: See ELETHIA.

Cathleen Burns: See EARTHSTAR.

Cindy Watson* (b. 1957) first came to the Pagoda in November 1991 in a motor home shared with her life partner Garnett Harrison. For nine months, they managed the Center in exchange for living on site in the motor home. During that time,

Cindy also managed the Alcove renovation project. That fall, they moved to Jacksonville to take jobs, but stayed in close contact with the Pagoda. When the Pagoda board reorganized in 1996, Cindy chaired the membership committee. In Jacksonville, Cindy has directed the non-profit LGBT youth center JASMYN (Jacksonville Area Sexual Minority Youth Network) since 1998.

Conni Ackerman Lieu: See LAVENDER LIEU.

Dean Brittingham* (spelled Deane in Pagoda records; b. 1950) came to the Pagoda to work on Crones Nest grants in 1982, and lived there off and on from 1982 to 1985. She grew up in Connecticut and became a feminist in 1968 through the New Haven Women's Liberation Center. After college in Vermont she helped found a women's center in Montpelier and was state coordinator for battered women's services in Vermont. She had lost that job because of her lesbian identity by the time she first visited the Pagoda, on vacation, and mentioned to Lavender that she had won grants for the battered women's shelters, including a Ms. Foundation grant. That led to her being invited back to the Pagoda as a grant writer. When interviewed in 2020, she had recently retired from a job at a senior center; she now lives in Santa Rosa, California.

Deborah Ennis: See FLAME.

Deborah Kotler: See FLASH.

Deirdre Doran (b. 1956) owned Cottage A (Dolphin) from 1996 to 1997, when she transferred ownership to her partner, Jackie DiLeo. Remembered as "the Boston women," they treated the cottage as rental property, although they did visit.

Dore Rotundo∞ (1935–2021) owned cottage 2 (which she called Judy Chicago) from 1981 to 1983. She performed in two plays at the Pagoda in the early years and was a lifelong musician. A professional architect, she designed Jean and Kay's beach house on Lot 4 ZZ (in 1984–1985) and the Alcove remodeling in 1992. She was

Martha Strozier (left) and Dore Rotundo in the early 1980s.

a founding member of the North Forty in Melrose, Florida, where she built a house. Her life partner was Martha Strozier.

Doris Wiegman: See NU.

Dorothy Campbell* (b. 1965) first visited the Pagoda in July 1991, performing feminist skits with her girlfriend Paula Arden as the Positively Revolting Hags. They returned with a play that December, then moved to St. Augustine in 1992. Dorothy briefly shared cottage A (Dolphin) with Paula, taught elementary school, participated in several singing groups that performed at the Pagoda, and directed Paula in a well-remembered staged reading of *The Second Coming of Joan of Arc* by Carolyn Gage.

Dorothy Mae French (1918–2012) was a St. Augustine resident and friend of Kay Mora. Both of them also had homes in Maine. Dorothy bought a beachfront lot, Lot 2 ZZ, in 1988, as part of the Pagoda expansion, but opted out of the shared mortgage and the North Pagoda Land Trust Association. She sold the lot in 1998.

Earthstar* (Cathleen Burns; b. 1959) was a St. Augustine resident who bought beachfront Lot 1 ZZ in 1988 and was part of the shared mortgage and the North Pagoda Land Trust Association. She paid off her share of the mortgage in 1993 and sold the lot in June 1996, three months before giving birth. She now lives in Washington State.

Edith George (1930–1999) bought cottage 2 in 1983 from Dore Rotundo and changed its name to Wild Patience. From 1986 until her death, Edith shared the cottage with her life partner, Joycie Myers. Edith retired from the army in 1972 after twenty years and had been a Pagoda supporter since 1981. She earned a computer science degree, was treasurer for Florida NOW for two years, and worked for five years as manager of the data processing department of a small Florida municipality. In her fifteen years residence at the Pagoda, she regularly attended Center business meetings and often handled maintenance issues. In the 1990s, she prepared financial reports for the Center, and in 1995 became the Pagoda Center bookkeeper. When the Pagoda board restructured in 1996, she became a board member and headed the Budget and Finance Committee. She soon resigned from the board, but continued as bookkeeper and kept up with membership and concert lists. After her death of cancer in February 1999, Pagoda friends accompanied her body to Arlington National Cemetery, where she had requested a military funeral.

Elaine Townsend* (b. 1962) first visited the Pagoda to do a concert in May 1984, returned several times for concerts, and became romantic partners with Karen J, who owned the upstairs of the duplex. They lived together there from 1990 through 1993 or 1994. She produced two recordings of her original songs, *Heartbreak Blues*, in 1987, and *Redemption*, in 2000. She stopped touring and performing full-time in 2002. Townsend now lives in Columbia, South Carolina.

Elethia* (Bonnie Lee; b. 1941) had just completed feminist studies with Mary Daly in 1980 when she learned about the Pagoda at the Michigan Womyn's Music Festival. She rented cottage 1, stayed for six weeks, and would live and work at the Pagoda off and on until 1993. She bought cottage 1 from Martha Strozier in 1983 and worked in both paid and unpaid jobs for the Pagoda—notably, as bookkeeper, newsletter editor, and Centerkeeper. In college, she had studied theology and psychology and later completed graduate degrees.

Ellen Spangler* (1934–2021) never lived full-time at the Pagoda but was closely involved with its work from the very beginning, spending many weekends there, coming from Jacksonville to build the Pagoda Playhouse stage and to repair cottages. For a time, she owned part of the duplex, and after her partner, Rose DeBernardo, bought cottage 8, they remodeled it and spent time there. Ellen and Rose met at the matriarchy conference and in December 1983 were the first women croned at the Pagoda. In the mid-1980s, Ellen moved to South Carolina, started a teaching and healing center there called Starcrest, and found a new life partner, Mary Alice Stout. In 1997 they moved to Alapine, where they built an earth-sheltered house.

Emily Greene* (b. 1946) first came to the Pagoda with her then partner, Wiggy, in the fall of 1978, and shortly thereafter bought cottage 8 in the first expansion of cottages. When the couple broke up, Emily sold her share to Wiggy (then called Nu) and cottage-hopped until she was able to buy cottage 6 (Lily) in 1982, living there until 1988, when she and her partner bought a house in town. She sold the cottage to Marie Squillace in 1995. Emily worked full-time as a nurse and did many volunteer jobs for the Pagoda, especially photography. A lifelong activist, she was part of the St. Augustine antinuclear group Seeds for Peace. She bought an Alapine lot and built a house there, but moved back to Massachusetts in 2013, where she continues her social justice work.

Fayann Schmidt* (b. 1951) first came to the Pagoda from Jacksonville in 1985, when her then partner was one of a group of lesbians who bought a house at the beach end of Beachcomber Way, near the Pagoda. Fayann moved to the Pagoda in 1987 and was Morgana's partner for thirty years (1987–2017). She ran a recycling business in St. Augustine and never did any paid work for the Pagoda but often volunteered, especially for maintenance work. During the time that the church was selling the Center and swimming pool, Fayann was the primary liaison with women living at the Pagoda. Today, she is an officer of Sheeba Mountain Properties, Inc., the corporation that bought and marketed the Alapine Village property.

Flame (Deb Ennis) moved from Connecticut to go to massage school in Gainesville and was a frequent enough Pagoda visitor to be part of a Pagoda "family portrait" of thirteen women taken in 1982. In the summer of 1986, she and Martine Giguère became partners at the Pagoda and moved to Cape Cod. She now lives on Cape Cod and is married to a man.

Flash Silvermoon* (Deborah Kotler; 1950–2017) was a musician and psychic who performed frequently at the Pagoda, including at the grand opening on November 19, 1977, and often for Pagoda birthday celebrations (July of each year). Initially, she was in the band Medusa Music with her then partner, Pandora Lightmoon; after June 1981, she performed solo.

Gaby Penning (1954–1991) was a visitor from Germany for several years, and for a time she shared cottage 6 (Lily) with Emily Greene. Gaby was Centerkeeper in the early 1980s, and is one of the thirteen women in the 1982 "family portrait." Emily and her partner visited Gaby in Germany in the fall of 1990, and Gaby was planning a Pagoda visit when she died suddenly of an aneurysm in Germany a few months later.

Garnett Harrison* (b. 1954) was a family law attorney in her home state of Mississippi when she was disbarred for issues associated with two clients who took their daughters underground when a judge granted custody to the ex-husbands they had accused of abusing the girls. She fled the state in fear of her life with a warrant out for her arrest for civil contempt. She was recovering from that trauma when she first visited the Pagoda in 1988–1989, staying with her sister Sallie Ann Harrison and Sallie's partner, Nancy Breeze. The Pagoda was a sanctuary for her then, and she returned there at Thanksgiving 1991 with a new partner, Cindy Watson, with whom she managed the Pagoda Center for nine months while living in their motor home on the grounds. They moved to Jacksonville at the end of the summer of 1992, and she started a new family law practice in nearby Kingsland, Georgia, since she was already a member of the Georgia bar. In 1996, she joined the thirteen-member restructured Pagoda board and was active in the attempt to continue the Pagoda in the face of financial and other challenges.

Inca: See LAURA FOLK.

Irene Weiss (1926–2016) first visited the Pagoda in 1984 from California with her partner, Marilyn Murphy, to give a workshop on classism and racism. They were on a cross-country tour in their motor home, Irene having retired from a successful career directing nursing homes that she also invested in. In 1988, the couple bought cottage B (Periwinkle) as part of the North Pagoda purchase and became very important Pagoda leaders for the next eight years, arranging private loans that allowed the church to greatly improve Center facilities.

Jacqueline "Jackie" DiLeo (or **Dileo**; b. 1950) now owns cottage A (Dolphin), originally owned by her partner, Deirdre Doran, who participated in the North Pagoda Land Trust. Deirdre transferred ownership to Jackie in 1997.

Jean Adele* (aka Jean Llewellyn, her married name; 1936–2019) first visited the Pagoda in 1981 from Maryland, where she was working as a prison nurse. She knew immediately that she wanted to live at the Pagoda and moved that same year, renting space until she bought cottage 8 (Amelia) from Wiggy/Nu in 1983. She met her life partner, Kay Mora, at a psychic fair in St. Augustine. They bought Martha Strozier's beachfront lot (next to cottage 5) and built a beach house, where they lived off and on until they sold it in 1994. They often hosted meetings at the beach house. When the Alapine community began in 1997, Jean bought a lot; she moved there in 2003.

Jennie Iacona (aka Jennie Lin; b. 1953) bought cottage B (Periwinkle) from Marilyn and Irene in July 1996. From 1996 to 1999 she worked closely with She Fay running the retreat business and managing the Center, mostly as Centerkeeper. She resigned as

Centerkeeper in the summer of 1999 and sold her cottage in 2000, the first sale of a Pagoda cottage to a heterosexual couple.

Jennifer Pritchett (b. 1953) was an actor connected to the Hippodrome in Gainesville when she bought cottage 2 (Wild Patience) from Joycie Myers. Jennifer later sold it to Lori Bonczek (not lesbian-identified), who still lives there.

Joycie Myers (1935–2016) was raised in a Georgia town where she and her parents were one of four Jewish families. After marrying at fifteen a man who became a Methodist minister, she converted to Christianity and was active in the church, playing the piano for services. She had four children, eventually completed a masters of education in counseling and guidance, and was a teacher and mental health counselor. She became a Pagoda supporter in 1986, when she partnered with Edith George and began sharing cottage 2, which they called Wild Patience. When Edith died in 1999, Joycie inherited the cottage. She sold it in February 2002 to Jennifer Pritchett, and moved back to Georgia to be near family.

Julie Eaton Morgan MacVicar: See MORGANA MACVICAR.

Karen J (b. 1951) bought cottage 6 with Leslie Eastman in 1978, naming it Mary McMillan and later Bastet. They lived there until 1982, when Leslie partnered with Morgana. Karen bought and lived in the upstairs of the duplex (named Isis) when she was with Elaine Townsend (from 1990 to 1993 or 1994). She eventually owned both floors of the duplex and sold it as a vacation rental in 2017, after the sale of the Center building and pool.

Katheryn "Kathy" Marsh (1954–2019) was an artist who rented the duplex upstairs in the 1990s for about seven years. For a time she was partnered with Karen J, who owned the building. In 1996, Kathy painted images on the fence that faces A1A.

Kathleen "Kathy" Clementson (1941–2018) was a visual artist who was partnered with Rena Carney in 1977, when Terpsichore bought the cottages that became the Pagoda. She never lived there, and in February 1978 swapped her cottage (#4) for Rena's share of their house in St. Augustine. She later became a successful Christian Science lecturer and healing practitioner until she married the love of her life, Suzanne Nightingale, in 2004 on the day that same-sex marriage became legal in Massachusetts. The church expelled her when she refused to renounce the marriage. Kathleen left a lasting legacy at the Pagoda in her artworks, such as the peach satin vulva that decorated the Pagoda altar for many years.

Kathleen Hannan* (b. 1951) is a singer-songwriter who lived in St. Augustine in the 1980s and participated in forming an antinuclear group, Seeds for Peace, there while partnered with a man. She spent time at the Pagoda, sometimes performing there, including at the Pagoda tenth-birthday celebration in 1987. During a later period, bisexual women were not invited to play on the Pagoda stage. Kathleen did come back and play at the Pagoda again in the 1990s. She has been partners for twenty-two years with the artist Jude Spacks (she/they). Hannan now lives in Hillsborough, North Carolina, where she directs two nonperforming choruses and continues her social and political activism.

Kay Mora (Kathleen Blaisdell, aka Kaimora; 1928–2003) was a practicing professional psychic for thirty-five years, dividing her time between Oquossoc, Maine, and St. Augustine. She founded the Metaphysical Mother Earth Church and was its minister, and also had a healing and learning center in St. Augustine and in Oquossoc. She did her first psychic workshop at the Pagoda in January 1983, soon after she met Jean Adele, who became her partner. They built and shared a beach house on Martha Strozier's beachfront lot, which they bought in 1984 and occupied or rented off and on until they sold it in 1994.

Laura Folk* (Inca; b. 1957) first stayed at Pagoda from 1979 to 1982, when she was known as Inca, lived in the Center building, and in 1980 was a greeter. She moved to Santa Fe to study polarity therapy (1982–1988), living one year of that on rural women's land known as Arf. When she returned to the Pagoda in 1988 or 1989, she had gone back to her given name. Laura was one of the first Pagoda women to buy a lot at Alapine, and now lives there.

Courtesy of Rainbow Williams

Lavender in her Isis swimsuit standing in front of her Pagoda cottage, #5, which she and her partner called Selket, for the Egyptian goddess of healing stings and bites.

Lavender Lieu (Constance Ackerman, aka Conni and Valentine; 1947–2005) was a Pagoda resident from 1978 until about 1992, sharing cottage 5 (Selket) with her then partner, Barbara Lieu. She did much legal work for the Pagoda, including the process that made them an incorporated, tax-exempt church. She was also an integral part of the business as a concert producer, guest greeter, and correspondent. With Barbara, she managed the Pagoda natural food store and started the library.

Leslie Ann Eastman (b. 1954) was Morgana's romantic partner from 1981 to 1987. Before that, she was with Karen J and lived in cottage 6 (Bastet) with her from 1979 to 1981, selling it to Karen in October 1981. Today she is partnered with Sherry Tamburo.

Lin Daniels* (b. 1954) first came to the Pagoda in 1987 with her then partner, Myriam Fougère, with whom she bought cottage 7. They lived there off and on for a few years, and Lin was Centerkeeper for a time in the 1990s. While living at the Pagoda, they produced the East Coast Lesbian Festival (ECLF), held in the northeast for several years starting in 1989, and involved many Pagoda women in that festival. Lin also produced the West Coast Lesbian Festival and Hawaiifest. She now lives in California.

Liz Daneman* (Elizabeth; b. 1956) first came to the Pagoda while in college at the University of Florida in 1978–1979 but was never active in the business of the Pagoda. In 1999, she was one of the four Pagoda women who formed Fairy Godmothers, Inc., in order to buy the cultural center and swimming pool from Pagoda-temple of Love.

Lois Bencangey (b. 1942), bought cottage A (Dolphin) with her partner, Maria Dolores Diaz, from Paulette Armstead in May 1990. They sold it to Deirdre Doran in 1996. Marilyn and Irene knew Lois and Maria from their work with Califia in California, where they lived.

Maria Dolores Diaz (c. 1939–unknown) bought cottage A (Dolphin) with her partner, Lois Bencangey, from Paulette Armstead in May 1990. They sold it to Deirdre Doran in 1996. Marilyn and Irene knew Maria from Califia, where she had organized antiracism workshops and spearheaded much greater participation of women of color as Califia leaders and attendees. Born in Honduras, Diaz immigrated to California with her family in 1940.[2]

Marie Squillace* (b. 1952) first visited the Pagoda in 1987 while living in Vermont. After her life partner's death in 1992, she returned and began renting at the Pagoda, buying Emily Greene's cottage, #6 (Lily), three years later. In 1999, she was one of the four Pagoda women who formed Fairy Godmothers, Inc., in order to buy the cultural center building and swimming pool from Pagoda-temple of Love. She still owns and lives in cottage 6.

Marilyn Murphy (1932–2004) first visited the Pagoda in 1984 in her motor home with her partner, Irene Weiss. They had driven from California to give a workshop on classism and racism, and they would return often and then be instrumental in forming the North Pagoda Land Trust, which bought the remaining Pagoda Motel lots in 1988. The couple bought cottage B (Periwinkle) and lived there from 1988 to 1995, becoming very important to the maintenance and remodeling of the cultural center and to life at the Pagoda.

Martha Strozier* (b. 1936), a psychotherapist with a master's degree in counseling, was not yet partnered with Dore Rotundo when she bought the beachfront lot that enabled a group of lesbians to assume a mortgage on the cottages on Lot 4 GG in April 1978. In June of that year, she helped Suzi Chance out of a financial crunch by buying cottage 1, which Martha named Lucy Stone. In 1981, she bought cottage 2 and later deeded it to Dore, and in 1983 they sold both cottages. Martha remodeled her cottage, lived there, and practiced therapy there for several years. She was Pagoda bookkeeper and a regular attendee at business meetings in the early years and was very important to its continued success.

Martine Giguère* (b. 1951) is from Quebec, Canada, and first visited the Pagoda in the summer of 1985 with her then partner, Myriam Fougère. She was part of a lesbian land group in Quebec, living on rural land with no utilities, when she met Myriam. They were also part of a Montreal lesbian co-op and a lesbian theatre group, and attended many women's music festivals, where Martine worked as a carpenter. On their first Pagoda visit, they stayed from May through July, and returned the following summer, when Martine exhibited collages on boxes and postcards. Martine developed further carpentry skills at the Pagoda and worked with Rena, Rainbow, and Dore on construction projects. The summer of 1986 she partnered with Deb Ennis (Flame) and moved to Cape Cod. In 1989, she moved back to Quebec and worked doing carpentry in the Montreal film industry for more than thirty years. In 1999, she and Myriam became partners again for twelve years. Both are now with other partners.

mica* (Meri Furnari; b. 1947) lived and worked at the Pagoda in 1980–1981, sharing the downstairs duplex, and was part of the group working on "going residential" in April 1981. She moved to San Francisco with a partner that September. mica now runs a writing and editing service in Oakland. She has been partnered with Angelica Chiong since 1987, and they married in 2008.

Morgana MacVicar* (Julie Eaton; b. 1947) cofounded the Pagoda in 1977 along with the three other members of the feminist dance troupe Terpsichore. She lived mostly full-time in her Pagoda cottage, #3 (Isadora), from 1978 until the early 1990s, when she began dividing her time between the Pagoda and the mountains of northeast Alabama, where she cofounded a new lesbian residential community, Alapine. Bellydancing was her specialty, and she often performed at the Pagoda, as well as doing Tarot readings and leading frequent Wiccan-influenced rituals in praise of the Goddess. She was the Pagoda's undisputed spiritual leader, and carries that on for the Temple of the Great Mother today.

Myriam Fougère* (b. 1955) is a multidisciplinary Quebecoise artist known for her vulva sculptures and her documentary films, especially *Lesbiana: A Parallel Revolution* (2012), which includes vintage footage from the Pagoda and interviews with former Pagoda residents. Myriam began visiting and exhibiting her art at the Pagoda in 1985, and still co-owns cottage 7, which she bought in 1988 with her then partner, Lin Daniels.

Nancy Breeze* (Nancy McAdams; 1932–2019) was partnered with Sallie Ann Harrison and living in Gainesville, Florida, when she began visiting the Pagoda frequently for weekends. In 1983, she moved to St. Augustine and started renting space at the Pagoda. In 1988, she bought cottage C (Coquina) as part of the North Pagoda land purchase. She served as trustee of the North Pagoda Land Trust until 1996, the year after she moved into St. Augustine to live with a new partner, Faye Quinlivan. She was a writer who is featured reading her work in two Pagoda videos: Rainbow Williams's video of December 25, 1987, readings; and Emily Greene's video of the sixteenth-birthday party, July 17, 1993, when Nancy and Paula Arden read Nancy's "Lesbian Persuasion" at the swimming pool.

Nancy Vogl* (b. 1950) was part of the Berkeley Women's Music Collective (BWMC), based in northern California, one of the first out lesbian bands. After the band played for the

Pagoda grand opening in November 1977, three of the four band members bought cottage 7 (Helva) with the intention of visiting to perform yearly and renting it the rest of the time. Although Nancy performed at the Pagoda only six of the next ten years, she soon bought out her partners, and held on to the cottage until 1988, when she sold it to Myriam Fougère and Lin Daniels.

Nu (sometimes "New," born Doris L. Wiegman, known also as Wiggy; 1947–1996) was a nurse and Emily Greene's partner when they found the Pagoda and bought cottage 8 in 1978, moving there from Orlando in 1979. When they broke up in 1980, Nu bought Emily's share of cottage 8, selling it to Jean Adele three years later. The last time Emily saw Nu, she had a new partner and was planning to move to Germany with her. Emily has since learned that Nu died of cancer in Orlando in 1996, at the age of forty-nine.

Pamela Grey (b. 1956), with a partner, bought cottage C (Coquina) from Nancy Breeze in 1995. An educator, she produced an album for Rainbow's band. She and another partner, Cecily Paige, heavily remodeled the cottage and sold it in 2006 to a heterosexual couple for an unusually big profit at the height of the real estate bubble.

Pamela Shook* (b. 1953) is an actor who first came to the Pagoda from Atlanta to perform in summer theatre in 1979, and later returned to live in St. Augustine for two years to work at the Florida School for the Deaf and Blind, often volunteering as ASL interpreter for Pagoda events. She lived at the Pagoda one other summer, house-sitting for Morgana. Pamela grew up in a conservative Southern Baptist family in South Carolina, where she attended Presbyterian College, earning a fine arts degree with a minor in theatre (1973). She found feminism at Columbia's feminist bookstore, Sojourner, where she got into a consciousness-raising group through which she came out as bisexual. While living in St. Augustine, she and several Pagoda residents were involved in the antinuclear group Seeds for Peace. Today she is married to a man and living in Waynesville, North Carolina.

Pat Crouse (b. 1934) was part of the first expansion in April 1978, when a group bought the second strip of cottages (Lot 4 GG). Pat bought in as an investment in lesbian community, but owned her cottage (#6) for less than a year, selling in January 1979 because of serious disagreements over rental arrangements.

Paula Arden* (b. 1960) first came to the Pagoda in July 1991 to perform comedy sketches that she and her girlfriend Dorothy Campbell had written. They returned with *Same Ship, Different Day*, a full-length play, that December. The following February, Paula was suspended from her high school teaching job in Cobb County, Georgia, when her lesbian identity became an issue. The couple moved to Florida and then to the Pagoda, where Paula rented cottage A from 1992 until she left in 1995, working many Pagoda jobs during that time. She is remembered especially for her performance in the title role of Carolyn Gage's *The Second Coming of Joan of Arc* at the Pagoda in 1993, and then on tour in 1994.

Paulette Armstead* (b. 1950) became a Pagoda supporter in 1984 and was part of the North Pagoda purchase in 1988, buying cottage A (Dolphin). A Tampa attorney, she and her partner treated the cottage as a vacation home and were active in Pagoda work parties. Paulette owned the cottage for two years, and was the only African American who ever owned a Pagoda cottage.

Rainbow Williams* (Sue Parker Williams; 1934–2022) was a multidisciplinary artist who first visited the Pagoda in 1978, became a $600 temple supporter in 1979, bought the downstairs duplex in 1982, and North Pagoda cottage D (Amelia) in 1988, serving as trustee for the North Pagoda Land Trust starting in 1996. She often organized art exhibits at the cultural center, and she illustrated Pagoda publicity brochures. The store sold her postcard drawings of Pagoda scenes. In 1989, she drew a twenty-foot mural of twenty Pagoda women to take to the East Coast Lesbian Festival. She kept many Pagoda photos and documents, including videotapes, especially those with her band, the Amazing Almost All Girl String Band, performing at Pagoda events. In 1999, she was one of four women who formed Fairy Godmothers, Inc., in order to buy the Center building and swimming pool.

Rena Carney* (b. 1950) graduated from the University of Florida in English and theatre, went on to graduate school at Florida State University, and moved to St. Augustine in 1975 for an internship with the Florida School for the Deaf and Blind to complete her master's degree in speech and language pathology. She persuaded Morgana MacVicar to join her to start a dance theatre company, and they and their partners cofounded the Pagoda in 1977. From 1977 through the summer of 1980, she was the driving force behind theatre at the Pagoda Playhouse, living full-time there, first in the two-story house that became the theatre and cultural center, then in cottage 4 (Sappha). In that time, she was active in Pagoda Productions, producing events and performing in plays. In the fall of 1980, due to expanded separatist rules, she moved to Gainesville to perform regularly at the Hippodrome, a regional theatre, and took a speech pathology job there. In 1996, she joined the restructured board of the Pagoda and worked to continue the cultural center and guesthouse. Three years later, she was one of four Pagoda women who formed Fairy Godmothers, Inc., to buy the cultural center building and swimming pool. She still owns her Pagoda cottage and now lives there half-time.

Rose DeBernardo* (b. 1933) met Ellen Spangler at the matriarchy conference in 1978, which she had been encouraged to attend by Barbara Deming, who was at that time neighbor to Rose's brother on Sugarloaf Key. (Later, Deming bought his house for the Sugarloaf community.) Rose bought cottage 8 from Jean Adele in 1984, sharing it with Ellen for some of the time that Rose owned it. Rose is prominent in Emily Greene's video of a 1994 New Year's Eve concert.

Rosemary Curb (1940–2012) was a Rollins College English professor and theatre specialist who became well-known for *Lesbian Nuns Breaking Silence* (1985), a book she co-edited. She was living in Winter Park and newly partnered with Rainbow Williams when the two attended a November 1979 Pagoda variety show; Rosemary then wrote about it for *Changes*, Rainbow's newsletter. The couple broke up in July 1981, but Rosemary continued a strong connection with the Pagoda.

Sandi Macik (b. 1957) bought cottage 5 (Selket) from Barbara and Lavender in June 2000. Before that, she had been a longtime Pagoda cottage-hopper, especially during the 1990s. She first came to the Pagoda in 1982 with her then partner, She Fay, and often performed with musical groups with She Fay. She still owns cottage 5.

Seaweed: See TRUDY ANDERSON.

She Fay* (Sheila Fay Thompson; b. 1957) lived in various cottages and a neighboring Beachcomber Way beach house from 1982, and rented cottage 8 (Amelia) from Rose DeBernardo for about seven years before buying it in 1998. Before that, she and Sandi Macik had lived in almost every cottage at one time or another. From 1996 to 1999, She Fay was very important in keeping the cultural center going, working closely with Jennie Iacona in maintaining the building, booking guests, and producing events. She still lives in her Pagoda cottage.

Sherry Kliegman (b. 1944) was part of the first expansion when a group bought the second strip of cottages (Lot 4 GG) in April 1978. Sherry owned the downstairs duplex (#9, Sojourner), renting it out; she sold it in November 1978 because of rental disputes and differences over separatism.

Sherry Tamburo* (b. 1952) is a fabric artist and set designer who lived at the Pagoda, renting cottage 4 (Sappha) from Rena Carney, from about 1990 to 1992, when she moved into town with Leslie Eastman. Sherry was active in Wiccan circles and ritual theatre, playing Demeter in *Rites of Spring*, a ritual theatre performance in 1991. She made the St. Augustine skyline that features in many photographs of the Pagoda stage. Emily Greene's video of the Pagoda sixteenth-birthday pool party (1993) shows Sherry bellydancing with Morgana. She is married to Leslie Eastman.

Shyne* (b. 1963) was a frequent Pagoda visitor and sometime resident from 1982, when she was graduating from high school in St. Augustine. (The only longtime Pagoda woman younger than Shyne is Dorothy Campbell, born 1965.) Shyne rented Nancy Vogl's cottage, #7 (Helva), as soon as she was eighteen, staying for a year. "I felt like I had been freed, that this was me. . . . I went from being a shy kid to just laughing and smiling and being free.

That's what the Pagoda did for me. It felt safe at the Pagoda." Trained as an LPN, Shyne had known Emily Greene since she was sixteen through working as a nursing assistant at the geriatric center where Emily worked. She moved into town with a girlfriend, Wendy, then to Gainesville for massage school, then to Atlanta. She moved back to St. Augustine in 2001 and rented various Pagoda cottages until 2004. She now lives at Alapine.

Sue Parker Williams: See RAINBOW WILLIAMS.

Suzanne "Suzi" Chance* (b. 1950) was a cofounder of the Pagoda, the one who saw the ad that took them out to Vilano Beach to look at those beach cottages. Not a dancer or artist, Suzi ran lights and did other technical work for Terpsichore, but she also lived with Morgana, her romantic partner, in the two-story building they were leasing as their dance theatre, and perched on scaffolding to help paint that big building. She and Patty Johnson co-owned the sailboat *The Matriark,* and Suzy did excursions for guests during the matriarchy conference. One of thirteen investors in the cultural center building, she had to sell her cottage to take care of a financial crisis, and spent little time at the Pagoda after moving to Gainesville. Trained as a social worker, she held several jobs in that field, as well as mariner jobs. She now lives near Athens, Georgia.

Tinker: See TRUDY ANDERSON.

Trudy Anderson (Seaweed; Tinker) was Pagoda's resident playwright from December 1978 through the summer of 1982, writing and producing several plays during her time there. Her theatre work at the Pagoda was all unpaid, and she supported herself through various Pagoda jobs, at one time earning $100 a month for these jobs. She rented space at the Center as well as several cottages, attended the "going residential" meeting in April 1981, and attempted to buy a cottage. She partnered with Rena Carney for a time and was with Karen J when the July 1982 Pagoda newsletter announced that they were leaving the Pagoda. Except for an October 1982 reference to a disputed debt, she disappears from Pagoda records after that, and we have not been able to locate her. Her last play at the Pagoda, *A Rose Is a Rose Has Arose*, was produced in the spring of 1982.

Valentine Lieu: See LAVENDER.

Vicki Wengrow* (b. 1942) had just finished massage school when she and two other women living in Ellen Spangler's housing collective in Jacksonville were part of the group who bought Lot 4 GG, with four cottages and a duplex. She and her then partner, Pat Crouse, owned cottages 6 and 8, expecting tenants to cover their expenses, but sold their cottages within the year because of serious disagreements about rental arrangements.

Wiggy: See NU.

Zoe Franks* (b. 1996) is the adopted daughter of Marie Squillace and Bridget Franks. Zoe was a child of Pagoda who still visits Marie there, but knew nothing of the Pagoda as a cultural entity before being interviewed. Zoe and her sister Rowan will inherit Marie's cottage.

Backmatter

Interviews

All Pagoda interviews were conducted by Rose Norman by phone or in person; and most were recorded and are now archived at the Sallie Bingham Center for Women's History and Culture in the Rubenstein Rare Book & Manuscript Library at Duke University. All interviewees had the opportunity to correct and revise transcripts or interview notes before archiving. Unless otherwise noted, all interviews were recorded, audio only. (Some interviewees requested that the recording not be archived or that the interview not be recorded.)

Group Interviews

Barbara Lieu and Morgana MacVicar, Alapine Village, Alabama, November 28–29, 2016, and November 3–4, 2018. Fayann Schmidt joined them for part of the November 3, 2018, interview.

Cindy Watson and Garnett Harrison, Jacksonville, September 14, 2021.

Flash Silvermoon and Pandora Lightmoon, Melrose; interviewed together at their home on November 12, 2012, but not specifically about the Pagoda experience. The interview focused on Flash's varied career.

Pagoda Performers at Dykewriters Friendship Gathering in Georgia, November 14, 2020. Barbara Ester described her experience attending the grand opening of the Pagoda in November 1977 and her return there as a performer in November 1987. She has a recording of her 1987 concert. Beth York and Phyllis Free recalled their performance with the band Anima Rising at the Pagoda in September 1979.

Pagoda Regulars at Dykewriters Friendship Gathering in Georgia, November 13, 2020. Rose Norman held a workshop for Dykewriters to talk about their Pagoda experience and recorded their memories. Attending were Barbara Ester (Spartanburg, South Carolina), Beckie Dale (Gainesville), Beth York (Spartanburg), Drea Firewalker (Marietta, Georgia), Leaf Cronewrite (Marietta), Madeline Davidson (Gainesville), Phyllis Free (Fernandina Beach, Florida), and Woody Blue (Gainesville). Robin Toler was present but had not been to the Pagoda. Three women recorded another group interview that day, sharing more Pagoda memories: Drea Firewalker, Woody Blue, and another Friendship Gathering attendee, Trey Anderson (Archer, FL).

Pagoda Women at Alapine: six women who had lived at the Pagoda and were then living at Alapine Village, Alabama, were interviewed at the Alapine Community Association house on April 14, 2013. The women were Barbara Lieu, Ellen Spangler, Emily Greene, Fayann Schmidt, Jean Adele, and Morgana MacVicar. This interview was also videotaped by Emily Greene and is part of her collection at the Lesbian Home Movie Project. All six were later interviewed individually, although Jean Adele's interview was not recorded.

Individual Interviews

Abby Bogomolny, Santa Rosa, California; interviewed by phone May 26, 2017.

Alix Dobkin, Woodstock, New York; interviewed by phone January 21, 2020.

Ann Gill, Gainesville; interviewed by phone July 28, 2018.

Ann Harman, Archer, Florida; interviewed by phone July 9, 2022.

Barbara Lieu, Alapine Village, Alabama; interviewed at Alapine April 13, 2017, and June 28, 2020; via Zoom on June 28 and August 4, 2020.

Beth Hodges, High Springs, Florida; interviewed at Alapine Village, Alabama, September 29, 2019.

Bonnie Netherton, Sugarloaf Women's Village, Sugarloaf Key, Florida; interviewed at Sugarloaf November 4–6, 2013, and July 2017; and by phone June 24, 2022.

Carole Etzler Eagleheart, Rio Rancho, New Mexico; interviewed at Rena Carney's Pagoda cottage January 30, 2019.

Cathleen "Earthstar" Burns, Friday Harbor, Washington; interviewed by phone October 1, 2020 (not recorded).

Cindy Thompson, St. Augustine; interviewed at Rena Carney's cottage February 3, 2019 (not recorded).

Dean Brittingham, Santa Rosa, California; interviewed by phone June 9, 2020.

Dore Rotundo, Melrose, Florida; interviewed at her home on the North Forty March 20, 2016, although the interview touched only peripherally on her Pagoda experience.

Dorothy Campbell, St. Augustine; interviewed at her rented Pagoda cottage (#7) October 10, 2016.

Elaine Townsend, West Columbia, South Carolina; interviewed by phone October 4, 2018.

Elethia, Herndon, Virginia; interviewed by phone September 6, 2016.

Ellen Spangler, Alapine Village, Alabama; interviewed five times: October 3, 2016, by phone; November 29, 2016, at the Alapine community house; September 29, 2019, at her home; February 29, 2020, with her partner Mary Alice Stout, at their home; and online via Zoom, again with Mary Alice, June 23, 2020 (video recorded). Some interviews focused on her work in South Carolina.

Emily Greene, Greenfield, Massachusetts; interviewed at the Alapine community house September 27–29, 2019, and followed up with several email recollections that are archived.

Fayann Schmidt, Fort Payne, Alabama; interviewed twice after the 2013 group interview: at a restaurant in Menlo, Georgia, April 11, 2017; and at Rena Carney's Pagoda cottage January 29, 2019.

Flash Silvermoon, Melrose, Florida; interviewed November 22, 2015, a follow-up to her 2012 group interview with Pandora (see above). This follow-up interview was not recorded.

Frank Halman, St. Augustine: grandson of Jane Schilling and resident of the Pagoda Motel from 1970 to 1974; interviewed by phone and at his home August 5, 2022.

Garnett Harrison, Jacksonville; interviewed by phone November 16, 2012, about her activist experience and the resulting trauma in Mississippi. (Also group interview in 2021 with Cindy Watson—see above.)

Kathleen "Corky" Culver, Melrose, Florida; interviewed at her home November 10, 2012.

Kathleen Hannan, Hillsborough, North Carolina; interviewed by phone November 16, 2020.

Kay Hagan, Santa Fe, New Mexico; interviewed by phone November 20, 2018.

Helen Renée Brawner, Arden, North Carolina; interviewed at her home July 21, 2015.

Jamie Anderson, Ottawa, Ontario; interviewed by phone October 2, 2018.

Jean Adele, Alapine Village, Alabama; interviewed with the group in April 2013, and again by phone November 19, 2016, after her move to Pennsylvania (phone interview not recorded).

June Parlett Norsworthy, St. Petersburg, Florida; interviewed by phone October 15, 2020.

Laura Folk, Alapine Village, Alabama; interviewed at her home March 1, 2020.

Lin Daniels, Los Altos, California; interviewed by phone April 20, 2020.

Liz Daneman, Melrose, Florida; interviewed at the home of Corky Culver, Melrose, October 13, 2016.

Margo George, Oakland, California; contacted by email in January 2021, but did not remember enough to answer any of the interview questions. She did review and correct my description of her.

Marie Squillace, St. Augustine; interviewed twice at her Pagoda cottage, October 10, 2016, and January 24, 2020.

Martha Strozier, Gainesville; interviewed at her home May 2, 2022.

Martine Giguère, Montreal, Quebec; interviewed by phone April 12, 2022.

mica-Meri Furnari, Oakland, California; responded to interview questions by email; also interviewed by phone March 12, 2022.

Morgana MacVicar, Mentone, Alabama; interviewed twice in group interviews (see above), and did lengthy recorded interviews on November 28–29, 2016. She then rewrote the 100-page interview transcript and requested that only the written version be archived.

Myriam Fougère, Montreal, Quebec; interviewed at her Pagoda cottage, January 29, 2014.

Nancy Breeze, Deland, Florida; interviewed at a restaurant in Deland, December 29, 2016.

Nancy Vogl, Santa Rosa, California; interviewed by phone October 27, 2016.

Pamela Shook, Waynesville, North Carolina; interviewed by phone October 17, 2020.

Paula Arden, Trion, Georgia:; interviewed at her home February 29, 2020.

Paulette Armstead, West Palm Beach, Florida; responded to interview questions via email September 2021.

Rena Carney, St. Augustine; interviewed at her St. James Beach home October 7, 2016; many follow-up interviews after that, but only the 2016 interview was recorded.

Rose DeBernardo, Anthony, Florida; interviewed by phone April 6, 2022.

She Fay, St. Augustine; interviewed at her Pagoda cottage, #8, October 10, 2016. Follow-up interviews were not recorded. Requested no archiving.

Sherry Tamburo, Shreveport, Louisiana; interviewed by phone November 12, 2018.

Shyne Oldham, Jacksonville; recorded at a library in Jacksonville January 14, 2020.

Sue Parker "Rainbow" Williams, St. Augustine; interviewed at her home November 9, 2013; several follow-up interviews after that, but only the 2013 interview was recorded.

Suzanne "Suzi" Chance, Athens, Georgia; interviewed by phone April 4 and 8, 2020.

Vicki Wengrow, Jacksonville; interviewed by phone September 22, 2016.

Zoe Franks, Gainesville; interviewed at her home December 29, 2016.

Endnotes

Introduction

1 Rosemary Curb, writing for *Changes,* the feminist newsletter edited by her then partner Sue "Rainbow" Williams. Curb, a college professor, would later become well-known as co-editor of *Lesbian Nuns: Breaking Silence* (1986).

2 Known always as Kathy in Pagoda days, Kathleen abandoned that nickname in later years, and I have respected her widow's wishes by calling her Kathleen throughout.

3 *Collected,* a Smithsonian-sponsored podcast launched in 2022, explores the roots of concepts like these in Black feminist thought. The "Combahee River Collective Statement," written collaboratively in 1977 by Barbara Smith, Beverly Smith, and Demita Frazier, was first published in *Capitalist Patriarchy and the Case for Socialist Feminism* (1979), ed. Zillah Eisenstein, under the title "A Black Feminist Statement," signed only by the Combahee River Collective. The text is online at https://www.blackpast.org/african-american-history/combahee-river-collective-statement-1977/.

4 The four lots containing the cottages, the duplex, the Center, and the swimming pool form a big square, 240' x 240' which is 57,600 square feet or 1.32 acres. The four beach-front lots total 15,250 square feet, adding about a third of an acre for a grand total of 1.67 acres. Three of the beach-

front lots remained vacant during almost the entire time the Pagoda was active.

5   This moniker appeared in 2011 in "The Pagoda . . . An Historic Lesbian Paradise," on the blog "St. Auggieland: The Strange, the Weird, the Auggie" (https://stauggieland.wordpress.com/2011/11/08/a-lesbian-paradise/). The blogger is identified as Alyssa, a Flagler College student from Kansas City.

6   Vilano Beach, where the Pagoda is located, is just outside the city limits, although residents have a St. Augustine address. Census records show that St. Augustine's population stood at 11,985 in 1980 and 14,329 in 2020 (https://stauggieland.wordpress.com/2011/11/08/a-lesbian-paradise/). While St. Augustine has grown less than 20 percent in forty years, the county in which these towns are located, St. Johns, has seen its population quintuple, from 51,301 in 1980 to 273,425 in 2020. In the decades when the Pagoda was active, St. Augustine's population declined slightly; it was only after 2000 that real estate began to boom and populations increased there.

7   Zachary Lashway, "UF Has Confederate Statue Removed from St. Augustine Before Dawn," News4Jax, April 24, 2020, https://www.news4jax.com/news/local/2020/08/24/uf-has-confederate-statue-removed-from-st-augustine-before-dawn/

8   Dr. Martin Luther King, Jr., had asked Young to go there to quell the civil rights riots in the summer of 1964. The path Young walked is now memorialized in a St. Augustine sidewalk. "Andrew Young Crossing Dedication Today," *Historic City News*, June 11, 2011. https://historiccity.com/2011/staugustine/news/andrew-young-crossing-dedication-today-15674. *Crossing St. Augustine* was part of *Andrew Young*

Presents, a quarterly series produced for Accord, Inc. Part 1 aired on Martin Luther King Day 2022: https://www.accordfreedomtrail.org/youngdoc.html. An earlier documentary film, *Crossing in St. Augustine* (2010), was made about the time that the sidewalk memorial was built at the site where the mob attacked Young.

9   The best introduction to Vilano Beach is Vivian C. Browning, Sallie L. O'Hara, and John T. Pilecki, *Vilano Beach and the North Beaches.* Images of America Series (Charleston, SC: Arcadia Publishing, 2015).

10   Heckscher tried to save it by building bulkheads, but in 1938, it had to be razed. On the Grand Vilano Casino, see Jackie Feagin, "Grand Vilano Casino Victim of Ocean," *St. Augustine Record,* February 7, 1987. Feagin says the casino was damaged by hurricanes, but I could not confirm that. A later story calls them "strong storms" ("Vilano Beach's name is 70 years old," *St. Augustine Record,* December 17, 1996). From Vilano Beach clippings file, St. Augustine Historical Society.

11   "L.G. Rees' Surfside Cottage Colony Grows, 'Flamingo' Being Completed: Others Are to Be Built Later," *St. Augustine Record,* August 5, 1936, news clipping and typescript without page numbers. This newspaper clipping is the only documentation about the original construction. It names all four cottages and says that Flamingo was just being completed. Flamingo is #3, the next-to-last cottage on Lot 3. It seems unlikely that Rees skipped a space and went back to build that cottage, so the reporter got the name wrong, the name plaques got changed later on, or Rees did not originally build them on Lot 3 perpendicular to the ocean. Barbara Lieu reports a possibly apocryphal story that they were built on the beachfront lots, facing

the ocean, and that Rees moved them after a hurricane or bad storm. It might be that he moved them after the storm that irreparably damaged the Grand Vilano Casino in 1937, or before the storm, responding to a forecast of very bad weather coming their way.

12   Rena Carney heard that Rees built each cottage a little bigger as he went along, and thinks that her cottage, #4, was originally the smallest and the first built. St. Johns County Property Appraiser (sjcpa.us) gives 480 sq. ft. for the cottages with enclosed garages but no heated additions (cottages 1, 2, 5, 6, and 7). For the cottages on Beachcomber Way, it gives 616 sq. ft. for the two cottages with no additions (Cottages A and C).

13   The Schillings bought Lots 1-5. Lot 5 was vacant, and they sold it to a Vilano Beach developer, Louie Dickinson, in 1976. Dickinson built a three-story apartment building known as the "triplex" behind the Lot 4 cottages, to the dismay of the Pagoda women.

14   Obituary, *St. Augustine Record*, March 5, 2003. https://www.findagrave.com/memorial/42336136/jane-elizabeth-schilling. Pappy Schilling's obituary does not turn up on an internet search.

15   Jane Schilling's grandson Frank Halman says that fire was in 1975 and that Jane was devastated by it. She had a deep fear of fire from a childhood experience of a house fire.

16   The Schillings lived at the Pagoda from 1971 to 1982. Jane Schilling had four children by a previous marriage, and those children were the parents of the grandchildren who lived at the Pagoda in the 1970s. Jane and Pappy had two children together, Frederic (Rick) and Dolores; Rick lived in the duplex and later in a Beachcomber Way cottage.

17 One or two people were knighted each year from 1969 to 2018: "St. Augustine Easter Week Festival," http://www. oldestcityeaster.org/history.html

18 Obituary, *St. Augustine Record*, March 5, 2003.

19 See Sherry Ortner's classic essay "Is Female to Male as Nature Is to Culture?," widely anthologized, but first published in *Feminist Studies* 1, no. 2 (1974): 5–31.

20 *Maize* has been published more or less quarterly since 1983 and is still active. Dr. Jean Boudreaux, "Shewolf" (1932–2020), published six editions of *Shewolf's Directory* between 1993 and 2016, traveling around the country collecting information. See Kate Ellison, "She Put Landykes on the Map: *Shewolf's Directory*," *Sinister Wisdom* 98 (Fall 2015): 113–14, and https://slfaherstoryproject.org/contributors/ shewolf-dr-jean-boudreaux/. Joyce Cheney's *Lesbian Land* was published in 1985 by Word Weavers, sponsored by Lesbian Natural Resources.

21 Kate Ellison, "Living Feminism," *Sinister Wisdom* 93 (Summer 2014): 92–94.

22 The Pagoda's difference from other women's land communities may account for its surprising absence from the academic literature about women's communities, and even about separatism. Nancy C. Unger gives some attention to the Pagoda in *Beyond Nature's Housekeepers: American Women in Environmental History* (New York: Oxford University Press, 2012, 176–87), mostly repeating what she had written in "From Jook Joints to Sisterspace: The Role of Nature in Lesbian Alternative Environments in the United States," in *Queer Ecologies: Sex, Nature, Politics, Desire,* ed. Catriona Mortimer-Sandilands and Bruce Erickson (Bloomington: Indiana University Press, 2010, 173–98). Dana R. Shugar

barely mentions the Pagoda in her *Sep-a-ra-tism and Women's Community* (Lincoln: University of Nebraska Press, 1995, 105), and then only to quote Morgana in *Lesbian Land,* describing the Pagoda's legal agreements.

23 Lesbians in land groups have embraced the term "landyke" since Jae Haggard started using it in *Maize* in 1995.

24 [Unsigned], "St. Augustine: Our Place in the Sun," *The Matriarchist* 1, no. 3 (November 1978): 7. In that same article, Morgana is quoted as saying they were "four women who loved the ocean and wanted to live together to combine our art and politics" (7), but that came later. Living together was not their original intention.

25 Corky Culver, "The North Forty: Florida (1972–Present)," *Sinister Wisdom* 98 (Fall 2015): 20.

26 On LEAP, see Corky Culver, "Transforming Lesbian Cultural Politics in Gainesville, Florida," *Sinister Wisdom* 109 (Summer 2018): 24–28.

27 A life-changing experience for many of these women was a 450-mile peace walk from Gainesville to Key West. Before that peace walk, Gainesville/Melrose and Sugarloaf women had spent sixteen days in a South Carolina jail after an antinuclear protest there. Corky Culver tells this story in "Into the Grueling Duelings of Consensus Dances Sweet Meditation," *Sinister Wisdom* 93 (Summer 2014): 23–26. See also an extended interview about the peace walk online at slfaherstoryproject.org.

28 Rose Norman, "Sugarloaf Women's Village: 'Some Ground to Stand On,'" *Sinister Wisdom* 98 (Fall 2015): 63–73.

29 Now the Barbara Deming Memorial Fund, demingfund.org.

30 "The Pagoda, Florida, 1982, Conversation Between Morgana and Elethia," in *Lesbian Land,* ed. Joyce Cheney (Minneapolis: Word Weavers, 1985), 111–15.

Chapter 1

1   From an unpublished story "Journey to the Pagoda." Quotations about this trip are from that story.

2   See pp. 247-49 for a list of plays performed at the Pagoda Playhouse. It is probably not complete, since some photos survive for which no one can recall the play.

3   After the summer 1979 production, Barbara Deming objected strongly to using the punning title *An Afternoon of S&M*, making light of sadomasochism, so Trudy agreed to change the title to *An Afternoon of Sophie and Myrtle*, and that title was used in publicity thereafter. Both surviving scripts, however, retain the original title, and it appears in the Pagoda Theatre entry in the *Chrysalis* directory of feminist plays (1980) as *An Afternoon of S and M*. The Holiday Inn sketch is not named in the news clipping from *The Traveller* that mentions winning a prize. It says the women performed a "20-minute comic skit directed and written by Trudy Anderson." The clipping is dated January 24, 1979 (p. 11) and includes a photo that looks like Sophie and Myrtle.

4   Pagoda advertised Trudy's *Crazy Ladies in a Junkyard* for the last weekend in August, but Pamela Shook thinks Trudy never got it written, and that's why they did *The X Miss Copper Queen on a Set of Pills* that August.

5   *Changes,* February 1979, p. 9.

6   Rosemary Curb, "The First Decade of Feminist Theatre in America," *Chrysalis* 10 (1980): 63–75. This article includes an "Annotated List of Feminist Theatres," which has an entry for Pagoda Playhouse (p. 74). The entry also says that in fall 1979 the Pagoda women toured New York, Boston,

Washington, D.C., and Atlanta, presumably an aspirational statement about a tour that both Morgana and Rena are positive never happened.

7   Quoted from June 10, 1979, meeting notes.

8   I have been unable to locate either Trudy Anderson or Anna Rallo, after numerous internet searches and posting queries in *Lesbian Connection*.

9   Emails from Emily Greene to author, September 2 and 7, 2018; quoted with permission.

10 The deed signing over this house, on Oneida Street, from Rena to Kathleen is dated February 10, 1978. Kathleen sold that house three years later.

11 "The Pagoda, Pagoda Temple of Love, Pagoda by the Sea (1975-2014)," unpublished manuscript, p. 2.

Chapter 2

1   The Schillings had sold Lot 4 GG and Lot 4 ZZ to these couples in 1976.

2   The column was "Doing the Charleston," and Ashley Cooper (pen name of Frank B. Gilbreth Jr.) was the columnist. This comes from Elaine Townsend's interview.

3   "Berkeley Women's Music Collective," http://queermusicheritage.com/olivia-bwmc.html, has pictures of the band, a 1975 songbook with music and lyrics by all the band members, a short 1975 music video featuring Suzanne (then known as "Susann") Shanbaum, and two stories about the band. Nancy bought the cottage from Suzanne and Debbie after the first year or two, when they found they could not get enough time off to visit.

4   Their total monthly mortgage payment was $241.83, divided into six units (the duplex counted as two), with the

shares based on whether the unit had two bedrooms or needed a new roof. The downstairs duplex had two bedrooms, and some cottages had enclosed the garage to make a second bedroom. The bank agreed to release the beachfront lot (4 ZZ) at the closing, with Martha paying $23,000 cash for that lot. That left the nine others with a $28,523 mortgage at 9 percent, which was paid off by about 2000. By that time, only Barbara and Lavender remained from the original group of nine, other women having taken their places.

5   The names on that deed are as follows: Elizabeth L. Hodges (Beth), Vicki Lee Wengrow, Patricia F. Crouse, Barbara H. Lieu, Susan [sic] Shanbaum, Nancy Vogl, Debbie Lempke, and Conni Lieu. Sherry Kliegman's name is not on the deed because Barbara Lieu signed for her. Martha Strozier had a separate deed for Lot 4 ZZ.

6   *Lesbian Land,* p. 111.

7   Notes for three Pagoda House meetings survive, dated May 6, 1978; June 3, 1978; and June 23, 1978. The ten women attending the first meeting about buying what they then called the Pagoda House were Pat, Vicki, Lavender, Barbara, Sherry, Rena, Morgana, Ellen, Martha, and Beth. All but Ellen were cottage owners, and Ellen would buy Beth's share of the duplex in September. Of the thirteen shareholders in November, one couple had bought a single share (one cottage), leaving twelve shares. If all twelve put in $620 each, they would have had $7440, which would have gone to down payment, closing costs, and a Pagoda House account. Insurance and real estate taxes were not included in their mortgage payment.

8   "Big" in that the house was over four times the square footage of the cottages. The house was advertised as 1,810 sq.

ft., including the attic, when it was being sold in 2016. The online property appraiser site gives "actual area" as 2,104 sq. ft. and "conditioned area" as 1,200 sq. ft.

9 From a fund-raising brochure, probably written toward the end of the summer of 1978, when the Pagoda women decided to keep going even though they already knew they could not make a profit. Donations were to be made to Women in the Arts, which indicates that the Pagoda did not yet have nonprofit status, which came in 1979.

10 On feminist activism in Gainesville and around the South, see the special issues of *Sinister Wisdom* by the Southern Lesbian Feminist Activist Herstory Project, sinisterwisdom. org/oralherstorians. The first ten stories concern lesbian-feminist activism in Florida, seven of them about activism in Gainesville.

11 Today, there is disagreement about whether they could have made a profit on cottage rentals with different business practices.

12 Later, to keep the prices affordable, the Pagoda women formalized the cottage sale price as the amount that the owner had paid plus a calculated percentage and assuming a share of the mortgage. Today, these cottages rent for $950–$1400 a month, mostly to women only, and selling prices have ranged from $100,000 to $350,000, the latter at the height of the real estate bubble.

13 In November (they had bought the cottages in April), Vicki sold cottage 8 to Emily Greene and Wiggy, and Sherry sold the downstairs duplex. In January 1979, Pat Crouse sold cottage 6 to Karen J and Leslie Eastman. Disagreements about the selling price added to the hard feelings.

14 Vicki's 2016 interview.

15   The $162 figure is from scribbled notes among Pagoda papers. Rena's copies of monthly financial reports on her cottage in 1980 and 1981 show monthly expenses ranged from $65 to $228 a month, not including the mortgage (which was paid off in 1982). The higher months were when fire insurance came due (in two installments), or there was a major purchase, like a bed ($50 in September 1980).

16   From a handwritten, undated letter from Conni (Lavender) to Morgana ("as womager"). It seems to have been written after August 9, 1978, when Lavender attended the closing on the purchase of the Center building, and before her return to the Pagoda in October. The festival is not named but Barbara Lieu says it was the Michigan Womyn's Music Festival. Rosemary Curb was at that 1978 festival and mentions having gotten a Pagoda flyer from Barbara there (see her November 1979 *Changes* review mentioning that).

17   May 6, 1978, new moon, WomeNotes & Decisions #3, notes by Vicki.

18   "The pig in the head" comes from Mary Daly's 1978 book *Gyn/Ecology,* frequently cited to describe internalized patriarchy. Vicki's first quotation is from an email to the author, June 11, 2022; the second quotation is from her phone interview of September 22, 2016.

19   In addition to Vicki, Pat, and Sherry's units on Lot 4, on Lot 3 Kathleen swapped her cottage for Rena's share of their St. Augustine house, and Suzi sold hers to Martha Strozier because of a financial emergency. Beth Hodges sold the upstairs of the duplex to Ellen Spangler in September 1978, but Beth was not involved in the dispute about tenants. She had simply followed a romance to Boston and would not move back south for many years.

20   Surviving documents include the agreements for 1977, 1980, 1982, and 1983, all of them describing the property in legal language and closing with witnessed, sometimes notarized, signatures. It appears that the owners of the second strip of cottages did not write a formal agreement until 1980, which may account for the disruption around tenants in 1978.

21   April 22, 1979, minutes. In the original arrangement, if you already owned a cottage, you had to make a $600 donation to the temple before you could buy another one. Later on, anyone buying a cottage was expected to also make a $600 donation to the temple, a requirement that shows up in meeting notes, but is not tracked in Cottage Eligibility Lists after 1983.

22   See April 22, 1979, meeting notes for the first list and the statement about how to prioritize who can buy a cottage. The women decided that year that the fairest way to prioritize cottage eligibility among supporters was by date of "first involvement"; however, the December 1981 version of the list is the first to include the date when people became monthly supporters and therefore eligible to buy a cottage. That December 1981 list is the first freestanding list (not embedded in meeting notes). Sometimes couples shared a membership. Ellen and her partner, Rose De-Bernardo, were designated "lifetime members" after Rose donated some property in Interlachen, a town fifty miles southwest of the Pagoda, to the church (it later sold for almost $1800). A few entries are marked "exchange" in the payment column. The last list, dated March 27, 1994, has 67 names, with over half of them (#27–67) dating eligibility from 1990 to 1994. This final list has no notation as to who

has paid $600, whether they are "involved" in the community, or how much they are paying monthly, as in many earlier lists.

Chapter 3

1　See Charlene Ball, "ALFA: Intersections, Activism, Legacies 1972–1994," *Sinister Wisdom* 93 (Summer 2014): 58-64. Some lesbians lived in the group's house, but it was more of a meeting place than a cultural center.

2　Margo doesn't remember how much the share cost, but the asking price at that time was $600.

3　The only place I have found the thirteen co-owners listed is in meeting notes for November 25, 1978. Barbara and Lavender together put in $600, while the other eleven women put in $600 each. Only one name appears on the deed: Conni Lieu (Lavender), as Trustee.

4　On this ambivalence about separatism, see Alma Rose's letter to Lavender of November 5, 1979. Alma was then partnered with filmmaker Arian Sanz, who was a member of the North Forty land group in Melrose. I have found nothing from Darcey Ortolf in the files. People recall her as a Rolfer at the Gainesville Women's Health Center (Rolfing is a physical therapy technique).

5　There is no evidence that the trust of which Lavender was Trustee was ever created. Notes from the November 25, 1978, meeting say that Lavender has not had time to set up the trust and that Margo George offered to do it. Margo says she was not yet in law school, but may have offered to have one of her lawyer parents do it.

6　Undated fund-raising brochure.

7 Pagoda Productions Finances 1979.

8 The Pagoda Productions account was closed in June 1981 (June 6, 1981, meeting notes).

9 Two of the 1979 plays are Trudy Anderson plays listed in Rosemary Curb's feminist theatre directory but may not have actually been performed. These are *Alleys* and *Crazy Ladies in a Junkyard.*

10 Tickets to Holly Near's Pagoda concert were five dollars apiece and by reservation only; there were sixty seats and all profits went to the antinuclear campaign, except for 2 percent to the Money for Women Fund, the Barbara Deming charity that Morgana worked for. Rosemary Curb reviewed the December 2 performance for the January 1980 *Changes* (pp. 3–4), illustrated with a Rainbow drawing of Holly performing, with J. T. Thomas on the piano and Susan Freundlich signing. Records say that Holly also did a private concert at the Pagoda on Monday, December 3.

11 That big year, Pagoda also sponsored four workshops: Martha Strozier did two sexuality workshops (January and March), Flash Silvermoon did a Tarot workshop in May, and Dore Rotundo did a drawing workshop in December.

12 "St. Augustine: Our Place in the Sun." *The Matriarchist* 1, no. 3 (1978): 7; "First Regional Matriarchy Conference: A Cultural High," *The Matriarchist* 1, no. 4 (1978): 12. These hard-to-find newspapers are archived at various research libraries: I found them at the University of Oregon, Feminist and Lesbian Periodical Collection, box 34, folder 10 (see also Duke University, ALFA periodical collection, box 27). In later years, Barbara Love would distance herself from the study of matriarchy, saying that it was mostly Liz Shanklin's great interest, that she was just following her

lead, and that Liz resented Barbara being asked to speak on the topic instead of her. Shanklin refused feminist appeals to change "matriarchy" to a different term that did not suggest patriarchy with women in charge. See an interview with Barbara Love by Kelly Anderson, Voices of Feminism Oral History Project, Sophia Smith Collection, March 6, 2008; transcript of video recording, https://www.smith.edu/libraries/libs/ssc/vof/transcripts/Love.pdf. This is the best description of the matriarchy organization that they started that I found. Love describes a New York City forum held two weeks after the regional conference at the Pagoda, but says nothing about the conference at the Pagoda, where she led a workshop.

13 "The Answer Is Matriarchy," a pamphlet distributed at a September 16, 1978, forum on the future of the women's movement, and reprinted in *Our Right to Love: A Lesbian Resource Book,* ed. Ginny Vida (Englewood Cliffs, N.J.: Prentice Hall, 1978).

14 The first Womonwrites was in 1979, and the conference continued annually through 2019. See Merril Mushroom and Rose Norman, "Womonwrites," *Sinister Wisdom* 93 (2014): 127–32; and Rose Norman, Merril Mushroom, and Kate Ellison, "Womonwrites, Lesbian-Feminist Cultural Cauldron," *Sinister Wisdom* 116 (2020): 88–92.

15 I interviewed Susan Robinson by email in August 2020. Her detailed answers to questions about the workshop are archived with other Pagoda interviews. All planning with Rich was done by phone, so there is no written correspondence about it. Robinson recalls having no interaction with Pagoda residents other than Lavender, who had made the arrangements, which included meals at the Center.

16 In the end, there were sixteen attendees, since Robinson's partner Betty Bird was present. She did not write poetry but had been instrumental in planning the workshop. Attendee Helen Renée Brawner writes her personal recollections of the workshop in "The Southern Women's Poetry Workshop with Adrienne Rich at the Pagoda, St. Augustine, FL," *Sinister Wisdom* 116 (2020): 105–7.

Chapter 4

1 Margot Adler traces the complex history of modern pagan and neo-pagan beliefs (earth-based religions) in *Drawing Down the Moon* (Boston: Beacon Press, 1979; rev. eds., 1986 and 2001). Feminist spirituality is one segment of that larger movement. For stories of some of the many feminist spirituality circles in the South, see *Sinister Wisdom* 124, *Deeply Held Beliefs: Spiritual/Political Activism in the South* (2022).

2 Matriarchal studies as a field of academic study has weathered much controversy but remains robust. Feminist scholars often draw on the work of the archaeologist and anthropologist Marija Gimbutas, whose books include *The Goddesses and Gods of Old Europe, 7000 to 3500 BC: Myths, Legends and Cult Images* (London: Thames and Hudson,1974), *The Language of the Goddess* (London: Thames and Hudson, 1989), and *The Civilization of the Goddess* (London: Thames and Hudson, 1991).

3 See Krista Schwimmer, "Z Budapest: Feminist Witch Who Fights Back," *Free Venice Beachhead,* August 1, 2014, https://freevenicebeachhead.com/z-budapest-feminist-witch-who-fights-back/

4   "Witch Trial," *Womanspirit* 1, no. 4 (1975): 51, online at https://voices.revealdigital.org. The Reformed Congregation of the Goddess, International (RCG-I), has claimed credit as the first Goddess church to be both incorporated and to obtain federal tax-exempt status. Founded in 1983 by Jade River and Lynnie Levy, RCG-I may just not know about the existence of the much smaller Pagoda-temple of Love, which has the paperwork for its incorporation dated 1978 and its tax-exempt status in November 1979.

5   Her legal name was Dorothy G. Head. Her death in 1984 is reported in the Pagoda newsletter, but not elsewhere.

6   Toni Head, "Changing the Hymns to Hers," *Heresies* 2, no. 1 (Spring 1978): 16.

7   Conni Lieu to "Dear Sisters," November 3, 1978. Toni Head's enthusiastic reply is dated November 7, 1978.

8   Head, "Changing the Hymns to Hers," 17.

9   Vicki Mariner, "An Interview with Toni Head," *Tallahassee Feminist History Project*, a special issue of *Spectrum: A Cooperative Newspaper for the Tallahassee Community* 28 (1981): 7; available at http://seaah.org/spectrum/spectrum198112.pdf.

10 See letters from Toni Head. The IRS letter granting 501(c)(3) status is with Crones Nest grant proposals. The June 6, 1979, annual report, naming the four officers, is filed with 1979 papers and comes from Barbara Lieu. The other dates come from Barbara Lieu's notes. Incorporation data are available online at dos.myflorida.com.

11 Originally published by Luna Publications, *The Feminist Book of Light and Shadows* was revised and reissued as *The Holy Book of Women's Mysteries, Part 1* (1979) and then as *The Holy Book of Women's Mysteries: Feminist Witchcraft, Goddess Rituals,*

Spellcasting and Other Womanly Arts (Wingbow, 1989), which was superseded by *The Grandmother of Time: A Woman's Book of Celebrations, Spells, and Sacred Objects for Every Month of the Year* (HarperOne, 1989).

12 Folder "Facility Files" contains Pagoda's Articles of Amendment, dated January 3, 1980.

13 The warranty deed and quit-claim (Conni Lieu, Trustee, to Pagoda-temple of Love) are both dated August 25, 1980.

14 Meeting notes for July 22, 1979, say that taxes were then $316 annually and insurance $576, adding that the women have calculated they can't afford both taxes and insurance with the current assessment from thirteen owners.

15 The Pagoda-temple of Love bylaws identify a "Circle of Wise Women" where the Mother Church bylaws had a Board of Directors. It is the decision-making body, but how members of the Circle are chosen is not stated. It's not clear whether the "Council of Wise Womyn" named in meeting notes for February 16, 1980, is the same thing, but in case it is, they define the Council of Wise Womyn "as those womyn who own, live, and work at the Pagoda." The first annual report (June 6, 1979) lists board officers as president, Barbara Lieu; vice president, Julie Morgana [Morgana MacVicar]; treasurer, [name withheld]; secretary, Conni Lieu. For nearly all of the following years, Morgana was president of that board, and the other offices rotated among a core of residents. In 1996, after a reorganization, board and procedures changed, but Morgana remained president. Note that the board that was running the Center over the years was a management board, and only the officers are named in the corporation's annual report.

16 Berkeley, CA: Moon Books, 1978, rpt. Beacon Books, 1984.

17 Morgana's revised transcript of her November 29–30, 2016, interviews, p. 9.

18 Ffiona Morgan (1941–2020) later bought a lot at the lesbian community founded by Pagoda women at Alapine, in northeast Alabama, but never lived there.

19 The conference was officially called "Through the Looking Glass"; its program is online at https://jwa.org/sites/default/files/jwa032c.pdf.

20 November 29, 2016, interview.

21 In the 1980s, Ellen Spangler founded a teaching and healing center in South Carolina. See Rose Norman, "Ellen Spangler and Starcrest," *Sinister Wisdom* 124 (Spring 2022): 64–69.

22 In the video of this performance, Rainbow credits Jean Sirius's meditations for lyrics. This author and text do not show up on an internet search, except for a garbled recording cited as Charles Hutchens, Jean Sirius, "Meditations for Women" (1981) at https://charleshutchins.bandcamp.com/track/meditations-for-women.

23 Rainbow performed this on dulcimer, then sang it a capella at Christmas Day readings at the Pagoda, which she videotaped, but did not arrange to archive. With her permission, I had that VHS tape digitized, and after her death, I sent a digital copy to the Lesbian Home Movie Collection. As of this writing, the original tape has not been recovered.

24 "Take a Picture" is published in *Sinister Wisdom* 104 (Spring 2017): 89. It follows Flash's memoir "Flashbacks of Flash Silvermoon, Lesbian Musician in Gainesville," *ibid.*, 84–88.

25 Emily Greene's video of Pagoda's eighteenth-birthday, July 8, 1995, includes this performance by Flash and Morgana, and is archived with the Lesbian Home Movie Project.

26 Flash writes about this in "Creating the Rainbow Goddess Tradition," *Sinister Wisdom* 124 (Spring 2022): 33–37.

Chapter 5

1 Email to author, November 16, 2021. With Emily's permission, I have collected her emails about her life as a memoir archived with her recorded interviews.

2 Much of the Melrose/Gainesville lesbian-feminist activity in the 1970s and early 1980s took place at an old house that Corky Culver rented on 500 acres, the Red House, where many women lived and cooked up projects like the North Forty, as well as cultural projects like Ferron concerts or Minnie Bruce Pratt poetry readings. Touring musicians often stayed there, and the Red House hosted legendary parties. Ferron stayed at the Red House the week she performed at the Pagoda.

3 Gaby appears frequently in Pagoda meeting notes from 1981 until the summer of 1985, when the newsletter says she returned to Germany. She visited again in March and December 1986, and Emily and her partner visited Gaby in Europe in the summer of 1990. Gaby had married a man by then. She was planning another Pagoda visit in 1991, when she suffered an aneurysm and died suddenly that January. She was thirty-six.

4 March 8, 1981, meeting notes.

5 Meeting notes say that fifteen attended but do not identify attendees.

6 The letter is undated, but presumably was mailed in April or May 1981. Financial records do not call out postage expenses, but probably it went out in the mailing with monthly meeting notes.

7   The financial connection between cottage rentals and the cultural center is hard to track. They kept those financial records separate, since the cultural center was owned by a tax-exempt church, while the cottages were privately owned and not tax-exempt. Only one document refers to 20 percent of cottage rental income going to "management," and what that covers is not explained.

8   These rates are from a brochure that says they are effective September 1, 1979; the rates are the same in a newer brochure (with a temple graphic on the cover) in Rena's 1982 folder. Rates from 1988 and later advertising are for sleep space in the Center, so are not comparable to cottage rental rates, though sometimes cottage owners rented a single bedroom with kitchen and bathroom privileges. For comparison, $20 in 1980 was worth about $73 in purchasing power in 2023.

9   Minimum wage was $2.90 in 1979, $3.10 in 1980, $3.30 in 1981, and not raised again until 1990, to $3.80. Adjusted for inflation, $5.00 would be about $18 in 2023 dollars.

10   Meeting notes for September 30, 1979, say "Sue Williams, from Winter Park, a good friend of Emily and Wiggy, would like to become a Big House owner/member." Rainbow announces in the November 1979 *Changes* that she is a new member of the Pagoda "collective," presumably meaning the group who bought the building in August 1978.

11   From Rainbow's unpublished memoir, where she also says that Edith ran for state treasurer of NOW and was one of the first women croned in Orlando.

12   Biographical information on Joycie Meyers comes from her obituary, posted at Tribute Archive by Berry Funeral Home and Crematory, https://www.tributearchive.com/

obituaries/837320/joycie-marilyn-meyers/elberton/georgia/berry-funeral-home-crematory. The obituary says she died March 11, 2016, in Elberton, Georgia.

13 This one-hour video is in Rainbow Williams's collection and contains readings by Nancy Breeze, Marilyn Murphy, Rainbow Williams, and Katy Wildsister (who organized the event), and others. Rainbow plays her dulcimer and sings original music.

Chapter 6

1 Daughters of Bilitis, founded in San Francisco in 1955 as a social alternative to bars, had chapters in some large cities and reached some women through its nationally distributed newsletter *The Ladder*, which lasted until 1970.

2 For an analysis of different ways of defining "lesbian culture," see the introduction to *Lesbian Culture: An Anthology: The Lives, Work, Ideas, Art and Visions of Lesbians Past and Present* (Freedom, Calif.: Crossing Press, 1993), edited by Julia Penelope and Susan Wolfe. They see lesbian culture as both depending on lesbian identity and at the same time a source of lesbian identity, and argue that establishing a "positive Lesbian identity" requires a communal context (p. 8, elaborated p. 10).

3 *Dance of Birth: Belly Dancing as Natural Childbirth Conditioning* (St. Augustine, Fla.: Patriachild Press, 1981); photographs by Morgan Gwenwald.

4 In the six years following *A Rose Is a Rose Has Arose*, only two plays, both one-woman shows, appear in Pagoda records: Yvonne Vogel's *I Wanna Live Don't Wanna Die* (February 1985) and Terry Baum's *One Fool* (January 1988).

5   Emily Greene's videos include both Rainbow's band and Flash performing solo at the Pagoda, as well as Cecily Jane, Lyn Thomas, and Karen Beth (1995). See lesbian-homemovieproject.org.

6   The show was advertised for May 15–29, 1985; the Pagoda newsletter later says they extended the exhibit to June 2. Myriam and Martine stayed until July 28.

7   Publicity from June 1978 shows "films by Arian & Alma" (Alma Rose) and describes their Mountain Movie Company as "Exploring female consciousness." Films by Arian & Alma show up again in July 1979 publicity (fifteenth-birthday scrapbook). The meeting notes for July 22, 1979, say that Arian Sanz wants to move to the Pagoda and live in her eleven-by-four-foot trailer there in September. I'm just inferring that she moved it there, because the 1982 meeting notes say the trailer is there, but not necessarily Arian herself. I found nothing about Arian in fall 1979 meeting notes. Her partner, Alma Rose, had been involved with the Pagoda in 1978, when she was a shareholder in the cultural center building.

8   See emails from June Parlett Norsworthy to author October 2020, and her phone interview of October 15, 2020. At the Pagoda, she was using her witch name, Orinda.

9   The salon that Edie Daly started in St. Petersburg lasted more than twenty years. See Daly's "Salon in St. Petersburg, Florida: A Living Prose Poem," *Sinister Wisdom* 93 (Summer 2014): 37–41.

10   Shari Benstock, *Women of the Left Bank: Paris, 1900–1940* (Austin: University of Texas Press, 1987).

11   The Wimmin's Salon was in December 1984; quote from January 1985 newsletter.

12 Correspondence with Olivia Records shows that they attempted to become an Olivia distributor but could not meet the requirements (four letters, Conni Lieu to Ginny Berson, November 9, 1978, to March 27, 1979). Olivia required distributors to be stores open full-time.

13 Barbara and Lavender had been trying to sell the store since December 1987, when Lavender's family began having health problems, and they needed to spend more time in South Carolina. Lavender's younger brother, Harry Ackerman, age thirty-eight and her only sibling, had a chronic illness and died of a staph infection in 1988. It was a blow to the whole family.

14 *Daughters of a Coral Dawn* is a utopian novel, the first of a trilogy by Katherine V. Forrest (Naiad Press, 1984). In it, nine women start a women-only community on another planet.

15 Nancy Breeze, "Crone," *Southern Breeze* (March–June 1985): 100–101.

16 From the photographs, it looks like Rose and Ellen's croning had about twenty-three people attending. The only other croning photographs are from the 1996 winter solstice, when Claudia Cole, Faye Quinlivan (Nancy Breeze's partner), and Kay Mora are wearing robes in the photos.

17 It is spelled Crone's Nest (on various planning documents), Crones' Nest (on the logo), and Crones Nest (in the 1985 *Cronicle* newsletter and a 2000 brochure). I have used Crones Nest, their final choice.

18 "St. Augustine: Our Place in the Sun," *The Matriarchist* 1, no. 3 (1978): 7. The use of both "wimmin" and "women" is per the original.

19 Morgana worked part-time as administrator for Deming's Money for Women Fund, but records indicate that funds

for Dean Brittingham's visit came directly from Deming, her friend and lover Mary Meigs, and others, rather than from the Money for Women Fund. Meigs was a Canadian author who often stayed in the Sugarloaf guest cottage. The amount donated is not given in records. Dean (then spelled Deane) lived at the Pagoda off and on from 1982 to 1985.

20   Originally, the grantwriters were funded for October–December 1982, and Sue Schein completely left the project in January 1983 to take a teaching job in Montreal.

21   Quoted in the Crones Nest committee's mid-1984 press release and reprinted in *Cronicle*, p. 2 (the newsletter was published just this once).

22   Dozens of slides taken by Sue Schein for the Eastman grant project have been donated to the University of Florida, along with other Pagoda records that include grants and grant charts, but no rejection letters. Considering that over two-thirds of residents of senior living facilities (including nursing homes as well as assisted living and other senior housing) are women, it seems likely that an all-women senior housing facility would be unremarkable. Of those in assisted living, 71 percent are women; https://www.consumeraffairs.com/assisted-living/statistics.html.

Chapter 7

1   Rainbow Williams's words, from a 2020 unrecorded interview.

2   "Letter from Florida," *Lesbian News,* April 3, 1988.

3   Murphy, *Are You Girls Traveling Alone?* (Los Angeles: Clothespin Fever Press, 1991), 20. Unless otherwise noted,

biographical information about Marilyn comes from "Color Me Lavender," the opening chapter of the book.

4   Much of Irene's biographical information comes from her interview for the Old Lesbian Oral Herstory Project (OLOHP), which is archived at Smith College: https://find-ingaids.smith.edu/repositories/2/resources/963. Irene's interview, conducted by Arden Eversmeyer, was published in *A Gift of Age: Old Lesbian Life Stories*, ed. Arden Eversmeyer and Margaret Purcell (Houston: Old Lesbians Oral Herstory Project, 2009), 223–32.

5   *A Gift of Age*, 228.

6   According to Clark Pomerleau, Califia cofounder Betty Willis Brooks attended Sagaris with Marilyn. Pomerleau's *Califia Women: Feminist Education Against Sexism, Classism, and Racism* (Austin: University of Texas Press, 2013) is the best source I have found on both Califia and Sagaris. Most writings about Sagaris focus on the disrupted second summer session that followed the session that Marilyn and Betty Brooks attended. Pomerleau describes Sagaris, including the controversies they had and what the Califia cofounders learned from them (pp. 37–41). On Sagaris, there is very little else, other than what Marilyn herself wrote, but see Sara M. Evans, *Tidal Wave: How Women Changed America at Century's End* (New York: Free Press, 2003), 109; and Alice Echols, *Daring to Be Bad: Radical Feminism in America, 1967–1975* (Minneapolis: University of Minnesota Press, 1989), 268.

7   Marilyn writes about both Sagaris and Califia in essays republished in *Marilyn Revisited* (Serafina, N.M.: Women, Earth, & Spirit, 2013): "Off the Deep End: Sagaris," 12–16; and "Califia: An Experiment in Feminist Education," 17–35. Both essays were originally published in *New Direc-*

tions for Women, where Murphy began publishing a column called "Lesbianic Logic" in 1992. (Elsewhere she says she continued writing for *Lesbian News,* but Pomerleau says the column ran in *Lesbian News* from August 1982 to June 1991 [p. 75].) Marilyn's Califia story ends with a list of eighteen collective members in 1983 and a list of over thirty women who had been members of the collective. She writes that the Califia Community Collective dissolved in December 1986, but Pomerleau explains that Califia continued under leadership of women of color for two more years (Pomerleau, 164-66). Until 1979, the collective was all white (Pomerleau, *Califia Women,* 124).

8   "Califia," 34.

9   The number of sessions per summer is from Pomerleau, *Califia Women,* 43. The rest is from Murphy, "Califia," 17–35.

10   Pomerleau, *Califia Women,* 50.

11   Pomerleau, *Califia Women,* 58. He does not say which women were involved in that collective.

12   Rainbow's North Pagoda files include a variety of corrective deeds that followed, e.g., when Ann Harman quit-claimed the swimming pool part of Lot 2 without providing an easement for access to the remaining lots, thus creating a cloud on that title. It was a more difficult cloud that turned up when the church sold the building and swimming pool, involving Pappy Schilling's name on the deed and his will not having been probated.

13   Rainbow, Nancy Breeze, and Marilyn and Irene had all made the $600 temple donation. Paulette Armstead does not remember whether she had done that, but given her Christian faith it is doubtful that she donated to a Goddess church.

14   Cottage A, like the duplex on Lot 4, is next to a vacant lot. Records do not show how ownership of the vacant lot west of cottage A was handled. In Pagoda's active days, it was used as access to the Center and for RV parking. Today, it belongs to the owners of cottage A (sjcpa.us).

15   The Cottage Eligibility List was not as vast as Myriam supposed. Myriam's name was #49, and none of the Pagodans that I have interviewed has ever complained that Lin and Myriam jumped the list, so it must have been perceived as fair. Four of the women who bought the North Pagoda cottages in April 1988 were ahead of Myriam: Rainbow, #11; Nancy Breeze, #25; Irene and Marilyn, #39. Earthstar, who bought a beachfront lot on the North Pagoda Land Trust mortgage, was #48. The list and rankings applied only to cottages on Lots 3 and 4.

16   Notes for the August 1987 business meeting show that Pagoda planned to use that $600 toward savings to make the Center more accessible. Myriam borrowed the down payment from her mother.

17   The magazine's full title was *Music Women: A Newsletter Especially for Managers, Producers & Distributors*. The California newsletter *Lesbian Tide* announced its birth in its January–February 1978 issue.

18   The first East Coast Lesbian Festival was held on Labor Day weekend of 1989 in western Massachusetts. Lin also produced the West Coast Lesbian Festival, which started June 5–7, 1992, in Malibu, California, and Hawaiifest.

19   Marilyn mistakenly writes that the fire happened after the lesbians bought the building: see "Pagoda: Temple of Love, 1994," *Lesbian Ethics* 95, no. 2 (1995): 19. Morgana, Rena, and Suzi are all quite certain there was never a fire there

when they owned it, and they tell the story of Jane Schilling and the fire demon. They also recall bringing in someone to banish the fire demon and what seemed to be a poltergeist.

20   See Pomerleau, *Califia Women*, chapter 5, for details on Califia's antiracism work. Pomerleau says it took seven years to bring leadership to 50 percent women of color and to improve racial diversity in attendance (131–32). Even so, Califia remains "one of the very few U.S. groups where people of color ever made up 50% of the leadership" (ibid., 132). In February 1986, white Califia Community Collective leaders turned the organization all over to women of color, who kept Califia gatherings going for another two years (ibid., 164–66).

21   On January 31, 1996, Diaz and Bencangey sold the cottage to Deirdre Doran, who lived in Massachusetts and treated it as rental property.

22   One proposal they considered was for the temple to buy one floor of the duplex and make it available to a resident woman of color, but they never followed through, maybe because of the tokenism of that gesture.

23   Online in an excerpt from the 2010 documentary film *Crossing in St. Augustine* https://www.youtube.com/watch?v=_yEl7LbFrTQ.

24   The loan came in the form of five $5000 promissory notes, each for fifteen years at 9 percent interest. Monthly payments were about $250, more than the $197.75 a month mortgage that they paid off with the loan. The original Center building mortgage documents do not specify the term of that 1978 loan from the Schillings, only the interest (7 percent) and monthly payment. Their total payoff in April 1992 was $5055.66, including a prepayment penalty

and payoff fee of $461.33. Presumably, it was a twenty-year mortgage that would have paid off in 1997.

25   There were actually two child custody cases in which ex-husbands were accused of sexually assaulting their daughters but were given sole custody of the abused child. In both, Harrison's clients (the mothers) took the disputed child underground, and a whole movement grew up around it. B. Leaf Cronewrite tells part of the story in "Garnett Harrison: Freedom Fighter in Mississippi," *Sinister Wisdom* 93 (Spring 2014): 71–77. See also Eleanor J. Bader, "Court Gives Kids to Abusive Dads," *New Directions for Women* 17, no. 2 (1988): 1, 20; M. Laurino, "Custody Wars: Moms Held Hostage," *Ms. Magazine*, December 1988, 88–96; "Two Cases That Gave Birth to a Movement, *People*, January 23, 1989; and Francis Wilkinson, "Witchhunting in Hattiesburg," *American Lawyer*. May 1988, 104–10.

26   June 1992 newsletter.

27   The temple owned the vacant lot just east of the duplex, known as Persephone's Pit/Garden in the active Pagoda days. A few years after selling the Center and swimming pool, they sold the Persephone's lot to She Fay, who had bought Cottage 8, next door to it.

28   Emily Greene's video collection is archived with the Lesbian Home Movie Project (LHMP). LHMP provides limited access to excerpts from videos for which they have permissions; see Lesbianhomemovieproject.org. Rainbow Williams also videotaped the eighteenth-birthday party as well as some events that are not part of Emily Greene's collection. Rainbow's videos were digitized but have not yet been archived.

29 Townsend would return to South Carolina to earn advanced degrees in social work (a master's in 1998 and a PhD in 2009).

30 Looking back today, she realizes that it was also a time of grieving for her as she came to realize that "professional music wasn't going to be my path."

31 It may be poetic justice that Nancy Schaefer was murdered by her husband in 2010.

32 Paula emceed the eighteenth-birthday party afternoon talent show at the pool party (July 1995) and is very prominent in Emily Greene's video of that event.

33 "Herstory of OLOC, Old Lesbians Organizing for Change, 1989–2007," compiled by Arden Eversmeyer, Mary Henry, and Margaret Purcell, 2008, posted at OLOC.org, OLOC-Herstory_1989-2007_long.pdf. Both Rainbow and Barbara Lieu recall this OLOC meeting, but neither was old enough to attend (the minimum age for OLOC participation was then sixty). In 2020, I spoke with Arden Eversmeyer, a longtime OLOC member, and the only attendee then still living. She believes the steering committee was mainly planning OLOC's part in the 1993 March on Washington, which OLOC led. Then a California-based organization in its fourth year of existence, OLOC was probably drawn to Pagoda by Marilyn and Irene. The previous year, the steering committee had met in Atlanta in association with the National Lesbian Conference.

Chapter 8

1 July 1982 newsletter.

2 By 1985, the price of Lot 2 had dropped to $40,000, but the women decided to just raise the $10,000 needed for

the pool. Two supporters and all ten cottage owners had already put in $100 each, so they needed eighty-eight more subscribers; they scouted other sources of funds as well. The April 1987 newsletter announces that Rose DeBernardo has donated three lots in Interlachen, and there is discussion of selling them and using the proceeds for the swimming pool. They were up to sixty-six subscribers by January 1988, while they were beginning to close on the North Pagoda land deal, which included all of Lot 2, including the swimming pool. The March 1989 financial report shows them selling the Interlachen lot for $1787.82; those funds were escrowed immediately and then raided in November when the big liability insurance bill came in.

3   The relationship between the pool fund and the North Pagoda mortgage is muddy. Meeting notes from April 1989 say that the swimming pool was bought by the Pagoda Community of Womyn, which would be making mortgage payments. (The escrow account for lifetime pool memberships was identified as the Pagoda Aquatic Association. The Pagoda Community of Women appears to be the same group with a new name, later referred to as Womyn of the Pool.) Having sold ninety-six shares at $100 apiece, one wonders why they needed a mortgage on the pool? Partly that was because they could not separate the swimming pool from the rest of Lot 2 before the sale. But they had no trouble doing so after the sale. (After quit-claiming the pool to the church, Ann's share of the North Pagoda mortgage payment did not change). Financial statements for the Center list the pool mortgage as $38.75 a month. When the temple sold the swimming pool to Fairy Godmothers, Inc., in 1999, sale documents value the pool at $9141, less than they had raised from memberships by 1988, and the temple still owed $1300 on the pool mortgage. As a sidenote,

the remaining, vacant portion of Lot 2 GG was valued at $18,889 in 1988 and sold in 2005 for $153,000.

4   November 1983 minutes show liability insurance jumping from $364.80 to $1500 annually because of the swimming pool.

5   See the June 5, 1989, newsletter with a letter from Martha Strozier arguing to close the pool, and a report from the Womyn of the Pool (yet another name for the Aquatic Association?) by Irene Weiss, responding to Martha's letter and arguing that "it is not productive or even relevant to think of money and energy spent on the pool as being in competition with money spent for accessibility, outreach, painting, etc." The newsletter includes a form to fill out soliciting opinions about what to do with the pool.

6   From an unpublished memoir in Rainbow Williams's private papers, donated to the University of Florida. This is the only place that I have found the different cottage sale rules discussed in any detail. Not mentioned in this memoir is a dispute about the possible sale of Nancy Vogl's cottage in 1988 to a supporter who had been accused of battering her partner. This dispute raised new and challenging issues around the use of the Cottage Eligibility List. That particular dispute was resolved when the supporter withdrew from the Pagoda.

7   Pomerleau, *Califia Women*, 106, citing Marilyn Murphy, "One of the Murphy Girls," in *Out of the Class Closet*, ed. Julia Penelope (Seattle: Seal Press, 1994), 300.

8   Marilyn Murphy "Did Your Mother Do Volunteer Work?" in *Marilyn Revisited* (Serafina, N.M.: Women, Earth, & Spirit, 2013), 36–50, where it is not identified as coming from any publication. Pomerleau cites this essay as being in the personal files of Califia member Betty Jetter.

9 Barbara Lieu says that their quiet voices in meetings were in response to women who had been raised in violent households and had asked them not to raise their voices in meetings. In her writings, Marilyn Murphy expresses the same comment about quiet versus loud behavior, attributing it to class differences, as Elethia does. Marilyn asserts that middle-class women are "more severely conditioned to be 'ladies' than the rest of us" ("Did Your Mother Do Volunteer Work?", 41).

10 From Elethia's unpublished memoir, "My Pagoda Experience," p. 3. At first, it might seem these were regional differences, with the Southern women being taught silence and indirectness, the northerners the opposite (or so it might seem to a Southerner). But Barbara, Elethia, Marilyn, and Lin were all raised in New York, Lin and Marilyn in New York City. Their differences do seem to arise from class and privilege differences.

11 April 1988 meeting notes. The first consultant was Kay Hagan, who visited from Atlanta. Pagoda supporter Olivia Stryker's notes from that weekend are in Hagan's archives at Duke and in the Pagoda archives. The second consultant was Anne Rhodes, a friend of Marilyn's who came from Ithaca, New York. Morgana's notes from that weekend are in Pagoda archives, and Marilyn writes about it in her "Lesbianic Logic" column for *New Directions for Women* (July–August 1993), p. 22.

12 It is puzzling that Elethia signed as president of the Pagoda board, since Morgana was nearly always president of the corporation. It would make more sense for Elethia to have been treasurer. I have found no corporate records to confirm any of this (online state records go back only to 1995), but

there are copies of all five promissory notes with Elethia's signature over the words "President, Board of Trustees." From 1994 to the present, Morgana was president. Barbara Lieu found records back to 1993 and found Marilyn as president in 1993, so Elethia might have been president in 1992, but Elethia is not an officer in any corporate filings found so far.

13 Marilyn Murphy gives her version of this episode, without mentioning names, in "Pagoda, Temple of Love, 1994," *Lesbian Ethics* 95, no. 2 (1995): 24–25.

14 Murphy, "Pagoda, Temple of Love, 1994," 18–26; quotations are from 20–21. This essay has numerous factual errors, such as that a fire in the Center destroyed their work on remodeling it as a theatre, and that "some of the original buyers were uncomfortable with the women-only policy and rented to men." The fire happened before they bought the building and began remodeling, and the original Pagoda women owners who complained about evicting the male tenants were not opposed to the women-only policy and did not thereafter rent their cottages to men (see chapter 2).

15 Arden Eversmeyer and Margaret Purcell, eds., *A Gift of Age: Old Lesbian Life Stories* (Houston: Old Lesbians Oral Herstory Project, 2009), 231.

Chapter 9

1 The January 1996 newsletter just says the wreck happened "late at night" and that it was the "second time," giving no date. It could have been December but was recent. This driver had insurance.

2 None of the thirteen earliest cottage owners were living at the Pagoda full-time in 1996. Those were Rena Carney, Morgana MacVicar, Kathleen Clementson, Suzi Chance,

Barbara Lieu, Lavender Lieu, Vicki Wengrow, Pat Crouse, Beth Hodges, Ellen Spangler, Sherry Kliegman, Emily Greene, and Wiggy (Doris Wiegman), owners of the buildings on Lots 3 and 4 in 1977 and 1978. In 1996, only four of those even still owned their cottage: Rena, Morgana, Barbara, and Lavender.

3 This comes from Morgana's "Pagoda Herstory," one legal-sized typed sheet dated 1998. The statement is confirmed by the records, which show only sixty-seven supporters in 1995, compared with more than one hundred in 1988. By 1998, the annual amount received from guests was almost twice that of supporters ($10,857 from guests, $5493 from supporters, according to a scribbled sheet of "credits").

4 See Emily Greene's video of the 1995 Pagoda birthday party and Rainbow Williams's video of the 1996 Pagoda birthday party.

5 See Rose Norman, "Alapine: Morgana's Magical Mountain (1997–Present)," *Sinister Wisdom* 98 (Fall 2015): 146–49. Morgana, Barbara, and Fayann had formed Sheeba Mountain Properties and bought 275 acres in northeast Alabama. Part of that had previously been subdivided into two-acre lots by a developer who called the property Alapine. It took them three years to get clear title to what would become Alapine Village, a lesbian residential community comprising forty-five buildable lots. In 1997, Sheeba began selling two-acre lots to lesbians, many of them former Pagodans, including Emily Greene, Jean Adele, Rose DeBernardo, Martha Strozier and Dore Rotundo, She Fay, and Ellen Spangler (and her life partner, Mary Alice Stout).

6 The December 1995 newsletter names these four women as organizers, but provides little other detail. Corporate officers in 1996 were Morgana MacVicar (president), Edith

George, and Garnett Harrison. Edith had been secretary in 1995, and moved over to treasurer, replacing Irene Weiss, with Garnett stepping in as secretary. No one replaced Marilyn Murphy, who had been vice president.

7   Only two full-time residents attended the meeting. Five attendees were cottage owners, and five were supporters who lived in St. Augustine or Jacksonville. One attendee was a new tenant.

8   The survey went along with Cindy Watson's March 25, 1996, letter. March 1996 business meeting minutes say that of the forty surveys returned, thirteen were from supporters and other women not involved.

9   The number of supporters whose names remained on the Cottage Eligibility List, and the number who were current with their monthly donation, were a moving target. Probably, there were never as many as one hundred caught up with their monthly donation.

10 During 1995, meeting attendance was unusually high. The March, July, and September meeting had eighteen, sixteen, and fourteen attendees, respectively.

11 The other three board members were Emily's partner and two local supporters, Claudia Cole and Nancy Gardner. Striking absences from the board include Marilyn and Irene, Lin and Myriam, Rainbow, and Nancy Breeze, all of them strongly associated with North Pagoda. Also absent is Lavender, who had moved to Atlanta. In February 1996, Nancy Breeze resigned as trustee of the North Pagoda Land Trust, and Rainbow took it over.

12 They started out proposing to meet four to six times a year, and wound up with yearly meetings "to oversee the legal and financial operations of the Pagoda-temple of Love" (Mor-

gana's 1998 "Pagoda Herstory"). Officers are not mentioned in these documents, but Morgana is president for all of these years. Nancy Gardner and Garnett Harrison were not listed on any committee in these minutes. Garnett had become unelected secretary. She officially became secretary of the corporation in 1996, replacing Edith George, and remained in that office through 1999. Annual reports listing officers are online from 1995 to the present at dos. myflorida.com.

13 Garnett resigned from the Workers Support Committee but agreed to help Edith with the money issues. At that same April meeting, they decide to try a steering committee to handle things between board meetings. It would be composed of Garnett, Cindy, Jean, and Joycie until the June meeting.

14 She Fay posts videos of some twenty-first-century performances by SueShe on her YouTube channel, https://www.youtube.com/user/SheFayzable. These include covers and well as her original songs.

15 Other performers in those last four years included regulars like Carole Eagleheart (all four years) and Jane Yii (formerly of Cecily Jane), as well as Jamie Anderson (1999). These are just advertised concerts for which we have records. Unadvertised concerts would add to the numbers.

16 Joseph Verrengia and Allen G. Breed, "Judgement Day in Struggle Between Human, Plant Life," *Anniston (Ala.) Star*, July 12, 1998, 5A.

17 Mike Schneider, "Fewer Out-of-State Tourists Made Orlando Trip in 1998," *Tampa Tribune-Times*, August 12, 1999.

18 This is from "A Proposal for the Future of the Pagoda, Temple of Love," a four-page email to the board, April 11, 1999.

19 Quoting signs posted in the Center.

20 I have found no report or notes from the February 13 meeting of "Concerned Pagodesses" (to quote Rainbow), nor an attendance list, but we know that parts of the meeting were recorded, and there are several letters about it. The letters are in the Pagoda files, but the recordings have not surfaced. Rainbow's February 16, 1999, email to the Sugarloaf women is the source of the number of women attending the meeting. Rainbow also tells them that the board will meet on April 10 to hear proposals about the Pagoda's future. Both She Fay and Elethia wrote letters about the meeting to Barbara Lieu, as did a Pagoda tenant named Merrill (who did not attend). Merrill expresses strong support for Jennie and disappointment in not being included in the meeting. She Fay has listened to a recording that Ellen made of the meeting and mentions that the tape was turned off several times. She is disheartened to have been excluded from the meeting, considering the jobs that she and Jennie have done between them for the past three years ("reservationist, maintenance person, center-keeper, bookkeeper, concert producer and keeper of the supporter/concert mailing list, past and present"). She tells Barbara that she and Jennie were not notified of the meeting in time to attend, and thinks that was deliberate and based on interpersonal issues and misunderstandings. She notes long discussions on the meeting recording with questions about reservations and the mailing list that could have easily been answered by either of them had they been present.

21 Cloudland, Georgia, is close to the rural property that the church bought in northeast Alabama, bordering the Alapine property. People often refer to the property as Cloudland, although all of the land is in Alabama. Elethia's letter to

Barbara Lieu also says that she thinks Jennie is "getting the short end of the stick" (March 17, 1999). Elethia's exact words about spirituality at the Pagoda are these: "The Pagoda does not have the Spiritual energy that it had for years and years. And, from what I know about it today, it may be years before it does . . . not that there aren't women who are spiritual but collectively it doesn't seem to exist" (ellipses in original). Earlier in her letter, Elethia reports that she has recently had a long talk with Jennie Iacona, and this conclusion about spirituality seems to stem from that.

22 Martine's addition to my edited notes from her April 12, 2022, phone interview. When I asked Martine whether she agreed with Elethia in this letter, she replied: "What I wrote about 'the ambient sacredness' of the Pagoda refers to the first times that I stayed at the Pagoda in 1985 and 1986. Later when there was a division and the community of Alapine started, it wasn't the same. In my point of view, some of the women who held the special Pagoda 'sacredness,' like Morgana and Lavender-Valentine had left. Yes there was still a spiritual expression and faith, but it was more subtle and personal. Rainbow's artwork reflected the Goddess's presence. The Pagoda had become a 'residential' community. So in a way I agree with Elethia even if I find her wording harsh, and it doesn't take into account the remaining 'Pagoda spirit.'"

23 It's not clear how this undated document was distributed, whether by hand, at a meeting, or sent to a mailing list. Since it sets an April 10, 1999, deadline, and mentions "now in 1999," it must have been written earlier that year.

24 Jennie estimates $50,000 repairs needed to get "proper licensing/permits from the city for a legal business," citing

expenses for wiring, pool, plumbing, roof, laundry room, drainage. It "needs to be upgraded to bring in more money . . . we are & have been just applying Band-Aids, which are just not holding any more!"

25   Jennie's resignation is July 12, 1999. On August 11, Barbara writes She Fay, beginning "Well it seems that it's just you and me now, about Center books."

Chapter 10

1   The Wikipedia entry for StoneSoup School says it was chartered in 1971 in Winter Park, and was based on the Summerhill School in England. It credits three founders: Sue Buie, Annette Chioma, and Rainbow Williams. It is now a boarding school in Crescent City, Florida.

2   Rainbow Williams, "Last Concert, Last Circles at Pagoda," 2017. She emailed this short essay to me and probably to many others.

3   Email from Rainbow Williams to Rena Carney, November 10, 2016.

4   The lot they called Persephone's Garden was a lot Ellen Spangler donated to Pagoda-temple of Love in 1984. The temple retained ownership until 2006, when they sold the lot to She Fay, whose cottage is next to it.

5   Property taxes totaled $7822 in 2005, $11,500 in 2006, and $13,293 in 2007. Online tax figures are reported separately for three parcels: the Center building, the lot in front of it, and the swimming pool. The swimming pool tax alone went from under $200 in 1999 to $715 in 2001, and was $2845 by 2005. In 2021, it was back down to $974.78. The house tax went from $146 in 2000 to $3806 in 2008. See sjcpa.us,

searching on parcel 1476400035 (the house), 1476400030 (the area in front of the house), and 1476400025 (the pool).

6   A March 3, 2009, letter from the FGI attorney gives these figures.

7   In 2008, both Marie and Liz wanted to sell their shares, or else take out a mortgage on the property, while both Rainbow and Rena remained opposed to incurring debt.

8   It's not apparent when cottages 6–8 and the duplex were zoned residential, or why cottage 5 was not included in that rezoning. It took years to untangle the various utilities that had been combined in motel days, and sometimes was not done as a group. FGI tried to deal with the easement problems for Lot 4 while working on Lot 3 easements, but the residents did not want to participate.

Chaper 11

1   Marilyn Murphy, "Lesbianic Logic," *New Directions for Women* (July–August 1993): 22.

2   Email from mica to author, February 14, 2022.

3   From a brochure directed to prospective residents. The seven-page document is not dated, but internal evidence suggests 1981 or 1982.

4   Marilyn writes about Group at length in her "Pagoda, Temple of Love, 1994," *Lesbian Ethics,* 95, no. 2 (1995): 18–26.

5   Written by Doreen Valiente, interpreted by Starhawk in *The Spiral Dance* (1979).

6   Marilyn and Irene wrote separate letters of protest dated February 1, 1994, when the other cottage association refused to invite them to a meeting.

7   As mentioned earlier, Pagoda residents Lin Daniels and Myriam Fougère produced the East Coast Lesbian Festival (ECLF), and several Pagoda residents were involved with it. Resistance to lesbian separatism, in particular to banning boy babies, was widely reported. Both *Sojourner* and the New York newsletter *WomaNews* published articles and letters about the controversy at ECLF. These publications are readily accessible online through Independent Voices (voices.revealdigital.org), searching for ECLF.

8   Audre Lorde (interviewed by Susan Leigh Star), first published as "Sadomasochsim: Not about Condemnation," in *Against Sadomasochism: A Radical Feminist Analysis*, ed. Robin Ruth Linden, Darlene R. Pagano, Diana E.H. Russell, and Susah Leigh Star (San Francisco: Frog in the Well, 1982), rpt. in Audre Lorde, *A Burst of Light: And Other Essays* (1988), 1–9.

9   *The Women's Review of Books* 4, no. 5 (February 1987): 11–12.

10   See *Sinister Wisdom* 93 (2014) for a story about how a lesbian couple in Kentucky, one of them an attorney, successfully brought domestic violence shelters to every county in the state.

11   "I Choose Vanilla" is a three-page, single-spaced, typed manuscript in the thick file of correspondence about the S/M controversy.

12   I was struck by this similarity in reading a 1990 interview with Andrea Dworkin, where the interviewer says that younger lesbians are saying they feel excluded if they do not practice S/M, much as young twenty-first-century lesbians are saying that LGBTQ youth shun them for identifying as "lesbian" rather than "queer." See Gail Dines and

Rhea Becker, "A Conversation with Andrea Dworkin," *Sojourner*, June 1990, 17–19.

13   Pyramid Mikrowave van Crowbar, letter to the editor, *Mama Raga* 6, no. 1 (January 1994): 10. Interestingly, Pyramid's name appears in the 1994 Cottage Eligibility List next to a $50 donation, so sounding off in print did not necessarily preclude supporting lesbian community. (Pyramid was not the author or recipient of the bloody handprint.)

14   When the S/M policy was made permanent in October 1990, the newsletter detailed the survey responses. Of the 34 supporters who wrote, 27 approved of the S/M policy, 2 disapproved, and 5 wanted a compromise. Eleven women who were not supporters wrote; this group was 7–4 in favor of the policy. The newsletter also says they lost 4 supporters over the policy and gained 7 new ones "because we have the policy." Without a list of supporters at that time, it's hard to replicate how they arrived at this tally. A note says they don't include the ones who dropped support in the 34 supporters, and do count the 7 new ones in the 34. In the letters file, I count 8 people opposing the policy on various grounds (their total is 6), some more strongly than others. Three supporters wrote a joint letter in July saying that they have attended all the meetings and are withdrawing their support because of the way it was handled—i.e., referring to the fact that cottage owners got one vote apiece (13 of 16 cottage owners voted for the policy), while all 60 supporters got just one vote on the policy.

15   Most cottage owners had donated $600 to the Center at some point. There are no good records of who donated $600 to the church as part of buying a cottage, although meeting notes refer to this practice several times and some

early Cottage Eligibility Lists have a column for the $600 donation.

16   Karen J's letter is undated but probably January 1988, since it refers to a letter from Marilyn Murphy about the Cottage Eligibility List, and that letter was published in the January 13, 1988, newsletter.

17   Nancy Breeze, "Lesbian Persuasion," *Common Lives/Lesbian Lives* 40 (Fall 1991): 108.

18   Handwritten, undated document. Internal evidence suggests it was written in 1995 or 1996.

19   From the Pagoda at Alapine group interview in 2013.

Chaper 12
1   Beach Break is now booking through VRBO.com.

Timeline of Key Pagoda Events
1   Barbara says that Lavender was enrolled in a graduate program, not massage school.

Plays Produced at the Pagoda
1   Rosemary Curb, "The First Decade of Feminist Theatre in America," *Chrysalis* 10 (1980): 63–75.

2   This play was advertised, but may have been replaced by another performance of *The X Miss Copper Queen*.

3   The entry in Rosemary Curb's directory is the only evidence that this play was produced.

4   Meeting notes also show March 21, 1982. They probably changed the date, but may have performed it in both March and April.

Pagoda Concerts

1   This and the following three concerts (covering October 5 through November 28) are advertised on one flyer with dates but not year. It could be 1985 or 1991, based on November 28's being a Thursday. But Elaine Townsend was living at the Pagoda in 1991, so 1985, when she was living in South Carolina, is more likely.

2   From an undated page with the October 1986 newsletter.

Pagoda Women

1   My interviews are archived at the Sallie Bingham Center for Women's History and Culture in the Rubenstein Rare Book & Manuscript Library at Duke University. OLOHP interviews are archived at Smith College, and some are published in two volumes: Arden Eversmeyer and Margaret Purcell, eds., *A Gift of Age: Old Lesbian Life Stories* (Houston: Old Lesbians Oral Herstory Project, 2009) and *Without Apology: Old Lesbian Life Stories* (Houston: Old Lesbians Oral Herstory Project, 2012). Jean Adele, Nancy Breeze, Rainbow Williams, and Irene Weiss all did OLOHP interviews, and Irene's interview is published in *A Gift of Age* (223–32).

2   Because the name Maria Dolores Diaz is very common, it was difficult to find reliable online information about our Maria. The census record states that she was born in Honduras and was a year old when she appears with her parents and four siblings living in Los Angeles: https:// www.ancestry.com/1940-census/usa/California/Maria-Dolores-Diaz_2kqtwg. Clark Pomerleau's book about Califia has substantial information about her work there, and he confirmed that she had died but did not know when.

References

Adler, Margot. *Drawing Down the Moon*. New York: Penguin Books, 1986.

"Andrew Young Crossing Dedication Today." *Historic City News*, June 11, 2011, https://historiccity.com/2011/staugustine/news/andrew-young-crossing-dedication-today-15674.

Ball, Charlene. "ALFA: Intersections, Activism, Legacies 1972–1994." *Sinister Wisdom* 93 (Summer 2014): 58–64.

Benstock, Shari. *Women of the Left Bank: Paris, 1900–1940*. Austin: University of Texas Press, 1987.

Brawner, Helen Renée. "The Southern Women's Poetry Workshop with Adrienne Rich at the Pagoda, St. Augustine, FL." *Sinister Wisdom* 116 (Spring 2020): 105–7.

Breeze, Nancy. "Crone." *Southern Breeze* (March–June 1985): 100–101.

————. "Lesbian Persuasion." *Common Lives/Lesbian Lives* 40 (Fall 1991): 105–10.

Browning, Vivian C., Sallie L. O'Hara, and John T. Pilecki. *Vilano Beach and the North Beaches*. Images of America Series. Charleston, S.C.: Arcadia Publishing, 2015.

Cheney, Joyce, ed. *Lesbian Land*. Minneapolis: Word Weavers, 1985.

Cronewrite, B. Leaf. "Garnett Harrison: Freedom Fighter in Mississippi." *Sinister Wisdom* 93 (Spring 2014): 71–77.

Culver, Corky. "The North Forty: Florida (1972–Present)." *Sinister Wisdom* 98 (Fall 2015): 19–24.

————. "Transforming Lesbian Cultural Politics in Gainesville, Florida." *Sinister Wisdom* 109 (Summer 2018): 24–28.

Culver, Kathleen "Corky." "Into the Grueling Duelings of Consensus Dances Sweet Meditation." *Sinister Wisdom* 93 (Summer 2014): 23–26.

————. "Sparks and Prairie Fires." *Sinister Wisdom* 93 (Summer 2014): 17–22.

Curb, Rosemary. "The First Decade of Feminist Theatre in America." *Chrysalis* 10 (1980): 63–75.

Daly, Edie. "Salon in St. Petersburg, Florida: A Living Prose Poem." *Sinister Wisdom* 93 (Summer 2014): 37–41.

Echols, Alice. *Daring to Be Bad: Radical Feminism in America, 1967–1975.* Minneapolis: University of Minnesota Press, 1989.

Evans, Sara M. *Tidal Wave: How Women Changed America at Century's End.* New York: Free Press, 2003.

Eversmeyer, Arden, and Margaret Purcell, eds. *A Gift of Age: Old Lesbian Life Stories.* Houston: Old Lesbians Oral Herstory Project, 2009.

————, and Margaret Purcell, eds. *Without Apology: Old Lesbian Life Stories.* Houston: Old Lesbians Oral Herstory Project, 2012.

Feagin, Jackie. "Grand Vilano Casino Victim of Ocean." *St. Augustine Record,* February 7, 1987.

"First Regional Matriarchy Conference: A Cultural High." *The Matriarchist* 1, no. 4 (1978): 12.

Head, Toni. "Changing the Hymns to Hers." *Heresies* 2, no. 1 (Spring 1978): 16.

Lashway, Zachary. "UF Has Confederate Statue Removed from St. Augustine Before Dawn." *News4 Jax,* April 24, 2020, https://www.news4jax.com/news/local/2020/08/24/uf-has-confederate-statue-removed-from-st-augustine-before-dawn/.

"L.G. Rees' Surfside Cottage Colony Grows, 'Flamingo' Being Completed: Others Are to Be Built Later." *St. Augustine Record,* August 5, 1936.

Marilyn Revisited. Serafina, N.M.: Women, Earth, & Spirit, 2013.

Mariner, Vicki. "An Interview with Toni Head." *Tallahassee Feminist History Project* special issue of *Spectrum: A Cooperative Newspaper for the Tallahassee Community* 28 (Solstice 1981): 7, http://seaah.org/spectrum/spectrum198112.pdf.

Murphy, Marilyn. *Are You Girls Traveling Alone?* Los Angeles: Clothespin Fever Press, 1991.

————. "Califia: An Experiment in Feminist Education." In *Marilyn Revisited,* 17–35. Serafina, N.M.: Women, Earth, & Spirit, 2013.

————. "Did Your Mother Do Volunteer Work?" In *Marilyn Revisited,* 36–50. Serafina, N.M.: Women, Earth, & Spirit, 2013.

————. "Lesbianic Logic." *New Directions for Women* (July–August 1993): 22.

————. "Letter from Florida." *Lesbian News,* April 3, 1988.

————. "Off the Deep End: Sagaris." In *Marilyn Revisited,* 12–16. Serafina, N.M.: Women, Earth, & Spirit, 2013.

————. "One of the Murphy Girls." In *Out of the Class Closet: Lesbians Speak,* edited by Julia Penelope, 299–314. Seattle: Seal Press, 1994.

————. "Pagoda, Temple of Love, 1994." *Lesbian Ethics,* 95, no. 2 (1995): 18–26.

Mushroom, Merril, and Rose Norman, "Womonwrites." *Sinister Wisdom* 93 (Summer 2014): 127–32.

Norman, Rose. "Alapine: Morgana's Magical Mountain (1999–Present)." *Sinister Wisdom* 98 (Fall 2015): 146–49.

————. "Ellen Spangler and Starcrest." *Sinister Wisdom* 124 (Spring 2022): 67–72.

———— "Sugarloaf Women's Village: 'Some Ground to Stand On.'" *Sinister Wisdom* 98 (Fall 2015): 63–73.

Norman, Rose, Merril Mushroom, and Kate Ellison. "Womonwrites, Lesbian-Feminist Cultural Cauldron." *Sinister Wisdom* 116 (Spring 2020): 88–92.

"The Pagoda . . . An Historic Lesbian Paradise." *St. Auggieland: The Strange, the Weird, the Auggie*, http://stauggieland.blogspot.com/2010/10/pagodaa-historic-lesbian-paradise.html.

"The Pagoda, Florida, 1982: Conversation Between Morgana and Elethia." In *Lesbian Land*, edited by Joyce Cheney, 111–15. Minneapolis: Word Weavers, 1985.

Penelope, Julia, and Susan Wolfe, eds. *Lesbian Culture: An Anthology; The Lives, Work, Ideas, Art and Visions of Lesbians Past and Present*. Freedom, Calif.: Crossing Press, 1993.

Pomerleau, Clark. *Califia Women: Feminist Education Against Sexism, Classism, and Racism*. Austin: University of Texas Press, 2013.

Schneider, Mike, "Fewer Out-of-State Tourists Made Orlando Trip in 1998." *Tampa Tribune-Times,* August 12, 1999.

Schwimmer, Krista. "Z Budapest: Feminist Witch Who Fights Back." *Free Venice Beachhead,* August 1, 2014, https://freevenicebeachhead.com/z-budapest-feminist-witch-who-fights-back/.

Shugar, Dana R. *Sep-a-ra-tism and Women's Community.* Lincoln: University of Nebraska Press, 1995.

Silvermoon, Flash. "Creating the Rainbow Goddess Tradition." *Sinister Wisdom* 124 (Spring 2022): 36–40.

————. "Flashbacks of Flash Silvermoon, Lesbian Musician in Gainesville." *Sinister Wisdom* 104 (Spring 2017): 84–88.

"St. Augustine: Our Place in the Sun." *The Matriarchist*, 1, no. 3 (1978): 7.

Unger, Nancy C. *Beyond Nature's Housekeepers: American Women in Environmental History.* New York: Oxford University Press, 2012.

_____. "From Jook Joints to Sisterspace: The Role of Nature in Lesbian Alternative Environments in the United States." In *Queer Ecologies: Sex, Nature, Politics, Desire,* edited by Catriona Mortimer-Sandilands and Bruce Erickson, 173–98. Bloomington: Indiana University Press, 2010. One of the few published descriptions of the Pagoda.

Verrengia, Joseph, and Allen G. Breed. "Judgement Day in Struggle Between Human, Plant Life." *Anniston (Ala.) Star,* July 12, 1998, 5A.

Vida, Ginny, ed. *Our Right to Love: A Lesbian Resource Book.* Englewood Cliffs, N.J.: Prentice Hall, 1978.

"Witch Trial." *Womanspirit,* 1, no. 4 (Summer solstice 1975): 51, https://voices.revealdigital.org/.

Acknowledgments

This narrative relies heavily on the memories of Old Pagodans, longtime residents or cottage owners whom I have interviewed many times over the years that I have been compiling this Pagoda story. Whenever possible, I have tried to bolster memories with documentary evidence such as journal entries, scrapbooks that Pagoda guests wrote in over the years, and most especially the meeting notes and newsletters that the Pagoda published to Pagoda supporters monthly during the 1970s and 1980s (with some gaps), and then less and less regularly in the 1990s. Rena Carney, Morgana MacVicar, Barbara Lieu, and Rainbow Williams kept many documents from those years. Morgana saved the program from opening night in 1977, and many more programs from events at the Pagoda. Barbara Lieu had guest books, lists of Pagoda supporters, newsletters, financial reports, and grant proposals, as well as legal papers and copies of deeds and quit-claim documents for the cottages. Rena Carney had meeting minutes and financial reports for the cottage association and the Center—not a complete run for the whole period, but nearly complete for the 1980s and some other years. She also had all of the Fairy Godmothers, Inc., records for the final period, when she, Rainbow, and two others owned the Center building and pool. Rainbow Williams created a large line drawing done to scale and showing all the cottages, the Center, the pool, the sundeck

347

(long gone), and the beachfront lots. She also saved a twenty-foot colored mural she drew depicting twenty Pagoda residents in 1989, as well as all the documentation for the North Pagoda purchase. While working with these documents, I arranged for a significant number of Rainbow's and Barbara's Pagoda files to be archived at the University of Florida.

While all of those Old Pagodans had photographs, Emily Greene had by far the biggest still photograph collection, precisely because she was the one who made it her business to compile photo albums during the years she lived there. She even provided many negatives that could be digitized, capturing much that was lost in aging prints. Emily also videotaped many Pagoda events, mainly concerts and parties, starting in 1993, and videotaped my 2013 interview with a group of former Pagoda residents then living at Alapine. She has archived these videos (seventeen VHS tapes from the Pagoda alone) with the Lesbian Home Movie Project, which had them professionally digitized. I was able to view several of these.

Many, many people have given generously of their time and their memorabilia to help put together the story of the experience that was Pagoda. Morgana has had a traumatic head injury and other physical challenges that make her memory sometimes unreliable, but contributing to this project has compelled her to make extensive editorial revisions and additions to her own recorded interview transcript. When Barbara Lieu found an unfinished poem by Kathleen "Corky" Culver about the Pagoda, written in the 1980s, I asked Corky to finish it for this book, and she did so, brilliantly.

Kelly Wooten, archivist at the Sallie Bingham Center for Women's History and Culture at Duke University, assisted several interviewees whose papers are archived there, retrieving valuable documents, as well as archiving all of the Pagoda interviews. Flo Turcotte, archivist at the University of Florida Smathers Libraries, has assisted in many ways, most especially in taking charge of archiving boxes and boxes of Pagoda files from Morgana, Barbara, and Rainbow, and in scanning some of Rainbow's architectural drawings. Staff at the St. Augustine Historical Society have been helpful in researching background on Vilano Beach, Shorty Rees, and the Schillings. Cheryl Ruppert, the last editor of Jacksonville's newsletter COE (Calendar of Events), went through old issues pulling out all the Pagoda concerts advertised there.

Julie Enszer, editor of *Sinister Wisdom*, has been crucial to this entire project. Working with the Southern Lesbian Feminist Activist (SLFA) Herstory Project, I had published one special issue of *Sinister Wisdom* (vol. 93, Summer 2014), and was working on a second (vol. 98, Fall 2015) when I realized that I had collected a mountain of interview material about the Pagoda, and that it needed to be a book. Little did I know how much more was to come. Throughout the ten years of interviews and research about the Pagoda, Julie has been my guiding light, advising and encouraging me along the way, reading several long, encyclopedic drafts, and providing invaluable review comments.

Merril Mushroom was my co-editor on the six special issues of *Sinister Wisdom* that we published (with others) during the ten years that I have been working on this book. The Herstory Project itself was her idea, brought up at workshops at Womonwrites: the Southeast Lesbian Writers Conference. A team of Womonwriters began working on the Herstory Project in 2009, the year before my retirement from college teaching, and that project led me to doing interviews with lesbian-feminists in the South, starting in Gainesville, Florida, which soon led me to the Pagoda and an immense treasure trove of archival materials about this amazing residential community and cultural center. Merril has been endlessly available and supportive of my deep dive into the Pagoda project.

Many others have reviewed various iterations of the manuscript. Rena Carney, Morgana MacVicar, and Barbara Lieu have reviewed many drafts of the manuscript. Merril Mushroom and Beth York both read the fourth and almost final draft, and She Fay, Cindy Watson, and mica Furnari have commented on chapters. Many others have read and corrected parts of chapters. Dykewriters and Lesbians Write On members have listened to me read excerpts from chapters in progress and helped me find people to interview. The pandemic came just in time to force me to begin putting the pieces together into drafts. Out of the pandemic was born Fun with Quarantina, a Zoom weekly reading group organized by friends in Huntsville, Alabama, who have now heard many five-minute readings from my work in progress. There is nothing like a live audience to reveal what is interesting and what is not.

Several people have contributed to technical aspects of the project. John Ramey, a recent master's graduate of my university, scanned several large boxes of musty documents that Morgana and Barbara had unearthed from storage. The digital files he created and organized allowed me to keep track of records and search documents more thoroughly than if I had relied on handling those allergy-triggering papers. My friend Suzanne Barbara has contributed her PhotoShop skills to improving old, faded photos and labeling the aerial view of the Pagoda property.

Rena Carney, whose Pagoda documents I pursued for three years before she decided to share them with me, has become a dear friend and close companion. She has opened her Pagoda cottage to me on many occasions, allowing me to write there for extended periods and to interview several previous Pagoda residents in her cottage. Rena's perspectives include thoughtful analysis of formal and informal business procedures, issues of feminism and separatism, and the importance of the arts in the Pagoda's herstory. It has been a rare privilege to work on the site of this amazing community with a person who was there from the beginning, in a cottage filled with memorabilia from those days.

Index

Page numbers in italics represent photographs and captions.

photography exhibitions, 125; poetry readings, 154; salons, 125–26; St. Augustine skyline backdrop, *156*, 284; Trudy Anderson's one-act feminist plays, 43, 45–47, 50–51, 116, 285–86

"The Pagoda Pool" (Phyllis Free), 161

Pagoda Productions, 46–58, 80–83, 247–49, 282. *See also* Pagoda Playhouse; logo, *108*; plays produced, 247–49; workshops, 83, 86, 308n11, 309n15, 310n16

Pagoda "Reclaimers" (1996–99), 32, 171–85; call for proposals to continue the Pagoda, 184–85, 190; concerts, 180; February 1996 retreat meeting to brainstorm ideas for continuing the Pagoda, 176–77, 331n7; February 1999 meeting to discuss finances and interpersonal issues, 182–83, 333n20; feminist spirituality and spiritual activities, 180, 183, 333–34n21, 334n22; financial problems and declining number of monthly supporters, 175–76, 181–85, 330n3, 331n9, 334–35n24; Florida wildfires (July 1998), 181; guest prices, 175–76; Morgana's message announcing move of the church operations to Cloudland, 183–85; the new Usina Bridge and traffic problems near Pagoda front gate, 173, 174–75, 329n1; the Pagoda-temple of Love's restructured board and board meetings, 177–78, 182–85, 331n11, 331–32n12, 333n20

Pagoda-temple of Love, 12, 79, 87–100. *See also* Temple of

the Great Mother; Circle of Wise Womyn and by-laws, 90, 91, 177, 312n15; credo, 90–91; incorporation as Goddess church, 13, 17, 26, 88–91, 143, 311n4; logo with channeled motto, *95*; Morgana and, 17, 77, 89–99, *93*, 331–32n12; Morgana's message announcing move of the church operations (1999), 183–85; residents' required $600 temple donations, 70, 91, 112, 145, 147, 306n21, 321n13, 322n16, 338–39n15; restructured board and board meetings, 177–78, 182–85, 331n11, 331–32n12, 333n20; rituals, 91–92, *93*, 100; and sale of the property to Fairy Godmothers, Inc. (FGI), 189, 193–94, 326n3; separatism, 90–91; and Toni Head's Mother Church, 88–89, 90

Paige, Cecily, 119, 280

Pamela Grey, 280

Pamela Shook, 46–47, 80, 280–81

Pandora Lightmoon, 40, 42, *99*, 271

Pass-A-Grille Beach, 59

Pat Crouse, 281, 286; as co-owner of the cultural center, 77, 303n7; as early cottage owner, 63, 70–72, 281, 286, 303n5, 304n13

Paula Arden, 32, 157–58, *249*, 281, 325n32; and feminist theatre at the Pagoda, 157–58, 267, 281; move away from the Pagoda, 170; staged reading of *The Second Coming of Joan of Arc* (1993), 158, *249*, 267, 281; suspension from teaching, 158, 281; today, 228

About the Author

Photo by Beth Karbe

Rose Norman is a retired professor who taught English at the University of Alabama in Huntsville for twenty-seven years. She directed the Business and Technical Writing Program, co-founded and was first Director of Women's Studies, and for her last four years chaired the English Department. She taught graduate and undergraduate classes in women writers, women's autobiography, and technical writing, and for four years was regional coordinator of a national high school poetry competition, Poetry Out Loud. Her work as general editor of the Southern Lesbian Feminist Activist Herstory Project (slfaherstoryproject.org) led her to over ten years' research on the Pagoda residential community and cultural center. During that time, she has interviewed over a hundred lesbian feminist activists and co-edited six special issues of *Sinister Wisdom*.